CRAFT
BEER
REVOLUTION

Viva la Revolution!

Joe Wul

JOE WIEBE

CRAFT BEER

REVOLUTION

THE INSIDER'S GUIDE TO B.C. BREWERIES

→ SECOND EDITION ←

DOUGLAS & McINTYRE

Allison—

*What a long, strange trip this has been. It may
have taken longer than either of us bargained
for, but I'm so lucky to have had you at my side
along the way. I look forward to many more
adventures with you in years to come.*

Love, Joe.

• •

Douglas and McIntyre (2013) Ltd.
PO Box 219, Madeira Park BC, Canada VON 2HO
www.douglas-mcintyre.com

Edited by Caroline Skelton
Typeset by Shed Simas
Maps by Eric Leinberger
Index by Daniela Hajdukovic
Printed and bound in Canada

 Canada Council   Conseil des Arts
for the Arts   du Canada

BRITISH COLUMBIA
ARTS COUNCIL
An agency of the Province of British Columbia

 Canadä

Douglas and McIntyre (2013) Ltd. acknowledges the support of the
Canada Council for the Arts, which last year invested $157 million to
bring the arts to Canadians throughout the country. We also gratefully
acknowledge financial support from the Government of Canada through
the Canada Book Fund and from the Province of British Columbia through
the BC Arts Council and the Book Publishing Tax Credit.

Cataloguing data available from Library and Archives Canada
ISBN 978-1-77162-062-8 (pbk.)   ISBN 978-1-77162-063-5 (ebook)

CONTENTS

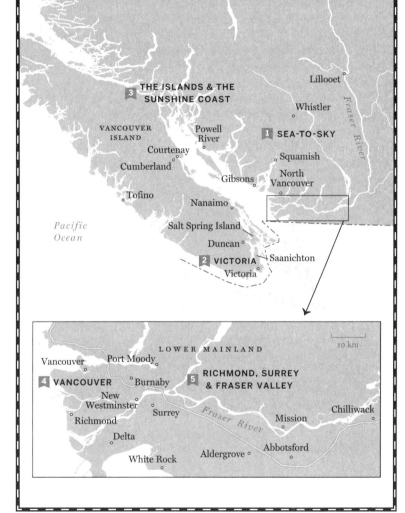

THE ISLANDS & THE SUNSHINE COAST

VANCOUVER ISLAND

Lillooet

Whistler

Powell River

SEA-TO-SKY

Courtenay

Squamish

Cumberland

Gibsons

North Vancouver

Tofino

Nanaimo

Pacific Ocean

Salt Spring Island

Duncan

Saanichton

VICTORIA

Victoria

Fraser River

LOWER MAINLAND

10 km

Vancouver

Port Moody

VANCOUVER

Burnaby

RICHMOND, SURREY & FRASER VALLEY

New Westminster

Surrey

Fraser River

Chilliwack

Richmond

Mission

Delta

Aldergrove

Abbotsford

White Rock

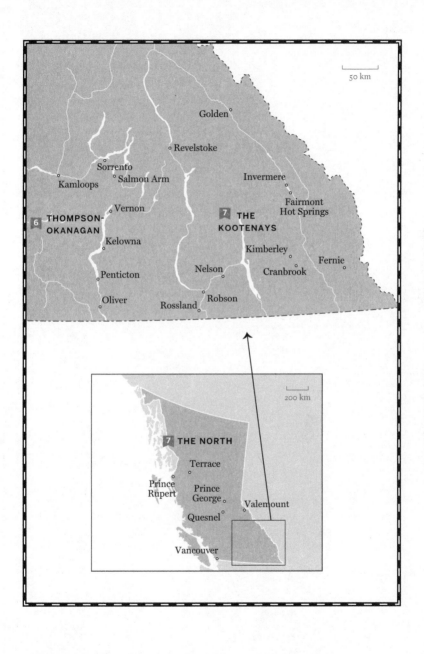

50 km

Golden

Revelstoke

Sorrento
Salmon Arm

Kamloops

Invermere

Vernon

Fairmont
Hot Springs

6 THOMPSON-
OKANAGAN

7 THE
KOOTENAYS

Kelowna

Kimberley

Nelson

Fernie

Cranbrook

Penticton

Rossland   Robson

Oliver

200 km

7 THE NORTH

Terrace

Prince
Rupert

Prince
George

Valemount

Quesnel

Vancouver

FOREWORD TO
REVISED EDITION
The Revolution That
Almost Didn't Happen

••••••••••••••••••••••••

THE FIRST EDITION of Craft Beer Revolution was published in May 2013. It was a big success right away—the publisher ordered a second printing just one month later and a third printing in 2014. The book spent much of 2013 on the B.C. bestseller list, and won the Gourmand Award for Best Beer Book in Canada for 2013.

To think it almost never happened.

Back in October 2012, after I had submitted the original manuscript to my editor and was just beginning to work on revisions, the publisher, Douglas & McIntyre—Canada's largest independent publisher at the time—went into bankruptcy protection and I spent the next four months in limbo. As Christmas passed and 2013 arrived, I figured the book would never get published, or if I was feeling optimistic, I imagined maybe it would come out a year late. Then, in early 2013, the announcement came that the Douglas & McIntyre imprint had been sold to the owners of Harbour Publishing, based on the Sunshine Coast. Within a week, an editor at Harbour called me up and asked me if I thought I could get the book done in time for a spring publication as planned. It took long hours—both from their staff and from me—but we pulled it off, and the book came out in May 2013, as originally scheduled, with almost no one the wiser to the feat we had just accomplished.

I launched Craft Beer Revolution twice—first at Spinnakers in Victoria and then at Yaletown Brewing as part of Vancouver Craft Beer Week. I finished off my speech at Yaletown by saying, "Unfortunately, I have to admit that this book is already out of date." And pointing to someone at the back of the room, I said, "You can blame it on Brent Mills because he just opened his new brewery in Delta." That was Four Winds Brewing, the newest brewery in B.C. for a few short weeks until the Heid-Out BrewHouse opened in Cranbrook. And then 33 Acres opened in Vancouver. And then Deep Cove. And Brassneck. And Persephone. And...you get the picture.

Nine craft breweries opened in 2013. That seemed incredible at the time, but what followed was mind-blowing: twenty-one new companies opened in 2014, with ten more ready to open early in 2015, bringing the total in B.C. at the time of this book's publication to ninety. I doubt if this unbelievable pace of growth will continue, but still it's very possible the total could surpass one hundred before the end of 2015. That means the industry will have doubled in size in just two-and-a-half years! If that isn't a revolution, I don't know what is.

After launching the book in Victoria and Vancouver, I hit the road, driving around the province, hosting events in conjunction with local breweries in more than twenty communities throughout B.C. I was amazed at the response from local beer lovers and honoured by the generosity of the breweries. I asked brewers to prepare a special batch of beer with "revolution" as the theme that we could serve at book launches, and I was blown away by their great ideas.

In Penticton, Cannery, Tin Whistle and Firehall (from nearby Oliver) collaborated on the Three Brewers Plot, a Belgian Wit cask conditioned with Valencia oranges soaked in

Cointreau, peppercorns and dark honey, and finished off with Amarillo hops. Needless to say it was stupendous.

In Fernie, the most remote community I visited on my tour, more than forty people in attendance at the Fernie Arts Station enjoyed food prepared by several local restaurants that all used Fernie's beer in the recipes.

There were too many great events to recount each one here, but another particularly good one comes to mind. In Powell River, Townsite Brewing decided to take the "revolution" theme to another level. First, they set up a throne for me made up of cases of beer, and then, figuring "What's a revolution without a little broken glass?" they set up a batting tee in the brewery (safely behind Plexiglas so the crowd of people could watch), placed a bottle of Budweiser on top, and encouraged everyone to take a swing with an aluminium baseball bat—protected from flying glass shards by a full-body rain suit and visored safety helmet, of course.

Everywhere I went with my book, I heard the same question: "When are you going to write a new version with all the new breweries in it?" For the first six months or so, I'd laugh and say, "Give me a break, this one just came out!" but I knew that with each new brewery that opened, the book was getting more and more out of date. So when 2014 arrived and I started to see just how big a year it was going to be, I told my publisher we needed to think about a revised edition, and the sooner the better. Pretty quickly, they agreed.

But revising this book was challenging: just to visit new breweries, let alone try to keep up with what was happening with the rest of them, including some very exciting places that were just getting going. And what about breweries that had been around for a while already? They deserved attention, too. And then there were the new breweries that had opened in places like Prince Rupert, Terrace, Quesnel and Valemount. A trip to visit each of those was a serious undertaking, one that I'll admit I was unable to accomplish before this book had to go to the printer. In the end, I wrote several brewery profiles in this book for places that I have not had the chance to visit in person, but in each case I interviewed the owners or brewers and did my best to taste some of their beer.

As the publishing deadline approached, I realized that although I had been visiting new breweries in and around Vancouver throughout the year, I still wasn't keeping up, especially with those outside the city. I needed to go on a blitz to get caught up. So, in the week leading up to the B.C. Beer Awards in Vancouver, I drove through the Lower Mainland, then up to Kamloops, down through the Okanagan and back through the Fraser Valley to Vancouver. All in all, I visited twenty-one breweries in five days, and came home with a trunk full of beer to sample.

This revised edition is up to date to the end of 2014, along with some breweries that were close enough to opening early in 2015 to be included, too. It contains profiles of ninety craft breweries, compared to the fifty covered in the first edition. Virtually every entry from the first book has been updated, and astute readers will also find several new essays and write-ups.

Thank you for joining me on this wild ride. It has been an exciting adventure so far, and it looks like it should continue to be a blast for a while yet.

Viva la Revolution!

Joe Wiebe
Victoria, B.C.
December 15, 2014

INTRODUCTION

Welcome to
the Revolution

••••••••••••••••••••••

BRITISH COLUMBIA'S CRAFT beer revolution began in 1982, in the tiny village of Horseshoe Bay, half an hour northwest of Vancouver, when a couple of persistent—one might even say stubborn—beer lovers built a small-scale brewery using old dairy equipment and began brewing an English-style mild ale for the Troller Pub across the street.

The Horseshoe Bay Brewery was Canada's first modern-day microbrewery. Its very creation went against the tide of the preceding seventy years. Until 1982, twentieth-century Canadian beer history was bleak: the Great War, Prohibition (yes, we did suffer from that malady, too, although not for as long as our American neighbours did), the Great Depression, and another world war squeezed much of the life out of the beer industry. In the post-war era, big breweries monopolized what was left, leaving consumers with almost no choice in what sort of beer they could drink: mainly it was yellow, fizzy and bland.

Although the Horseshoe Bay Brewery only survived for a few years, by building it, Frank Appleton and John Mitchell started a revolution. Since then, Canada's brewing landscape has changed radically and irrevocably. Governments have reformed archaic liquor laws and brewing regulations, often because tenacious brewers pushed them to do so. Where once it was nearly impossible to get anything other than a nearly flavourless version of Pilsner beer, there are now so many styles of beer available that many craft beer lovers are arguing for a return to simpler styles—like Pilsner.

The first twenty-five years of the microbrewing movement saw relatively steady growth. After the Horseshoe Bay Brewery broke the ice in 1982, there was an initial burst in 1984 with the arrival of three more breweries that are still flourishing today: Spinnakers, Granville Island Brewing and Vancouver Island Brewery (originally named Island Pacific Brewing). New breweries arrived in waves over the next two decades—and there were many closures, too, as start-up operations discovered the challenges associated with this nascent industry.

From an economic standpoint, craft beer has grown from nothing into a significant player in the marketplace—from about 6 per cent of the total beer market in B.C. in 2007 to 21 per cent in 2014. Sales in the sector have increased by $110 million over the past five years—more than $20 million per year on average. And much of this huge growth occurred during a so-called economic downturn. Today, small- and medium-sized breweries, producing less than 160,000 hL, account for almost $200 million in beer sales annually. By 2015, British Columbia will likely welcome its hundredth craft brewery.

The craft beer revolution has also spread beyond breweries and brewpubs to include restaurants and bars that are entirely focused on craft beer: so-called "taphouses" like the Alibi Room and St. Augustine's in Vancouver or the Churchill and Garrick's Head in Victoria that each have around fifty taps serving craft beer from the Pacific Northwest and Europe. Restaurants host beer-pairing dinners and hire certified cicerones (the beer equivalent of a wine sommelier). Beer festivals take place in Victoria, Penticton, Vancouver, Whistler and the Kootenays every year. Craft beer–focused tour operators have set up shop in Vancouver, and you can take a beer-themed bicycle tour in Victoria or Vancouver. Many private liquor stores have evolved into bottle shops that showcase craft beer above and beyond anything else, and there are several specialty distributors devoted to sourcing difficult-to-find craft beers from around the world.

If you don't know much about craft beer, you've come to the right place. This guidebook will get you started, and if you want to learn more, the community of beer lovers and brewers in British Columbia is very accessible and will happily welcome you into its fellowship. If you already consider yourself a hophead or a beer geek, then I hope you will learn something new from this book—perhaps an aspect of the history, an anecdote from a brewer, or even a beer you haven't tried yet.

Most of all, I hope this book will become dog-eared and beer-stained, its pages inked over with your own comments and tasting notes. Cheers.

WHAT IS CRAFT BEER ANYWAY?

The term "craft beer" is a brilliant piece of rebranding that was undertaken collectively by the entire microbrewing movement in North America. I have asked many different people—brewers, marketers and writers—who have been involved in the industry for decades when they first heard the term used, and most people point to the mid to late 1990s. Personally, I noticed it coming into vogue a little later than that, a few years after the turn of the millennium. Since then, it has expanded across North America and even beyond to the rest of the world.

This rebranding itself is a big part of the reason why craft beer has taken off in the way it has. Instead of "microbrewing" or "micro beer," which really just means small beer, the term "craft beer" carries much more meaning and value. By linking beer with the local food scene—something wineries thought to do a long time ago—craft brewers started to connect with vast new markets. The result has been a boon to the industry.

The original term, "microbrewery," comes from government

taxation law that divides the industry into groups based on their brewing capacity. Here in B.C., there is a three-tier system with micros coming in under 15,000 hL, a regional category that covers anything above that up to 150,000, and then everything else above that. (1 hectolitre, a commonly used measurement in brewing, is equal to 100 litres)

A craft brewery is a small-scale operation that produces less than 150,000 hL per year (or less than 1 million hL in the U.S.). The brewery must be independent, and it must be dedicated to brewing high-quality beer using only the best ingredients. Craft brewers are in business to make good beer, not just to sell a whack of it. As Garrett Oliver, the brewmaster at Brooklyn Brewery, writes in the *Oxford Companion to Beer*, "craft brewing universally involves boldly flavored beers coupled with a defiantly independent spirit."

When it comes down to it, you know it when you taste it.

A B.C. CRAFT BEER ODYSSEY

Over the course of two decades living in Victoria and Vancouver, I visited most of the craft breweries near those cities long before I started working on this book. As a freelance beer writer for newspapers and magazines, I travelled to many different communities to visit breweries for stories. And as I began writing the first edition of this book, I set out to visit the remaining B.C. breweries I'd never been to before. I undertook a big road trip around the bottom half of the province, what I called my Craft Beer Odyssey. I love driving, so the chance to drive across the province and back was a thrill for me, even if my schedule was jam-packed without much time to sightsee or spend more than a day in any one place. I drove 2,364 kilometres in a clockwise loop from Vancouver up through Squamish to Lillooet, then across through Kamloops, Sorrento, Salmon Arm and Revelstoke, down to Invermere, Fairmont Hot Springs and Fernie, and then back east to Nelson, Robson and Osoyoos before returning home to Victoria. In eight days I visited six breweries and three brewpubs, one winery, one hop farm and one craft beer–focused pub. I also went for one horseback ride (my first ever), relaxed in a hot spring, swam in a lake, and took the longest free ferry in North America, which crosses Kootenay Lake just east of Nelson.

I found even more evidence of the strong growth of the craft beer industry in B.C. than I was hoping for—many of the places I visited are smaller, somewhat isolated communities, so I wasn't sure if the burgeoning success the industry was enjoying in Greater Vancouver, the central Okanagan and Vancouver Island would be reflected in those places as well. But whether it was Kamloops, Revelstoke, Fernie or Nelson, the story was the same: local consumers were embracing craft beer like never before and the breweries were doing all they could just to keep up with demand.

B.C. is truly a spectacular province, even more so now with so many craft beer communities to seek out. Use this book to plan a beer-soaked adventure of your own. I'm sure you will not be disappointed.

THE THIRSTY WRITER

I began to develop a thirst for beer while living with my parents in Niagara-on-the-Lake, Ontario, in the mid-1980s. Surprise, surprise: most of my teenage beer drinking involved illicitly procured Molson or Labatt products. But luckily there were a few influences in my young life that inspired my interest in what was then the brand-new microbrewing movement.

One was my older brother, Pete, who had developed an interest in British and German beers while travelling and working overseas. When he visited from Toronto we'd often go out to see a movie, including a pre-show pint or two at a British pub next to the movie theatre—although I was only seventeen or eighteen, I never seemed to get asked for ID when I was there with my older brother. I remember enjoying the richer flavours of Bass, Double Diamond and Smithwick's, and was proud to take my own friends there later when we were all of age.

Another influence was my friend Ken, who learned home

brewing from his uncle. While still in high school, he actually arranged for a teacher to take him and a couple of his buddies, me included, on a field trip to a microbrewery—Wellington County Brewing in Guelph. This amazes me today since we were all underage, but the teacher must have seen the value of this for Ken. It certainly paid off since Ken went on to study brewing in Germany and then worked as a professional brewer in Canada and the United States for fifteen years.

Most craft beer aficionados have a "conversion moment," an event or episode in their life when they discovered craft beer and became hooked on it. Mine occurred on a backpacking trip to Europe with another buddy, Glen, in the spring of 1991 when Ken was studying in Germany. Glen and I landed in Frankfurt, found the train to Freiburg, and then walked with already-too-heavy packs to Ken's *Studentenwohnheim* (student residence). Ken took us to a pub and ordered three bottles of beer—something called Hefeweizen, which I'd never heard of back in Canada. Before he allowed us to taste it, however, he showed us the proper way to pour it. He carefully tilted the bottle so that the amber liquid flowed down the side of the tall, curvy glass. He stopped before the bottle was empty, leaving a couple of inches of beer in the bottom. Then he did something crazy: he turned the bottle on its side and rolled it back and forth on the top of the bar, stirring up the dregs at the bottom of the bottle. Finally, he poured the lees over the beer in the glass, leaving the cloudy yeast in suspension in the beer itself and a two-inch head of foam on top.

As interesting as this demonstration was, that wasn't my moment of epiphany. My first sip of the Hefeweizen was. I'd never seen or tasted anything like it before: yellowish-orange and cloudy with a thick, creamy head on top, effervescent almost like champagne, and with a fruity banana, bubble-gum flavour. I loved it immediately. That moment transformed me forever—suddenly I didn't just want to drink beer, I wanted to sample it in all its different forms. It was a revelation.

And that's what Glen and I did over the next eight weeks, all over Europe and the UK, often forgoing proper meals so that we could try another pint of beer instead. I can still remember, even taste, so many of them. Black beer in a pub next to the Charles Bridge in Prague. Guinness at the seven-hundred-year-old Brazen Head Pub in Dublin. Creamy Austrian lager in litre steins in a Salzburg castle cellar. A nondescript lager in a train station somewhere in France—the half-pints were so expensive we decided the glasses they came in must be included in the price and stuffed them in our backpacks. A long row of draught handles in a pub in Edinburgh with numbers for names (60/-, 70/-, 80/-), which we found out was traditionally based on the price in shillings of a hogshead of the beer in question—we tried them all. And on our final evening in London, pooling our few remaining coins for one last shared pint—we flew home from Heathrow the next morning with just a few pence in our pockets.

I moved to Victoria a few months after my trip to Europe, and after arriving here, I began exploring B.C.'s nascent microbrewing scene. I loved discovering a new brewery or brewpub, and I have always been on the lookout for something new at the liquor store. But I didn't seriously think about being a beer writer until I was walking through California's Sonoma vineyards for a travel story for the *Vancouver Sun* in 2008. I was there with a dozen wine writers. On the second night, they staged an intervention of sorts: I guess they'd had enough of me talking about beer all the time, so they sat me down and told me that I should do what they did—except I should write about beer. It seems obvious in retrospect, but it was as if a light went on in my head. From then on, while it hasn't been the only thing I write about, beer has increasingly become the focus of my stories. I branded myself as the Thirsty Writer and didn't look back.

The next step in that evolution is the book you are holding in your hands, now in its second edition. Hopefully, it will benefit from the knowledge I have gleaned in my quest for beer over the past twenty-five years or so. Thanks for joining me on this journey. May your thirst, like mine, be unquenchable.

GLOSSARY OF TERMS

••••••••••••••••••••••••

THERE ARE A few acronyms and terms in this book with which some readers may not be familiar. If you know them all already, consider yourself a certified beer geek. Otherwise, here are some definitions.

ABV
This stands for "alcohol by volume," the typical way alcohol in beer is labelled. The most common beer styles (Pilsners, pale ales, wheat beers, ESBs, etc.) generally average 5 per cent ABV, while IPAs and many stronger Belgian styles may range from 6 to 8 per cent ABV. Heavier imperial porters, stouts, barley or wheat wines and Belgian "quads" might top out over 10 per cent ABV.

ale
In its current definition, ale refers to a class of beers made using the top-fermenting yeast *Saccharomyces cerevisiae*, as opposed to lagers that use a bottom-fermenting yeast. There are dozens of styles of beer running the gamut of flavours and descriptions that all might be considered ales, from pale ales to porters, Saisons to stouts, and Hefeweizens to Belgian abbey ales. The word ale came into the English language from the Danish word "*öl*." Prior to the sixteenth century, British brewers disdained the use of hops and referred to foreign brews that did use hops as "beer," calling their own version made without hops "ale."

barrel aging

Craft brewers age certain beers in barrels for months or years before bottling, imparting flavours from the wood into the beer itself. Strong styles like barley wines and imperial stouts or porters are often aged in bourbon barrels, for instance. Sour beer producers use wine barrels that are infected with Brettanomyces yeast to purposefully sour their beers.

bomber

This is the colloquial name for the 650 mL bottle, which has become the standard size for single bottle sales in the North American craft beer industry. Craft breweries usually put their core brands in six-packs and their more unusual seasonal or limited release beers in bombers.

Brettanomyces

Brettanomyces ("Brett" for short) is a genus of yeast often referred to as "wild yeast" because of its ability to spoil conventional beer, and because of the characteristically funky flavours and aromas it can generate. It is purposefully used by Belgian Lambic brewers—indeed, the strain they use, *Brettanomyces bruxellensis*, is named for them. Conventional brewers live in fear of a Brett infection in their brewery, as it can ruin entire batches, but craft brewers are using it more and more to create Brett-conditioned IPAs, Saisons and other Belgian styles.

CAMRA

The Campaign for Real Ale was founded in the UK in 1971 and in B.C. in 1985. There are five regional branches in B.C.: Victoria, Vancouver, Powell River, the Fraser Valley and the South Fraser. (See "Getting Involved" on page 244.)

ESB

This stands for Extra Special Bitter, a popular British ale style that is also often referred to simply as "bitter."

growler

Growlers are 1.9-litre (half-gallon) refillable bottles that resemble mini moonshine jugs and can be refilled at many craft breweries and brewpubs in B.C.

Hefeweizen

A German wheat ale, usually cloudy with suspended yeast, that has an effervescent body and a fruity banana, bubble-gum aroma and flavour. Perfect on a summer patio.

hops

Hops are the flowers or cones of *Humulus lupus*, a climbing vine that grow vigorously up to fifteen metres tall. There are dozens of different varieties of hops, which are divided generally into two groups: bittering and aroma. Bittering hops are added early in the brewing process, as the wort (unfermented beer) is boiled, while aroma hops are added toward the end of the boil. Adding aroma hops to the fermented beer later on is called "dry hopping," and this results in a highly aromatic and flavourful hop character.

IBU

This stands for "international bitterness units," which is a measurement of the saturation of the alpha acids derived from hops in beer. Although it is not officially a scale out of 100, there is a theoretical saturation limit of 110, and anything past 100 cannot really be discerned by the human palate.

IPA

India Pale Ale—originally an English ale style that was brewed for export to British subjects living in India—it became very popular in the late nineteenth century and then lost its appeal when Pilsner lagers gained international prominence. Craft brewers began reimagining the style in the 1980s and 1990s, using hops grown in the Pacific Northwest that exhibit extreme bitterness as well as potent pine and citrus flavours and aromas. It has since become the flagship craft beer style by which breweries are often compared.

lager

As with ale, lager is a generic term for a class of beers made using a bottom-fermenting yeast (*Saccharomyces pastorianus*), which is best fermented at cooler temperatures than ale yeasts. In a general sense, lagers are considered cleaner and crisper than ales because the yeast tends to ferment more completely and produce fewer fermentation byproducts. The word comes from the German verb *lagern*, which means "to store" because lagers take longer to ferment than ales and had to be "lagered" in cold caverns during the warm spring and summer months prior to mechanized refrigeration. Today, 90 per cent of the beer consumed in the world is lager, primarily the generic international Pilsner style brewed in mass quantities all around the world.

Pilsner

What we now call Pilsner was originally an attempt by a Czech brewer in Plzen to re-create the brown lagers made in neighbouring Bavaria, but using Bohemian ingredients. The resulting happy accident was a new, golden lager with a sweet, malty body and an assertive floral, grassy hop character. The style caught on and eventually took the world by storm.

Saison

The French word for "season," this Belgian "farmhouse ale" style is very dry, highly carbonated, and fruity (thanks to the Belgian yeast). It is usually bottle-conditioned (refermented in the bottle), which can result in a cloudy appearance and sediment in the bottle. It can range from 5 per cent to 8 per cent ABV with a hop bitterness range of 20–40 IBUs. Delicious and refreshing.

sour beers

Prior to automated refrigeration and modern sanitation, most beers probably had some sour character or turned sour fairly quickly after fermentation, especially in warmer months when bacteria and wild yeasts were at their busiest. Certain intentionally sour beer styles, however, were developed in Belgium (Lambic, Oud Bruin, Flanders red) and Germany (Berliner Weisse), and have been embraced by contemporary craft brewers. Brewers usually employ *Lactobacillus* and *Pediococcus* bacteria to create acidity, and Brettanomyces (wild yeast), which contributes a range of pungent flavours and aromas, and can eliminate some undesirable off-flavours generated by the bacteria. Sour beers are generally aged for several months or years, often in oak barrels infected with Brettanomyces, with different batches or vintages carefully blended by the brewer to create the final product.

taphouse

These pubs with multiple taps (usually at least twenty, but often as many as forty or fifty) are ideal for craft beer lovers because of the variety they offer. Taphouses often sell sets of four sampler glasses, which give customers the opportunity to try different beers without having to buy a whole pint (or sleeve or glass) of each one.

Wit/white ale

Cloudy and effervescent, this is the Belgian equivalent of a German Hefeweizen, but the Belgian yeast imparts more of a spicy character that is often enhanced by brewers adding bitter orange peel, coriander or other spices.

SEA-TO-SKY

AT THE BREWERY	DRAFT	FOOD	GROWLERS	BOTTLES	TOURS	BEDS
Black Kettle Brewing	✪		✪	✪		
BrewHouse High Mountain Brewery	✪	✪	✪			
Bridge Brewing	✪		✪	✪		
Deep Cove Brewing & Distilling			✪	✪		
Green Leaf Brewing	✪	✪	✪	✪		
Hearthstone Brewery	✪	✪	✪	✪		
Howe Sound Brewing	✪	✪		✪		✪
Whistler Brewing			✪	✪	✪	

CRADLE OF THE
REVOLUTION

• •

I DECIDED TO open this guidebook with the Sea-to-Sky region because it is home to the town of Horseshoe Bay, where the craft beer revolution began in 1982. Although the Horseshoe Bay Brewery is no longer in existence, the region still represents a good starting point—for both the craft beer novice and the grizzled veteran who thinks he or she knows everything about beer already.

Sea-to-Sky refers to the highway that runs from North Vancouver up to Whistler. It's a rugged, winding route that is exhilarating to drive when it isn't bumper-to-bumper, but it can also be a dangerous road, especially in winter conditions. This is a region for all-season outdoor enthusiasts: you can hike, bike, climb, camp, dive, kayak, canoe, snowshoe, ski or board to your heart's content. And then when you've tired yourself out, you can relax with a great local beer.

The Sea-to-Sky region includes some of B.C.'s oldest and newest breweries. Whistler Brewing dates back, in various ownership configurations, to 1989, and Howe Sound Brewing in Squamish was established in the mid-'90s. Squamish, the midway point between Vancouver and Whistler, was also home to the Tall Ship Ales company, a brewery that was greatly respected for its high quality and innovation—they brewed the first bottled India Pale Ale in B.C. that I am aware of. Sadly, that company didn't survive, but its brewer, Bill Herdman, recently resurfaced in the industry, working with North Vancouver's Green Leaf Brewing for a time.

In the first edition of this book, I wrote that "North and West Vancouver seem primed for a brewing explosion." Well, I certainly got that one right. Since then, four more breweries have joined Bridge Brewing on the North Shore, and Bridge itself outgrew its original nano-sized operation, expanding into a bigger location. The opening of the Red Truck brewery in Vancouver led the Mark James Group to sell its brewery in the old Taylor's Crossing brewpub to the owners of the Mission Springs brewpub, who are using it to launch the Hearthstone Brewery there.

The craft beer scene in Whistler has improved immensely over the past couple of years, thanks in part to the Whistler Village Beer Festival, which was launched in 2013 (see "Whistler Village Beer Festival" on page 22). While it used to be virtually impossible to find good craft beer outside of the BrewHouse, you can now find a good range of options on tap or by the bottle at many of the village's bars and restaurants.

And although there is no brewery above Whistler, at least not yet, there is good incentive beyond the spectacular scenery for beer lovers to drive the circle route north through Pemberton and Lillooet and then east to Kamloops. Pemberton Distillery is an interesting and unique place to visit, and Lillooet is home to the biggest organic hop farm in B.C., the one-time Bitterbine Hop Farm, now known as Harvesters of Organic Hops (HOOH), which is supplying several small B.C. breweries with its harvest bounty.

Clearly, the Sea-to-Sky region has a lot going on in terms of craft beer. The only thing left for me to wish for is for B.C.'s craft beer revolution to come full circle with a new brewery in Horseshoe Bay. Maybe if we dream it, it will happen.

blackkettlebrewing.com
604-987-9989
Unit 106-720 Copping Street,
  North Vancouver
E-MAIL
  info@blackkettlebrewing.com

Black Kettle Brewing

||||||||||||||||||||||||||||||||||||||||||||||

Tap List

PALE ALE
5.4% ABV
A basic pale ale that won't
blow your mind.

IPA
6.4% ABV | 58 IBU
A basic malt-forward IPA
without much of a hop
profile.

PART OF A wave of five new breweries on the
North Shore, Black Kettle is, unfortunately,
the least interesting. It is a bit hard to find,
and even when you do, the beer probably will
not turn you into a return customer.

Black Kettle grew out of home brewing
dreams of two friends who worked on their
recipes on a half-barrel brewing system for
two years before making the leap to a full-
fledged brewery with a ten-barrel system. So
far, the brewery has produced two basic core
beers, simply named Pale Ale and IPA, and
some seasonals, similarly titled Wheat Ale,
Scotch Ale, Porter and Oatmeal Stout. Products are available as growler fills or 650 mL
bombers at the brewery.

The brewery's no-frills approach to naming and labelling might seem refreshing in
a market that is so saturated with clever
names and eye-catching designs, but the
beer inside is decidedly no-frills, too. That
said, Black Kettle is still very new so I hope I
will be rewriting this description very soon!

Facts & Figures

OPENED ▸ *2014* ✪ **STYLES PRODUCED ▸** *2 + seasonals* ✪
WHERE TO BUY ▸ *The brewery or private liquor stores in Greater
Vancouver* ✪ **ON TAP ▸** *North Vancouver and Vancouver* ✪
GROWLERS ▸ *Yes*

BrewHouse
High Mountain
Brewing Company ←

mjg.ca/brewhouseouse
604-905-2739
4355 Blackcomb Way, Whistler
E-MAIL brewhouse@shaw.ca

||||||||||||||||||||||||||||||||||||||||||||

THE BREWHOUSE CONTINUES to be the best place to enjoy craft beer in Whistler Village. Many of the village's pubs and restaurants have expanded their tap lists beyond Guinness and the usual industrial lagers to include craft beer, but nothing beats the quality and freshness of the beers carefully produced by Derrick Franche at the brewpub.

One of Derrick's strengths is cask conditioning, a skill he honed while working at Dix brewpub in Vancouver before it closed in 2010. He taps a special cask on the last Wednesday of every month and often contributes casks to seasonal festivals, such as Central City's winter and summer cask events.

The BrewHouse is part of the Mark James Group chain that includes Yaletown Brewing in Vancouver and Big Ridge Brewing Co. in Surrey. It has a prime location in Whistler, right next to the Olympic Plaza, and is divided into a family-friendly restaurant with a big outdoor patio right on the Village Stroll, and a pub side perfectly suited for après ski, après bike, après hike or après shopping if that's as active as you get. No judgments here.

Tap List

5 RINGS IPA
7% ABV | 60 IBU
Go for gold with this Olympic-calibre IPA. Winner of Beer of the Year at the 2012 B.C. Beer Awards and Best IPA in 2014.

BIG WOLF BITTER
5.4% ABV | 30 IBU
This is an ESB in the finest British tradition—creamy and bittersweet with caramel tones in the background.

Facts & Figures

OPENED ▸ *1997* ✪ STYLES PRODUCED ▸ *5 + seasonals* ✪ ON TAP ▸ *The brewpub* ✪ GROWLERS ▸ *Yes*

WHISTLER VILLAGE
BEER FESTIVAL
Held in Whistler every September

••••••••••••••••••••••••

THE WHISTLER VILLAGE Beer Festival launched in 2013, but I missed it the first time as I was visiting Bellingham, Washington, for its own Beer Week festival (which was excellent, by the way).

I made it to Whistler for the second annual festival in 2014, and I was really impressed. The organizer asked me to participate in its educational component so I hosted a seminar on B.C.'s Craft Beer Revolution (complete with six beer samples signifying different important points over the past three decades). And then I was free to enjoy the rest of the four-day festival, which included a variety of beer dinners, tap takeovers and cask nights held in various venues throughout Whistler Village.

The main event is the Saturday afternoon beer festival held outside at the Whistler Olympic Plaza, with more than fifty breweries from B.C. and the rest of the world ready and willing to serve their beers.

Even though September isn't ski season, Whistler has many other activities to enjoy outside of the beer festival itself, including mountain biking, hiking, golfing, visiting spas and, of course, shopping. Personally, I recommend checking out the Peak-to-Peak Gondola to clear your head on Saturday morning before the big beer fest.

www.wvbf.ca

Bridge Brewing

bridgebrewing.com
604-770-brew (2739)
1448 Charlotte Road,
    North Vancouver (new location)
E-MAIL info@bridgebrewing.com

||||||||||||||||||||||||||||||||||||||||||

BRIDGE BREWING'S STORY stands as a prototypical example of how to succeed in
the craft beer industry in B.C. Founded by
the husband-and-wife team of Jason and
Leigh Stratton in the summer of 2012, the
company opened as a nanobrewery in a
nondescript industrial park near the Iron-
workers Memorial Bridge, with Patrick Doré,
an elite chef Leigh had met while working at
a hotel, as the initial brewer.

Since then, Bridge has expanded considerably, first by adding bottle sales to private
liquor stores, and then by moving the brewery
to a bigger location with a higher-capacity
brewing system and expanding the staff to
eight people. The new location has a proper
tasting room—a big improvement on the
original's, which was so small that visitors
basically had to hang out in the brewery itself.
Doré has opted to return to cooking, so a new
brewer, Jeremy Taylor, has taken his place.

And the original brewing equipment has
been reincarnated in a way—the Rossland
Beer Company bought it for its new start-
up. Hopefully that company will have just as
good a story to tell a few years from now.

Tap List

NORTH SHORE PALE ALE
5.5% ABV | 27 IBU
A tasty Northwest-style
pale ale, well balanced with
a nice hop bite over top of a
solid malt base.

HOPILANO IPA (seasonal)
6% ABV | 59 IBU
This West Coast IPA is
definitely worth braving the
bridge traffic for.

Facts & Figures

OPENED › 2012
STYLES PRODUCED ›
    2 + seasonals
WHERE TO BUY › The
    brewery or private
    liquor stores in the
    Lower Mainland and
    Victoria
ON TAP › Greater
    Vancouver and Victoria
GROWLERS › Yes

deepcovecraft.com
604-770-1136
Unit 170–2270 Dollarton Highway,
  North Vancouver
E-MAIL info@deepcovecraft.com
TWITTER @DeepCoveCraft

Deep Cove Brewers & Distillers

Tap List

LOUD MOUTH PALE ALE

5.5% ABV | 56 IBU

A solid pale ale with a big
Northwest hop profile—
malt and juicy fruit in
perfect balance.

STAR STRUCK RYE IPA

7% ABV | 82 IBU

This was one of the earliest
rye IPAs on the B.C. market
and it continues to be one
of the best. It has tropical
citrus hop notes over a
spicy, toasty rye malt base.

Facts & Figures

OPENED ▸ *2013*
STYLES PRODUCED ▸
  5 + seasonals
WHERE TO BUY ▸ *The
  brewery or private
  liquor stores*
ON TAP ▸ *North
  Vancouver and Greater
  Vancouver*
GROWLERS ▸ *Yes*

||||||||||||||||||||||||||||||||||||||||||||||

DEEP COVE OPENED in the summer of 2013,
kitty-corner from Bridge Brewing's original
location but with a much more attractive
roadside location meant to draw in passersby
to its tasting room and growler station. The
brewery hosts live music events there and
invites food trucks to park outside, encouraging customers to hang out into the evening.

The brewery is partly owned by the Gib-
bons Hospitality Group, the folks who put on
the Whistler Village Beer Festival. It also has
a distillery on site, which has been producing
vodka and gin thus far, along with limited
batches of absinthe and a unique product
called Hilda, which is a brandy made from
distilled beer and aged in oak barrels for
nine months. The result is similar to rye
whiskey, apparently.

Kevin Emms, Deep Cove's original
brewmaster, moved on to Granville Island
Brewing midway through 2015. Brett Jamie-
son replaced him; he had already been
running the distillery side of things.

Late in 2015, it looked like Deep Cove was
finally getting its lounge endorsement, which
would allow it sell beer by the glass in its very
attractive tasting room.

Green Leaf Brewing ←

greenleafbrew.com
604-984-8409
123 Carrie Cates Court, Lonsdale
Quay, North Vancouver
E-MAIL
martin@greenleafbrew.com
TWITTER @greenleafbrew

||||||||||||||||||||||||||||||||||||||||

GREEN LEAF BREWING'S location just inside Lonsdale Quay as you enter from the SeaBus Terminal is about as good as it gets. Think of all the commuters who walk by in the morning and then dream about the beer all day, making them as thirsty as desert wanderers by the time they are on their return commute home. Cha-ching!

My first taste of Green Leaf's beer came before I actually visited the brewery, thanks to a friendly beer blogger who brought me some samples (thanks Mike). I was quite surprised by the diverse range of beers, each one progressively more challenging and interesting than the last. I became even more interested when I visited the brewery and met the brewer, Bill Herdman, who had previously founded Tall Ship Ales, a Squamish brewery that operated in the mid-1990s and is now seen as having been ahead of its time. Bill has since moved on but Green Leaf continues to brew interesting beers that stand out from the crowd.

The brewery opened an outdoor patio in the spring of 2015, which definitely makes the SeaBus trip from Vancouver even more enticing.

Tap List

LES SAISONNIERS
5% ABV | 25 IBU
A little darker than many other Saisons, this one is made with the benchmark Dupont Saison yeast and black pepper, lemon zest and coriander, which gives it a great zing to go along with the yeast character.

ANIMAL FARM IPA
7.4% ABV | 67 IBU
A bit messy thanks to a mix of yeasts including the ones used in the Saison, but the result is a unique hybrid Belgian IPA.

....

Facts & Figures

OPENED ▸ *2013*
STYLES PRODUCED ▸
2 + seasonals
WHERE TO BUY ▸ *The brewery or private liquor stores*
ON TAP ▸ *North Vancouver*
GROWLERS ▸ *Yes*

hearthstonebrewery.ca
604-984-1842
1015 Marine Drive,
   North Vancouver
E-MAIL
   info@hearthstonebrewery.ca
TWITTER @hearthstonebeer

Hearthstone Brewery

Tap List

HAZELNUT PORTER

5% ABV | 18 IBU

The hazelnut character is
subtle, not overwhelming,
giving this porter a
nice sweetness that is
reminiscent of a milk stout
along with roasty coffee
notes.

BOHEMIAN PILS

5% ABV | 20 IBU

I love a well-made Pilsner
and that's exactly what it
is: malty, hoppy, dry, crisp
and complex—in other
words, delicious.

Facts & Figures

OPENED ▸ *2015*
STYLES PRODUCED ▸
   5 + seasonals
WHERE TO BUY ▸ *At the
   brewery*
ON TAP ▸ *At the brewery
   and pubs in Greater
   Vancouver*
GROWLERS ▸ *Yes*

|||||||||||||||||||||||||||||||||||||||||||||||

YOU MIGHT RECOGNIZE the location of this new
brewery as Taylor's Crossing brewpub, which
operated there from 2004 to 2011. The Mark
James Group continued to use the facility to
brew its Red Truck line, but following the
construction of the Red Truck brewery in
Vancouver in 2014, it sold the North Vancouver operation to the owners of the Mission
Springs brewpub, who have opened Hearthstone Brewery there as an independent
offshoot. It is not officially a brewpub, but
rather a brewery with an attached taproom
and pizza restaurant.

Darren Hollett moved over from Mission
Springs and is working with George Woods,
who was a brewer with Scotland's notoriously rebellious brewers, BrewDogs. It will
be interesting to see how much of that brewery's "bad boy" style carries over with him.
Early on, Hearthstone's marketing certainly
is irreverent, as reflected in this description
of its Graham Cracker Ale, which explains
how graham crackers were created by a
Presbyterian minister trying to stave off
"unhealthy carnal urges"—masturbation.
"Google it," they write. "We couldn't make
this sh*t up if we tried."

Howe Sound Brewing

howesound.com
604-892-2603
37801 Cleveland Avenue,
  Squamish
E-MAIL
  hsibrew@howesound.com
TWITTER @howesoundbeer

||||||||||||||||||||||||||||||||||||||||||||||

JUST AS THE sheer rock face of the granite monolith known as the Stawamus Chief towers above the town of Squamish, one hour north of Vancouver, Howe Sound Brewing stands out in the B.C. landscape of craft beers—at least their unique, one-litre "potstopper" bottles do.

When siblings David and Leslie Fenn opened this brewpub, restaurant and inn in 1996, they thought it would be a case of "If we build it, they will come," but Leslie acknowledges it was a tough go at first. "The tourism scene wasn't here yet," she admits. But these early adaptors persisted, and as tourists began discovering this mecca of outdoor activities (and Vancouverites began noticing the low cost of housing), Howe Sound Brewing was ready to serve beer to them all.

The Fenns conscripted B.C. brewing legend John Mitchell, who lives relatively nearby in North Vancouver, to help design the brewhouse. Mitchell also developed their original recipes and still keeps his hand in the mix, dropping by every Friday to poke his nose in and point out to Leslie and the brewing staff what they're doing wrong. I say this with complete affection for John, but it's absolutely true! (See "John Mitchell" on page 29.)

In 2001, provincial rules that had kept

Tap List

BALDWIN & COOPER BEST BITTER
5.5% ABV | 52 IBU
John Mitchell's own recipe, this is a pitch-perfect ESB.

KING HEFFY IMPERIAL HEFEWEIZEN
7.7% ABV | 25 IBU
Like a picture of a solid German Hefeweizen seen with 3-D glasses, this beer explodes with flavour.

TROLLER BAY ALE
5% ABV | 25 IBU
This is a chance to taste B.C.'s original craft beer— John Mitchell's original recipe from the Horseshoe Bay Brewery.

TOTAL ECLIPSE OF THE HOP IMPERIAL IPA (seasonal)
8% ABV | 90 IBU
An incredible beer—not for the faint of heart, but definitely for the hophead!

brewpubs from selling their beer off-premises were loosened, and Howe Sound responded quickly by making its beer available on draft throughout the Lower Mainland. The company began bottling in their distinctive flip-top bottles in 2007, and grabbed attention among craft beer lovers with a wide range of offerings, surprising considering the limited size of their brewhouse. Thus far, Howe Sound has released more than thirty different beers, including obscure styles (Berliner Weisse), political critiques (Bailout Bitter), and cheeky brands such as the Three Beavers Imperial Red Ale that skated close to Olympic trademark restrictions with a label that showed off gold, silver and bronze medals won at brewing competitions draped around the necks of ultra-Canadian beavers.

Brewmaster Franco Corno has built off of Mitchell's original recipes and applied his own personal touch, which often leans toward the "imperialization" or amplification of traditional styles, as he has done very successfully with the King Heffy Imperial Hefeweizen, Total Eclipse of the Hop Imperial IPA, Pumpkineater Imperial Pumpkin Ale, and Pothole Filler Imperial Stout, all of which top out above 7.5 per cent ABV and offer big, robust flavour profiles.

That said, don't skip out on Howe Sound's regular brews in favour of trying the monster imperials—Mitchell's original bitter recipe, Baldwin & Cooper Best Bitter, is worth the trip to Squamish alone. For that matter, I do recommend going to the brewpub in person. Stay overnight, enjoy a meal in the restaurant and a nightcap at the pub listening to a local band. Wake up to the incredible views of the Chief, maybe even go for a climb or a hike, and then buy some bottles to bring home with you. Howe Sound is one of B.C.'s top craft beer getaways.

Facts & Figures

OPENED ▸ 1996 ○ STYLES PRODUCED ▸ 7 + seasonals ○
WHERE TO BUY ▸ Liquor stores throughout B.C. and at the brewery ○
ON TAP ▸ Throughout B.C. ○ GROWLERS ▸ No

JOHN MITCHELL

The Grandfather of Craft Beer
in British Columbia

••••••••••••••••••••••••

JOHN MITCHELL IS a crotchety curmudgeon. There is simply no
better way to describe him, except perhaps in his own words,
"A bloody, brainless fool," as he referred to himself several times
during our conversation at Howe Sound Brewing in August
2012, on the first day of my Craft Beer Odyssey.

At eighty-two years of age, having accomplished what he
has, much of it through sheer dogged determination, it's not
surprising he is cantankerous in his twilight years. But he also
has a great affection for Howe Sound, his "local," which he visits every Friday, as well as its co-owner and CEO, Leslie Fenn.
She treats him like visiting royalty every time and has seemingly infinite patience with him, even when he is critiquing the
beer and *tsking* over its serving temperatures after testing it
with the thermometer he carries in his shirt pocket.

Mitchell's beer of choice, a Baldwin & Cooper ESB, his original recipe when he set up the brewery there back in 1996, is
delicious: a pitch-perfect bitter, one of the best examples of the
style you'll find in B.C. And he still likes it, too—once it has
warmed up to "proper cellar temperature," that is.

Born in England, Mitchell trained as a chef at the Mayfair
Hotel in post-war London. He also spent three months working
in the cellar there, delivering Worthington's White Shield beer
to the various pubs, restaurants and dining rooms throughout
the hotel. This was bottle-conditioned beer that had to rest in
the cellar for forty-eight hours after delivery.

"You had to handle them like bloody bombs," Mitchell says.

That was when he first began to understand the idea of real beer as being alive. "For my pleasure, Stan the cellar man, bless his heart, would give me a bottle every day. That, to me, was the Rolls Royce of beer. I've never forgotten it."

Bottle-conditioned beer in England, though once the standard, has pretty much gone the way of the dodo, but thankfully, Mitchell's early experience with it contributed to the renaissance in "real beer" production he helped ignite in Canada some thirty years later.

When he immigrated to Canada in 1954, Mitchell says, "I thought I'd stepped back into Prohibition." The beer scene was horrible then, he says, with essentially no choice between the three dominant brewers, Carling, Labatt and Molson.

In 1978, Mitchell had been the bar manager at the Sylvia Hotel in Vancouver's West End for fifteen years when he and a neighbour had the opportunity to take over the Troller Pub in Horseshoe Bay, where he lived. Back then, he says, the liquor board assigned pubs one of the three big breweries to ensure balance between them, and the Troller was arbitrarily connected with Carling.

When brewery workers went on strike in 1979, "There was no beer in the middle of the summer," for several weeks. The Troller was forced to serve cider until the liquor board finally brought in Olympia Beer from the U.S. "I was so incensed," he says.

Remembering the beer culture he grew up in back in Britain, Mitchell "went on a pilgrimage" to the only four remaining traditional brewpubs in England in 1980. Back in B.C., he persuaded his business partners that they should build their own brewery. They grudgingly agreed to let him pursue it, but first he had to persuade Allan Gould, the manager of the Liquor Distribution Board.

As Mitchell puts it, he "ranted and raved" at Gould for forty-five minutes, expecting to be turfed out with a simple no afterwards, but instead, he says Gould's response was, "Well, John, I've been trying to think of reasons to turn you down and

I haven't thought of one. Now you have to put a proposal in to the minister."

Mitchell submitted his application in May 1981. As fortune would have it, the minister, Peter Hyndman, was already frustrated with apparent collusion between the three big national breweries, and he likely saw Mitchell's request as a positive PR opportunity. When one of the breweries raised its prices slightly that summer and the other two dutifully followed suit, Hyndman had had enough. According to Mitchell, the minister pulled out his proposal in front of reporters and said he was going to allow it. Mitchell first heard about it from a CBC reporter who called him up to ask about the new brewery, and then he received a call from Gould who told him he had to build his brewery now.

Knowing nothing about brewing, Mitchell turned to Frank Appleton, another British ex-pat who had written an article in *Harrowsmith* about brewing. Appleton had worked at Carling-O'Keefe's for several years before quitting over the inferior quality of the beers. Mitchell managed to persuade Appleton to join him in Horseshoe Bay and the two put together the rudimentary brewery using dairy equipment for about $35,000. They had to put the brewery in a separate building from the pub—federal law required it to be at least a roadway away.

His partners, aghast at the price tag, asked him how much beer they'd have to sell to break even. He thought one keg a day would cover it, but they were only selling two kegs of Carling per day at best.

The beer they brewed—arguably the first modern-day craft beer brewed in Canada—was Bay Ale, a British mild modelled after Fuller's London Pride. Mitchell says he delivered eight kegs to the pub on the first day. They sold seven. Now his partners insisted he had to brew a lot more, but the tiny brewery could only manage to produce thirty kegs per week, which meant the pub could only sell five per day, since it was open six days a week.

They rarely managed to keep up with demand. On one memorable evening, a soccer team from Richmond decided to hire a bus "to go to Horseshoe Bay for a decent pint." They showed up at 7:00 PM, but that day's five kegs were gone already so the team was out of luck.

Mitchell says the brewery paid back its $35,000 cost in just twelve weeks and was making the pub $500 per day in clear profit. He brewed all the beer for a while, but after a series of disagreements with his partners, he left at the end of 1982 to join Paul Hadfield and another business partner in setting up a new brewpub on the waterfront in Victoria. That was Spinnakers, which opened in 1984 and is still thriving today while the Horseshoe Bay Brewery only lasted for a few years.

Having learned his lesson with the cobbled-together brewing equipment he'd made do with at Horseshoe Bay, Mitchell bought a proper system from England for Spinnakers. He brewed four beers to start: Spinnakers Ale, a light ale meant for mainstream drinkers; Mitchell's ESB, which is still being served there today; Mt. Tolmie Dark Ale and Empress Stout. The brewpub was a big hit and continues to be to this day. In the 1988 edition of his *New World Guide to Beer*, famed British beer critic Michael Jackson describes Mitchell's ESB as "beautifully balanced," the Mt. Tolmie Dark as "a classic strong mild, of which Britain should be envious," and the Empress Stout as "a model of the style."

Unfortunately, Mitchell had another falling-out with this set of business partners and left Spinnakers after two and a half years. It must be said that he was probably not the easiest person to get along with, at least in his approach to business, considering the disputes he had with his partners at both Horseshoe Bay and Spinnakers—he certainly feels like he was taken advantage of in both situations. At least he ended his association with the microbrewing scene on a positive note when he helped set up Howe Sound Brewing in Squamish. Yes, he is quick to point out any flaw or inconsistency there, too, but he still shows up every Friday without fail and is welcomed with open arms.

B.C.'s craft beer revolution owes its start to the dogged determination of "this idiot Mitchell," to use another of his colourful self-descriptions. Arguably, taking on the brewing triumvirate of Carling, Labatt and Molson and the bureaucratic indifference of various levels of government in the early 1980s required someone who was stubborn almost to the point of being pig-headed, which is precisely what he was.

"My loud mouth got me some attention and it worked," he says now, looking back to thirty years ago when everything started at Horseshoe Bay. And of B.C.'s craft beer revolution and the part he played in it? "I'm very proud of what has happened. I couldn't be more pleased."

Mitchell's role in leading B.C.'s craft beer revolution has been commemorated in two ways since the first edition of this book came out. Howe Sound Brewing began brewing Troller Bay Ale, which replicates his original recipe from the Horseshoe Bay Brewery, giving us all a chance to taste Canada's original craft beer without the requirement of a time-travelling, stainless-steel DeLorean (and its hard-to-find plutonium fuel). And in 2014, CAMRA Vancouver honoured him with a Lifetime Achievement award. Personally, I was amazed no one had thought of doing that sooner.

Thank you, John.

whistlerbeer.com
604-962-8889
1045 Millar Creek Road, Whistler
E-MAIL tours@whistlerbeer.com
TWITTER @Whistlerbrewing

Whistler Brewing

||||||||||||||||||||||||||||||||||||||||||

Tap List

BLACK TUSK ALE
5% ABV
This dark mild has stood the test of time.

WHISKEY JACK ALE
5% ABV
A basic, inoffensive amber ale.

PARADISE VALLEY GRAPEFRUIT ALE (summer seasonal)
5% ABV
A twist on the idea of adding a slice of something citrusy to a wheat beer, this is a blonde ale with added grapefruit rind. Interesting.

LOST LAKE UNFILTERED IPA
6.8% ABV | 75 IBU
A step in the right direction—a solid West Coast IPA with some hop aroma and a decent flavour.

WHEN I FIRST arrived in B.C. in 1991, Whistler Brewing's Black Tusk Ale quickly became one of my favourite beers. Unfortunately, after a few short years, it seemed to disappear off the market. Over the two decades since then, Black Tusk and other Whistler beers have come and gone as the company has moved through several ownership changes, resulting in inconsistent brews and a lack of brand confidence among beer drinkers.

In 1999, the brewery merged with Bowen Island Brewing and the new company moved to Delta. By 2001, the Whistler brand was being produced by Bear Brewing in Kamloops. Alberta's Big Rock Brewery bought Bear and the other brands in 2003 as part of an attempt to gain a foothold in the B.C. beer market, but by 2005, Big Rock was disillusioned with that plan and sold the brands to the NorthAm Group, based in Vancouver, which revitalized the Whistler brand with an eye to the coming Winter Olympics in 2010. They still brewed the beer in Kamloops, but claimed to use Whistler glacier water, shipped all the way by tanker truck. I've heard from more than a few industry insiders that they really did ship water there from Whistler— but I still have trouble believing it myself.

Beer drinkers in Whistler were not impressed with the pretence of a beer with their hometown's name on it that was actually brewed three hundred kilometres away, so in 2009, just in time for the Olympics, the brewery opened a small brewhouse in the Function Junction industrial neighbourhood, about fifteen minutes south of Whistler Village and its world-famous ski hills. Most Whistler beer is still brewed in Kamloops, but at least some of it is now produced in the town itself. The Function Junction location has a taphouse with a basic food menu and a fun but surprisingly expensive tour that is geared toward people who know little or nothing about brewing. If you're a beer geek who already knows the difference between a lauter tun and a brite tank, forgo forking over $13.95 for the tour and buy a six-pack of Black Tusk Ale instead.

The current version of Black Tusk Ale is pretty good; Whistler claims it is the original recipe, but twenty years later, I have no way of knowing whether this is true or even possible. I doubt it, but regardless, it's their best beer.

In the first edition of this book, I quibbled over whether Whistler Brewing should even be considered "craft," but since then I have decided to step back a little from my criticisms of Whistler and other breweries that seem to pay more attention to marketing than they do to the beer itself, such as Turning Point/Stanley Park. Whistler officially fits the description of craft beer in B.C.—I just wish they'd work a little harder on what goes into their beers rather than how the packaging looks.

Facts & Figures

OPENED ‣ *1989 (& 1999 & 2001 & 2006 & 2009...)* ○
STYLES PRODUCED ‣ *5 + seasonals* ○ **WHERE TO BUY** ‣ *Liquor stores throughout B.C. and at the brewery* ○ **ON TAP** ‣ *Throughout B.C.* ○
GROWLERS ‣ *Yes*

BEST BEERS

Sea-to-Sky

....

BrewHouse High Mountain Brewing 5 Rings IPA
Voted Best IPA at the 2012 B.C. Beer Awards and Best IPA at the 2014 Awards: it's worth the trip to Whistler.

Bridge Brewing North Shore Pale Ale
A delicious pale ale with a solid Northwest hop profile.

Howe Sound Brewing King Heffy Imperial Hefeweizen
Warning: after one taste, you will not stop until this entire one-litre bottle is empty. And then you might want to open another...

Deep Cove Brewers Star Struck Rye IPA
Rich and fruity, with a complex depth thanks to the rye malts and Galaxy hops.

Howe Sound Brewing Total Eclipse of the Hop
This imperial IPA packs a wallop of flavour: a deep, rich, malty backbone supports a decadent array of hops.

VICTORIA

AT THE BREWERY	DRAFT	FOOD	GROWLERS	BOTTLES	TOURS	BEDS
4 Mile Brewpub	✪	✪	✪	✪		
Axe and Barrel Brewing (formerly Loghouse Brewpub)	✪	✪	✪	✪		
Canoe Brewpub	✪	✪	✪	✪		
Category 12 Brewing			✪	✪		
Driftwood Brewery			✪			
Hoyne Brewing			✪	✪		
Lighthouse Brewing			✪	✪		
Moon Under Water Brewpub	✪	✪	✪	✪		
Phillips Brewing	✪		✪	✪	✪	
Spinnakers Gastro Brewpub	✪	✪	✪	✪		✪
Swans Brewpub	✪	✪	✪	✪		✪
Vancouver Island Brewery	✪		✪	✪	✪	

CAPITAL CRAFT

• •

BREWING IN B.C. dates back to 1858, the year of British Columbia's birth, when William Steinberger opened Victoria Brewing
on the shores of Swan Lake, just north of Victoria. The German immigrant had come to North America in search of gold,
but he saw a business opportunity when he realized the burgeoning new capital of B.C. had no breweries of its own.

A similar opportunity was seized by Paul Hadfield, John
Mitchell and their business partners back in 1984 when they
opened Canada's first modern-day brewpub on the shore of
Victoria's picturesque Inner Harbour, kicking open the door
to the craft beer revolution in Canada that had been initiated
by Mitchell and Frank Appleton in Horseshoe Bay two years
earlier. While Hadfield initially saw Spinnakers mainly as an
architectural project, he later took over as publican there and
has been in charge of the seminal B.C. brewery ever since.

But the craft beer scene in Victoria goes way beyond Spinnakers. Three other excellent downtown brewpubs have
followed Spinnakers' lead over the years, all within an easy
mile-long walking loop around the Upper Harbour above the
fabled Blue Bridge. Add five top-notch craft breweries in the
city itself and a new brewery up in the Saanich Peninsula, plus
two new brewpubs on the West Shore, and the result is one of
the best beer destinations in the Pacific Northwest.

When I moved back to Victoria in 2012, I will admit I found
myself missing Vancouver's taphouses, the Alibi Room in particular. Victoria's pubs and restaurants are definitely devoted

to craft beer, but back then at least, it was hard to find any craft beer that wasn't brewed on Vancouver Island. To my relief, spots with more interesting and extensive tap lists began to emerge around the time the first edition of this book came out. First was the newly renovated Garrick's Head Pub with fifty taps. Then came its sister bar, the Churchill, with another fifty unique taps, right next door. The Yates Street Tap House and the Guild Free House also became options to consider. Finally, the Drake opened across from Swans. Although it "only" has about thirty taps, it is a very fine assortment that always includes something that will reduce my pangs of homesickness for my favourite barstool at the Alibi. Another cool aspect of craft beer culture in Victoria is that both Spinnakers and the Moon Under Water brewpubs have guest taps where they serve interesting and unusual beers from other craft breweries in B.C. and beyond.

Victoria hasn't kept up with Vancouver in one way, though— the brewery lounge model that has led to the advent of neighbourhood storefront breweries such as Brassneck, 33 Acres and Main Street Brewing across the water is nowhere to be seen in Victoria yet. As far as I can tell, none of the existing breweries has even bothered to ask the City of Victoria for a lounge endorsement so they can sell beer by the glass in their own tasting room (arguably only Phillips and Vancouver Island Brewery have the space for it anyway). I hope some daring entrepreneur will find the right space for this sort of brewery in downtown Victoria.

There are some great stories to go along with the excellent beer being crafted: the legendary Matt Phillips, who started his brewery by maxing out every credit card he could get when the banks all turned down his loan applications; the incredible success story of Driftwood Brewery, now regarded as one of the best breweries in Canada; and the long road Sean Hoyne took from brewing at Swans and the Canoe for more than twenty years before finally starting his own brewery in 2011.

Victoria's craft beer culture has been a model of stability

from the get-go; there has been none of the roller coaster ups and downs that Vancouver has experienced with its beer scene. New breweries open here in a reasonable manner, a year or two apart, giving everyone a chance to get to know the new players in between. Driftwood opened in 2008, followed by Hoyne in 2011 and Category 12 in 2014. In the future, a new brewery will be part of the Roundhouse redevelopment right next to Spinnakers, and I have been hearing about a couple other new breweries downtown, although it is too soon to confirm either of them as I write this.

You can sleep above the brewpub at Swans or next door from the pub at Spinnakers; canoe, kayak or take the Victoria Harbour Ferry between four brewpubs; check out the breweries with a tour and tasting at Phillips or Vancouver Island Brewing; and fill your growler at nearly every brewery and brewpub in town. Victoria is more than just the provincial capital—it's B.C.'s craft beer capital, too.

4 Mile Brewing

4milebrewingco.com
250-479-3346
199 Island Highway, Victoria
E-MAIL
  info@4milebrewingco.com

||||||||||||||||||||||||||||||||||||||||||

THE FOUR MILE House is a historic building—the fourth oldest house in Greater Victoria, dating back to 1858. Located in View Royal just outside of the city, it was a roadhouse that served stagecoaches in the nineteenth century and then automobile drivers until Prohibition caused it to close down. In the 1940s it re-opened as the Lantern House Inn— "the Coziest Cabaret on the Coast." Upstairs was an infamous brothel that was popular with sailors.

The building wasn't used commercially from the early '50s until 1979 when the current owners, Graham and Wendy Haymes, reopened it after extensive renovations. The pub is gorgeous and well maintained, embracing its history without ignoring modern updates.

Early in 2014, brewery consultant Alan Pugsley installed 4 Mile Brewing's Peter Austin Brick Kettle brewing system and created the original range of beers. Doug White is the resident brewer.

Generally speaking, the beer lineup is fairly cautious—mostly based in the British recipe book. None stands out as exceptional, and it's not uncommon to find off-flavours. But it's early days still, and I'm happy to keep trying if they are.

Tap List

BEST BRITISH ALE
4.25% ABV | 24 IBU
Naturally carbonated and unfiltered, this is a very authentic low-gravity Best Bitter.

PALE ALE
5.1% ABV | 38 IBU
This English-style pale ale has a bit of West Coast hop character.

....
Facts & Figures

OPENED › 2014
STYLES PRODUCED › 5 + seasonals
WHERE TO BUY › The brewpub or private liquor stores
ON TAP › The brewpub and elsewhere on Vancouver Island
GROWLERS › Yes

canoebrewpub.com
250-361-1940
450 Swift Street, Victoria
E-MAIL info@canoebrewpub.com
TWITTER @canoebrewpub

Canoe Brewpub, Marina and Restaurant

Tap List

DARK ALE
5.5% ABV | 20 IBU
Full-bodied and creamy but not heavy. Very drinkable and satisfying.

IPA
6.5% ABV | 65 IBU
This South Pacific IPA bursts with hops from Australia and New Zealand that offer tropical fruit–tinged bitterness.

GOLDEN LION BELGIAN ALE (seasonal)
5.6% ABV | 15 IBU
An exceptional Belgian golden ale with spicy, fruity flavours and a rich malt character.

....

Facts & Figures

OPENED ▸ *1996*
STYLES PRODUCED ▸
  4 + seasonals
WHERE TO BUY ▸ *In bottles at the brewpub*
ON TAP ▸ *The brewpub*
GROWLERS ▸ *Yes*

|||||||||||||||||||||||||||||||||||||||||||||

CANOE MIGHT JUST be the best place to drink a beer in British Columbia—architecturally speaking, at least. The brewpub is situated in a gorgeous heritage edifice, the brick-clad City Lights Building (built in 1894), which originally housed coal-fired generators that powered the city's streetlights. Following a $6-million restoration, it boasts dramatic vaulted ceilings and exposed beams. Out front is the city's best west-facing patio, right on the edge of the Upper Harbour with a great view of the old Blue Bridge—or its replacement if it is ever finished.

Sean Hoyne, the original brewer at Swans, was the first brewmaster at Canoe and stayed there for fourteen years before he launched his own brewery in 2011. His replacement, Daniel Murphy, brings an Australian accent and flavour to the place. Murphy apprenticed under Hoyne for several years before working at a brewery in Tasmania where he says there is an exciting craft beer scene.

The Canoe Brewpub has a top-notch kitchen with a strong focus on local ingredients to go along with its strong assortment of beers, making it a destination for foodies as well as beer lovers.

FROM SWAN LAKE
TO SPRING RIDGE
The Early Days of Brewing in Victoria

••••••••••••••••••••••••

WILLIAM STEINBERGER CAME to North America from Köln, Germany, seeking a lucky strike in the California gold rush. As he followed the crowds of prospectors north to B.C.'s Cariboo gold fields, he realized there was another, better way to make some money—brewing beer for the thirsty crowds in Victoria, a boomtown which had seen its population jump from three hundred to five thousand as it became the supply hub for prospectors heading north. So, in 1858, he purchased some excess grain from a local farm that had lost its Russian market because of the Crimean War, and established Western Canada's first brewery on the shores of Swan Lake, just north of Victoria.

The next year, he built a larger operation in downtown Victoria (probably because the murky waters of Swan Lake would not have been ideal for brewing) and within a few years his Victoria Brewing Company was joined by five others. It must have helped when the British Royal Navy set up its base in Esquimalt in 1865—then, as now, sailors proved a good source of thirsty customers. Steinberger himself did not stick around very long, but other brewers who followed him did and some became quite prominent citizens as Victoria grew from rugged fort to provincial capital.

The brewers' demand for ingredients led to a hop-growing industry on the Saanich Peninsula that became so large, the farms were even exporting their hops off-island for a time. Unfortunately, they were decimated by a hop louse infestation in the 1890s and the industry died out there. Barley was not a very successful crop because of the damp climate so it had to be imported.

Several breweries in Victoria set up shop on Spring Ridge—present-day Fernwood—to make use of the clean, flowing spring water there. The earliest recorded one was the Lion Brewery, which opened in 1862, but others also built breweries in the area, or piped the water to their operations downtown.

After the turn of the century, the most prominent breweries in the city were the Victoria-Phoenix (after the 1893 merging of Steinberger's original enterprise, which had changed hands several times already, with Phoenix Brewery) and Silver Spring Brewery, which was founded in 1902 in Vic West. Those two companies dominated the market until 1928 when they were amalgamated under the Coast Breweries banner and began brewing Lucky Lager to compete with Molson and Labatt.

Labatt bought Lucky Lager Breweries in 1958. They demolished the Silver Spring brewery in 1962, but continued to brew Lucky at the original Victoria-Phoenix plant downtown on Government Street until 1981. Even though the company had initiated a major heritage renovation in the '70s, Labatt levelled the historic building in 1982, ending local production of Lucky Lager, or any beer, in Victoria.

The city was only "dry" for two years, though, until 1984 when Spinnakers and Vancouver Island Brewery (then Island Pacific Brewing) opened.

Category 12 Brewing

category12beer.com
250-652-9668
Unit C – 2200 Keating Cross
   Road, Saanichton
E-MAIL
   info@category12brewing.com
TWITTER @C12beer

IIIIIIIIIIIIIIIIIIIIIIIIIIIIIIIIIIIIIIIIIIIIII

GREATER VICTORIA'S FIRST new brewery since Hoyne opened in 2011, Category 12 Brewing was founded by Karen and Michael Kuzyk. Michael is a scientist with a PhD in microbiology and biochemistry from UVic who has brewed at home for twenty years. Karen is a one-time oenophile (wine lover) whose conversion occurred when Michael started brewing with Belgian yeasts; she says she is fully committed to the brewery—as long as he brews Belgian beer.

Category 12 is meant to evoke mysterious science, as in Area 51 or District 9, as reflected by the website's "Welcome to the Lab" branding. Michael's passions are Belgian-inspired and "colossal West Coast" styles. The fact that C-12 launched with a Black IPA and a hoppy, North American-style Saison—two fairly challenging beers both up near the 7 per cent ABV mark— rather than the typical pale ale and ho hum lager—says a lot about his intentions.

The brewery is in the Keating Industrial Park just off the Pat Bay Highway and has a tasting room and growler station. The brewing equipment was all built by Specific Mechanical, just around the corner, and the building has lots of room for growth.

Tap List

UNSANCTIONED SAISON

6.9% ABV | 27 IBU

The addition of fruity, citrusy Zythos hops gives this dry Saison a West Coast edge. Delicious and dangerously drinkable—do not attempt any science experiments while under its influence.

DISRUPTION BLACK IPA

6.7% ABV | 77 IBU

When Michael gave me a sample of his home brewed version of this I knew he would open this brewery. It's very good—dark and roasty with a big dose of aromatic and flavourful West Coast hops.

....

Facts & Figures

OPENED ▸ *2014*
STYLES PRODUCED ▸
   2 + seasonals.
WHERE TO BUY ▸ *The brewery or in South Island private liquor stores*
ON TAP ▸ *Select South Island taphouses and pubs*
GROWLERS ▸ *Yes*

driftwoodbeer.com
250-381-2739
102-450 Hillside Avenue, Victoria
E-MAIL
  orders@driftwoodbeer.com
TWITTER @driftwoodbeer

Driftwood Brewery

IIIIIIIIIIIIIIIIIIIIIIIIIIIIIIIIIIIIIIIIIIIIIIIII

Tap List

FARMHAND ALE

5.5% ABV

A full-bodied Saison with a spicy Belgian yeast character and a peppery zing you'll feel in your sinuses. Unique and delicious.

FAT TUG IPA

7% ABV | 80 IBU

Arguably the best beer in B.C. A big hop profile featuring citrus and pine from a "shwack o' hops," as the label reads.

SARTORI HARVEST IPA (seasonal)

7% ABV | 75 IBU

Brewed with "wet hops" immediately after the harvest, this IPA features fresh, grassy, citrusy hop flavours. Exceptional and very popular.

SINGULARITY (seasonal)

11.8% ABV

This bourbon barrel–aged Russian imperial stout features complex flavours including plums, berries, chocolate, caramel and port. Simply incredible.

KEVIN HEARSUM AND JASON MEYER met while working together as assistant brewers at Lighthouse Brewing, where they spent a lot of time fantasizing about what they'd do if they had their own brewery. That dream became a reality when they opened Driftwood in late 2008. Even in their wildest fantasies, however, I doubt they ever expected to achieve such a level of success in such a short time. The brewery is now recognized as one of B.C.'s best—if not *the* best.

The brewing duo had a solid plan to set Driftwood apart. "We wanted to stake out our space as a brewer of Belgian beers in the Northwest," Meyer told me shortly after they opened. Of their first three beers, two were Belgians: a Wit called White Bark Ale and Farmhand Ale, a Saison brewed with 10 per cent sour mash and cracked pepper. The third was a Northwest pale ale, originally called Driftwood Ale but since rebranded as New Growth Pale Ale. That trio still represents the core of Driftwood's lineup, but since then the brewery has added Crooked Coast Amber Ale and several interesting seasonals. Oh yeah, I almost forgot, they also brew a little IPA you've probably never heard of called Fat Tug.

It was the addition of Fat Tug IPA in late 2010 that cata-pulted Driftwood to the upper echelons of B.C.'s beer scene. Before they launched it, Meyer told me, "There are a lot of good IPAs out there. We know that the bar has been set high, so we intend to try and set it just a little bit higher." Audacious words, perhaps, but that's exactly what they did. Fat Tug has quickly grown into their flagship beer, now accounting for more than half of Driftwood's sales. It is so wildly popular in the Vancou-ver area that the brewery had to open its own warehouse there and hire sales staff who just focus on the Lower Mainland.

Other Driftwood beers are extremely popular as well: its annual wet-hopped seasonal, Sartori Harvest IPA, is the most highly anticipated seasonal release in B.C. (see "Hopping Fresh" on page 48); and Singularity, a potent, barrel-aged impe-rial stout they release each January, is coveted and hoarded by craft beer cellarists. The brewery also has a well-developed sour beer program under the "Bird of Prey" banner, which has featured several different releases, including: Belle Royale Wild Sour Cherry Ale, Flanders Red, Mad Bruin Sour Brown Ale, and Lustrum Wild Sour Anniversary Ale (brewed with blackcurrants for the brewery's fifth birthday). One of my favourites is the uniquely refreshing Gose-uh, a tart and dry wheat beer brewed with *Lactobacillus* bacteria that is oh-so refreshing on a summer evening. The brewers also like to work with local maltster Mike Doehnel, and even named their first Pilsner after him.

The addition of a new centrifuge and a proper tasting room with additional front-line staff in 2014 shows that Driftwood is only getting better with age—just like many of its beers.

....
Facts & Figures

OPENED ▸ *2008* ○ **STYLES PRODUCED ▸** *5 + seasonals* ○
WHERE TO BUY ▸ *Liquor stores throughout B.C.* ○ **ON TAP ▸** *Throughout B.C.* ○ **GROWLERS ▸** *Yes*

HOPPING FRESH

The Most Popular
Seasonal Beer Style in B.C.

....

THERE ARE SEVERAL different seasonal beers brewed in B.C.,
including berry beers made with fresh, local raspberries in
summer and pumpkin beers fermented with sugar pumpkins in fall. But the single seasonal style that garners the most
excitement is tied into the annual hop harvest that occurs at
summer's end.

Fresh-hopped or wet-hopped beers, as they are sometimes
called, use hops that have just been harvested and are still
dripping with the succulent oils that contribute so much aroma,
flavour and bitterness to beer. Normally, hops are dried so
that they can be shipped and stored for several months without spoiling. Instead, fresh-hopped beers must be brewed as
quickly as possible after the hops have been picked.

The most sought-after fresh-hopped beer is Driftwood
Brewery's Sartori Harvest IPA, which the brewery first produced in 2009 and has released annually ever since. Although
Driftwood is on Vancouver Island, the brewers travel to the
mainland to load their truck with fresh hops from Sartori Hop
Farm in Chilliwack, then drive back to the brewery and brew
the batch first thing the next morning.

Driftwood adds fresh hops at multiple points during the
brewing process, with the result being a unique beer that showcases the hops' freshest qualities. In other words: a hophead's
wildest fantasy. But it is an ephemeral style, not ideal for cellaring, because the volatile hop oils and flavour compounds break
down quickly. This is a beer to drink soon after you get it. After

a few months, it won't taste nearly as good.

Driftwood Brewery may not have been the first B.C. brewery to release a wet-hopped beer, but Sartori Harvest IPA has quickly become the brand that is synonymous with the style in B.C., and rightfully so. While it is difficult to compare wet-hopped beers year to year, Driftwood's annual release has been excellent each fall.

Usually, Sartori features a big nose of sweet citrus and grassy aromas that are just as prominent in the flavour of the beer, too. Underneath all those fresh aromas, it's a solid IPA comparable to their incomparable Fat Tug IPA, but with a zing.

Several other B.C. breweries produce fresh-hopped beers, too. Salt Spring Island Ales actually has its own hops field on a farm. Located just over a kilometre from the brewery, they hold an annual harvest festival. The fresh hops are added to a different style each year. Spinnakers uses hops grown on its own farm in Sooke in a variety of fresh-hopped beers each fall. Persephone also grows its own hops at its farm-based brewery in Gibsons.

In the fall of 2015, two separate fresh-hopped beer festivals launched, one situated on a hop farm in Abbotsford and the other at the urban epicentre of craft beer, Driftwood and Hoyne's shared parking lot in Victoria. Hopefully, they will become annual events:

BC Hop Fest: Celebrating Fresh Beer
bchopfest.ca

Fresh to Death: Victoria's Harvest Celebration of Fresh Hop Beer
victoriabeerweek.com

hoynebrewing.com
250-590-5758
101-2740 Bridge Street, Victoria
E-MAIL info@hoynebrewing.ca
TWITTER @hoynebeer

Hoyne Brewing

Tap List

HOYNER PILSNER

5.5% ABV

An authentic Bohemian
Pilsner, this is bursting with
flavour well beyond its light
appearance.

DARK MATTER

5.3% ABV

Not a porter. Not a stout.
This mysterious brew is
surprisingly quaffable for
such a dark beer.

DEVIL'S DREAM IPA

6% ABV

A well-balanced West
Coast IPA with a solid malt
foundation that really
shows off the pine-citrus
hops.

GRATITUDE (seasonal)

9% ABV

Beautifully packaged in
seasonal paper, this full-
bodied winter warmer
is ideal for carolling
parties and late-night gift-
wrapping sessions.

IIIIIIIIIIIIIIIIIIIIIIIIIIIIIIIIIIIIIIIIIIIII

SEAN HOYNE HAS been a professional brewer
in Victoria longer than anyone else—surprising since he never planned on brewing
beer for a living. He was studying graduate-
level literature at the University of Victoria
and brewing beer at home on the side
back in 1989 when he saw an ad seeking a
brewer at the brand-new Swans Brewpub.
He applied on a whim and brought a six-
pack of his homebrew to the interview with
Frank Appleton, who designed and built the
brewery.

Appleton, who, together with John Mitchell, was one of the founding fathers of B.C.'s
modern craft brewing movement (see "John
Mitchell" on page 29), had helped with the
construction of the brewpub but was ready
to hand over the reins to a worthy apprentice.
Hoyne says that the interview with Appleton
amounted to drinking his homebrews and
chatting about them; by the time the bottles
were empty, he'd been offered the job.

Hoyne quickly realized he had found his
true calling. He spent several years at Swans
before moving on to open the Canoe brewpub just down the street, where he worked
for the next fourteen years. He wanted to
open his own brewery ever since he got into
the business, and the recent craft beer boom

in B.C. helped solidify his decision to finally make the leap.

It took him only eight months to get his brewery up and running in a building right next to Driftwood Brewery in the semi-industrial Rock Bay area of Victoria, which is also home to the Moon Under Water brewpub. Although the location isn't exactly trendy, the brewery sells a lot of beer in growlers—it's always busy at the filling station whenever I swing by to get a refill.

Hoyne is dedicated to each beer style he brews, envisioning his ideal consumer as someone who loves that specific style first and foremost. So, for instance, his Pilsner is a true Bohemian Pilsner that wouldn't be out of place in a pub in the Czech Republic. His IPA, though not as over-the-top hoppy as some other West Coast versions, still boasts a citrus-pine nose and a flavour with a great malt-hop balance.

The bottle labels feature poetic discursions, definitely showing off Hoyne's literary origins. Apparently, he still likes to catch up on the latest critical perspectives on James Joyce's *Ulysses*, but now, at least, it's with a glass of his own Dark Matter or Down Easy Pale Ale in hand.

....
Facts & Figures

OPENED › *2011* ✪ **STYLES PRODUCED ›** *5 + seasonals* ✪
WHERE TO BUY › *The brewery and in liquor stores throughout B.C.* ✪
ON TAP › *Vancouver Island and Vancouver* ✪ **GROWLERS ›** *Yes*

ROCK BAY MASH-UP

B.C.'s Craft Brewers Embrace Collaboration

· ·

"A RISING TIDE lifts all boats."

This old expression could serve as a motto for British Columbia's uniquely cooperative craft beer industry. Take, for example, the Rock Bay Mash-Up.

Two Victoria companies, Driftwood Brewery and Hoyne Brewing, are neighbours, sharing a parking lot in a light industrial complex in the Rock Bay neighbourhood. As is the case with most B.C. breweries, everyone involved in the two businesses is extremely friendly, even helpful, sharing ingredients when one or the other is short on something, and helping to troubleshoot technical problems or sharing on common freight needs.

But in March 2014, Driftwood and Hoyne celebrated their neighbourliness by literally connecting the two breweries to collaborate on a Baltic porter. They had each brewed a batch of the beer in their own facilities already—Hoyne's with a lager yeast and Driftwood's with an ale yeast—and when the beer was deemed ready, they hooked up nearly one hundred metres of hoses between the two breweries and pumped Hoyne's batch to merge with Driftwood's in one of Driftwood's larger fermentation tanks.

They weren't even sure if it would work; that is, if the pressure on Hoyne's side would be enough for the beer to travel slightly uphill through such a long pipe to Driftwood. But it did, of course. They bottled the beer in two separate batches, one for each brewery to sell, and called it the Rock Bay Mash-Up.

The beer was delicious, made even more special by the circumstances of its creation.

Collaboration in general is far from uncommon in B.C.'s craft beer community. Indeed, "community" sums up the craft beer industry perfectly since most of B.C.'s breweries see each other as partners rather than competitors. Sharing ingredients such as hops, malts and yeast is extremely common, as is borrowing an empty cask or two, or letting someone else know about some barrels that might be bought for a song.

Collaborating on beers also happens on a regular basis. Usually, one brewery hosts one or more others, and the visiting brewers bring certain ingredients to share in the recipe. Several Main Street–area breweries in Vancouver produced the Brewery Creek Collaboration Beer in the fall of 2013, and Parallel 49 Brewing and Central City Brewing even collaborated on the Mystery Gift advent calendar–style twenty-four-pack in 2014.

When I toured around the province launching the first edition of this book in the summer of 2013, I asked local breweries to put on a special Revolution-themed beer wherever I went. In Penticton, three local breweries teamed up to make a special cask in my honour. I learned it was the first time they had done so, but ever since, they have continued to kibitz and collaborate. When I went there to visit Penticton's newest brewery, Bad Tattoo, in late 2014, I found myself sitting at a long table nestled among the fermentation tanks in the brewery itself with twenty-three other people, including representatives from each of the local breweries. We toasted Bad Tattoo, of course, but we also toasted the announcement that its main competitor, Cannery Brewing, would be opening its own new facility in a few months.

A rising tide indeed!

lighthousebrewing.com
250-383-6500
836 Devonshire Road, Victoria
E-MAIL
  info@lighthousebrewing.com
TWITTER @lighthousebeer

Lighthouse Brewing

Tap List

**RACE ROCKS
AMBER ALE**

5% ABV

This dark amber ale is
very quaffable with a
lighter body than its
colour implies.

TASMAN ALE

5% ABV

A copper-coloured ale
tinged with tropical
flavours from exotic
Tasmanian hops. One of
the best labels around, too.

SHIPWRECK IPA
(previously Switchback)

6.5% ABV | 85 IBU

One of the top three West
Coast IPAs in B.C. with
a heady blend of citrusy,
aromatic Citra, Zythos and
Falconer's Flight hops.

**SIREN RED
ALE** (seasonal)

8% ABV | 70 IBU

A big, bold, boozy, malty,
yeasty and hoppy beer
that doesn't really fit
any stylistic description
I can think of other than:
delicious.

||||||||||||||||||||||||||||||||||||||||||||||||||

I WAS LIVING in Victoria in 1998 when Race
Rocks Amber Ale, Lighthouse's flagship beer,
first appeared, and it immediately became
my favourite local beer. It was dark but not
heavy, very drinkable with a malt character balanced between caramel and roasted
barley. I moved away from Victoria a few
years later and discovered other new beers,
but when my girlfriend and I decided to get
married in Victoria where we'd met, it was
an easy decision to serve Race Rocks at the
reception.

Lighthouse has grown significantly over
the years, and underwent a major expansion
in 2012. Up until a few years ago, though,
Lighthouse was dismissed by many craft
beer drinkers. Its core lineup was safe and
innocuous, and none of its beers reflected
the new trends in craft beer—West Coast
IPAs, Belgian styles and the like. Television
ads that featured guys ogling bikini babes
didn't help much either.

That all changed with the launch of the
Big Flavour series in 2010, which showcased
beer geek styles in 650 mL bombers—includ-
ing Shipwrecked Triple IPA, Navigator
Doppelbock, Deckhand Belgian Saison,
Overboard Imperial Pilsner and Uncharted
Belgian IPA—all with original labels painted

by local artists. And indeed, the beer geeks took notice. Each new release was met with much pleasure and discussion.

Then, in early 2012, Lighthouse took it up another notch with the release of Belgian Black in an all-black bottle featuring a skeletal pirate. As striking as the image was, what was in the bottle caught the most attention. Though it came out early in January, some beer bloggers declared it the year's best brew. The unique Ardennes yeast that brewer Dean McLeod used pulled plum and cherry flavours out of the dark malts and merged them with that spicy character unique to Belgian yeasts. Truly exceptional. A few months later, Lighthouse followed it up with Belgian White, an imperial Wit beer that used the same yeast along with Galaxy and Citra hops to impart a citrusy zing. And late in the year, they continued the colour theme with Siren Red Ale, which might just have been the best of the bunch.

Dean McLeod also made it a priority to mentor his assistant brewers; he encouraged them to brew their own recipes on a pilot system, and some of these brews made it on to the growler taps for public consumption. Building on that, Lighthouse held a unique event called Ramshackle in the summer of 2015 where attendees tasted beers created by four assistant brewers and then voted on their favourite. Matt Lyons won with his Belgo-American Mild, which was brewed as a full batch and released in bombers under the name Pacific Sunset.

Shortly afterwards, McLeod announced he was leaving Lighthouse to take a job opening a new distillery in Victoria. Although this came as a surprise, clearly his crew of brewers was well prepared to continue his legacy.

....
Facts & Figures

OPENED › *1998* ☉ STYLES PRODUCED › *8 + seasonals* ☉
WHERE TO BUY › *Liquor stores throughout B.C.* ☉ ON TAP › *Victoria-area restaurants and select spots in Vancouver* ☉ GROWLERS › *Yes*

GREAT CANADIAN
BEER FESTIVAL

Held every September on the Friday
and Saturday after Labour Day

••••••••••••••••••••••••

THE BIGGEST ANNUAL event on the B.C. craft beer calendar and one of the biggest in Canada along with Montreal's Mondiale du Bière, the Great Canadian Beer Festival celebrated its twentieth anniversary in 2012 and just keeps getting better and better—despite numerous obstacles thrown in its path by government bureaucrats over the years.

From its humble origins in the Victoria Convention Centre in 1993 to its mammoth current proportions on the soccer pitch at Royal Athletic Park, this festival has certainly come a long way over the years. These days, more than eight thousand people attend over two days, sampling beers from more than sixty breweries from throughout Canada and the U.S. The entry ticket includes a sample glass (unfortunately plastic because of liquor authorities concerned about breakage and injuries) and a program featuring profiles of all the beers on hand. Tokens for beer samples are sold inside the event.

Tickets go on sale in July and sell out very quickly. Plan a long weekend in barcVictoria around the GCBF and visit some of the excellent brewpubs and breweries B.C.'s craft capital has to offer.

---

www.gcbf.com

Axe and Barrel Brewing Co.

(formerly Loghouse Brewpub)

axeandbarrel.com
250-474-1989
2323 Millstream Road, Victoria
E-MAIL info@axeandbarrel.com

|||||||||||||||||||||||||||||||||||||||||||||||||

LANGFORD'S LOGHOUSE PUB has been a popular spot for locals since 1989. The building included an on-site private liquor store for a while, but when owners Ron Cheeke and Diana Kresier built the big, dinosaur-themed Liquor Planet store next door (complete with giant dinosaurs and "prehistoric prices," I kid you not), they decided to put a brewery into the newly vacant space in the pub.

Dave Woodward, previously of Tofino Brewing and the BrewHouse in Whistler before that, was brought in to set up the brewery and brew the beer. The ten-barrel (12 hL) brewhouse and the rest of the brewing equipment all come from local manufacturer Specific Mechanical.

When the brewery opened in September 2015, the name changed from Loghouse to Axe and Barrel, and the adjoined restaurant closed for renovations with the plan to re-open by December with a barbecue focus. In the meantime, the brewery's tasting room was open for growler fills and casks and kegs were being filled to go on tap at restaurants and pubs in Victoria.

Tap List

RYE PALE ALE
5.2% ABV | 30 IBU
This west coast pale ale has a spicy rye character and a big citrus kick from lots of "C" hops.

IPA
6.8% ABV | 70 IBU
This "Woodwardesque" IPA shows off brewer Dave's penchant for hops with a fruity, citrusy mix of Australian Topaz, Ella and Summer varietals.

....
Facts & Figures

OPENED ▸ 2015
STYLES PRODUCED ▸ 4 + seasonals.
WHERE TO BUY ▸ The brewpub
ON TAP ▸ The brewpub or select taphouses in Victoria
GROWLERS ▸ Yes

moonunderwater.ca
250-380-0706
350B Bay Street, Victoria
E-MAIL
  moonunderwater@shaw.ca
TWITTER @TheMoonBrewpub

The Moon Under Water

Tap List

||||||||||||||||||||||||||||||||||||||||||||||||

POTTS PILS
5.2% ABV | 38 IBU
An authentic, unfiltered
North German Pilsner:
light, dry and crisp. *Sehr
gut!*

CREEPY UNCLE DUNKEL
5.4% ABV
Dunkels are not very
well known here, but this
slightly sweet dark lager is
exactly what you'd find on
tap in Germany.

THIS IS HEFEWEIZEN
5.5% ABV
The best, most authentic
German Hefeweizen I've
had in B.C.—cloudy with
bubblegum and banana
yeast characteristics.

**THE VICTORIOUS
WEIZENBOCK**
8.2% ABV
Wow, this is a bold brew:
spicy yeast flavours
underneath a marvelously
complex malty body.

IF YOU ARE *asked why you favour a particular public-house, it would seem natural to
put the beer first, but the thing that most
appeals to me about the Moon Under Water
is what people call its "atmosphere."*
—**GEORGE ORWELL**, "The Moon Under Water,"
Evening Standard, February 9, 1946

The Moon Under Water brewpub was
originally founded in 2011 by Don and Bonnie
Bradley, who had founded the original Bowen
Island Brewing in the 1990s, along with their
nephew Ron. They focused on low-gravity,
British-style session ales, including a full-bodied bitter with only 3.8 per cent ABV, just as
one might expect to find in a British pub.

Then, just after the 2012 Great Canadian
Beer Festival, word came out that the Brad-
leys had sold the brewpub to a young couple
named Clay Potter and Chelsea Walker, along
with Clay's parents. The new owners immediately began tweaking the style of the place
to "turn it into craft beer central." Born and
raised in Victoria, Potter worked at Lighthouse and Driftwood before going to Scotland
to study brewing and distilling at Heriot-Watt
University (a route that several young B.C.
brewers have taken in recent years).

Potter fell in love with German beers

during an internship at a big Bitburger brewery and has shifted the Moon's beer lineup to mainly feature German styles (sometimes with North American twists, including his extra hoppy Potts Pils, Creepy Uncle Dunkel, and Victorious Weizenbock) alongside Tranquility IPA. His seasonal brews have included This Is Hefeweizen—the most authentic Hefeweizen I've tasted in B.C.—as well an Altbier, Maibock, Wheat Wine, Rauchbier and a Berliner Weisse.

With a very small brewing space, the brewpub has no room for a packaging line, so Potter decided to work with West Coast Canning, a mobile canning company, to release Light Side of the Moon in tall cans in the spring of 2014. He hoped to sell through one batch of cans that summer but the beer was phenomenally successful so WCC had to return several times to fill more cans so the Moon could keep up with demand (see "West Coast Canning" on page 60).

Supplementing the brewpub's own beers are several guest taps featuring unique beers from up and down the northwest coast. Potter likes to collaborate with other breweries, and also brings in guest brewers for special one-off brews, such as the Benchwarmer Belgian Blonde—so-named because it was created by two assistant brewers from other breweries who "came off the bench" to produce it.

Despite its location in a nondescript plaza across from a cement plant in the Rock Bay industrial area, the Moon Under Water has blossomed under new management into one of Victoria's most popular craft beer destinations.

....
Facts & Figures

OPENED ‣ *2011* ◉ **STYLES PRODUCED** ‣ *4 + seasonals + guest taps* ◉ **WHERE TO BUY** ‣ *The brewpub and private liquor stores in Victoria and Vancouver* ◉ **ON TAP** ‣ *The brewpub* ◉ **GROWLERS** ‣ *Yes*

WEST COAST CANNING

Mobile Canning Service Helps Small Breweries with Packaging Options

•••••••••••••••••••••••••

"SHORT AND TALL—we can it all." West Coast Canning's motto earns a chuckle when you meet the company's co-founders side by side. Kevin Pederson—Mr. 355 mL—looks way up to his business partner, Matt Leslie—Mr. 473 mL—who stands six foot seven. Both hail from Prince George originally, but Leslie now lives in Vancouver (just a couple blocks from Main Street Brewing and Brassneck Brewery in Mount Pleasant) after a stint in Victoria.

The two friends are business partners in Canada's first mobile canning company, West Coast Canning (WCC), which began operating in April 2014 with a first run at the Moon Under Water brewpub in Victoria. As is the case with many small breweries, the Moon had neither the space nor the money to install a permanent canning line, but brewmaster Clay Potter had the idea for a summer session lager that would be perfect for cans. So that's where WCC came in.

The basic idea is that WCC brings the canning line and the cans themselves to the brewery on the day (or days) when the beer needs to be packaged and then disappears once the job is done. Based in a Burnaby warehouse, Leslie and Pederson load their equipment into a twenty-four-foot box truck and drive it to the brewery. If all goes well, they can fill thirty-eight to forty cans per minute (355 mL can size) and thirty-three to thirty-five cans per minute (473 mL), up to 100 to 115 hectolitres per day.

The company also stores empty cans for breweries that do

not have the warehouse space, and because of its own bulk ordering, it can offer lower minimum orders to breweries that use its services.

When the Moon first used wcc's services to can its Light Side of the Moon beer in attractive tall cans with wraparound labels featuring a thirsty astronaut floating in space, Potter told me he hoped the beer would sell well enough to justify bringing the canning guys back a few more times that summer. It was such a success that the Moon reordered cans twice and had wcc back several times by mid-summer.

Since canning at the Moon Under Water, West Coast Canning has worked with several other B.C. breweries, including Old Yale, Postmark, Deep Cove and Tofino.

---

www.westcoastcanning.com

phillipsbeer.com
250-380-1912
2010 Government Street, Victoria
E-MAIL info@phillipsbeer.com
TWITTER @phillipsbeer

Phillips Brewing

Tap List

BLUE BUCK ALE
5% ABV

Phillips' flagship beer: a
solid, malt-forward pale
ale that you can find on
tap almost everywhere on
Vancouver Island.

BOTTLE ROCKET ISA
5% ABV

Bright and hoppy but light
and "sessionable," this is
part of a wave of new lower
alcohol India Session Ales
from B.C. breweries.

ELECTRIC UNICORN
WHITE IPA
6.5% ABV | 75 IBU

This beer is as delicious,
complex and original as
its label, which features
a unicorn shooting laser
beams from its eyes.

AMNESIAC DOUBLE IPA
8.5% ABV | 85 IBU

I love this beer. I think.
Wait a sec, I forget. No, I
do, really. It's big, strong
and hoppy, but so well
balanced.

||||||||||||||||||||||||||||||||||||||||||||||

LIFT A GLASS to the legend of Matt Phillips.

After working at a few different breweries,
including Whistler Brewing and Spinnakers, Phillips decided he wanted to start up
his own operation. All the banks and credit
unions turned down his loan applications,
but, undeterred, he filled out every credit
card application he could find and used that
capital to fund his start-up. He lived in the
brewery, showering at a nearby gym, and
began brewing in earnest.

The first few years were precarious finan-
cially, and Phillips had to do everything
himself. He even had to move his brewery
when a ruptured tank resulted in a flood
of Phoenix Lager (named in honour of
the Victoria-Phoenix Brewery from a century earlier), which greatly displeased his
landlord. Slowly but surely, though, his reputation grew, and so did his beer sales.

With growth came other challenges,
including one from within the province's
beer community. His flagship beer was Blue
Truck Ale, named after the blue-painted
milk truck he used to deliver his beer all over
B.C., but the Mark James Group didn't like
the similarity to its Red Truck brand. Phillips changed his beer's name to Blue Buck
and kept on trucking.

By 2008, Phillips needed to expand. He found an ideal space on Government Street in the heart of Victoria's Design District, just a few blocks from Vancouver Island Brewery and close enough to the Inner Harbour to be accessible by foot for beer-loving tourists (see "Victoria's Beer Mile" on page 70). The brewery has a storefront for beer and T-shirt sales, as well as a very popular growler filling station. With eight beers available for growler fills on a rotating basis, I keep my eye on their website for the occasions when an unusual seasonal style appears on the list: perhaps one of the Grow-Hop IPA series, which features a single hop such as Amarillo, Centennial or Cascade—or sometimes even the excellent Hoperation Tripel Cross Belgian IPA or Amnesiac Double IPA.

Phillips Brewing is one of the B.C. craft beer industry's big success stories. From those early days of overdrawn credit cards to the domination of Blue Buck Ale throughout British Columbia, it's a tale worth celebrating. Best thing is it's based on great beer, consistently brewed without skimping or cheating. And it's all true. If you think I'm telling tales, take a brewery tour (Tuesday to Saturdays—check the website for hours) where you will see the old blue truck, now retired, in the back lot.

Update: In September 2015, Phillips opened its own malting facility behind the brewery. The brewery had been working with farmers to grow barley and wheat on the Saanich Peninsula, north of Victoria. The first two harvests (from 2014 and 2015) worked out to about 30% of the brewery's annual needs, but they hope to encourage enough farmers so that all of the grain they need is eventually grown locally.

....
Facts & Figures

OPENED ▸ *2001* ✸ **STYLES PRODUCED** ▸ *12 + innumerable seasonals* ✸ **WHERE TO BUY** ▸ *Liquor stores throughout B.C.* ✸ **ON TAP** ▸ *Throughout B.C.* ✸ **GROWLERS** ▸ *Yes*

GROWLIN' FOR BEER

• •

A GROWLER IS a big glass bottle with a handle on the neck that resembles a moonshine jug. The regular size is 1.89 litres, which is half a gallon. That is a little less than a six-pack or about four 16 oz U.S. pints, which is the size of a "sleeve" of beer in B.C. (unless the pub is serving authentic British pints, which are 20 oz). The concept behind growlers is that you buy the jug itself (usually five dollars) and then pay for a fill of whatever beer you like (ten to twelve dollars per fill). Depending on how it is filled, it may stay fresh unopened anywhere from a week to several months in the fridge at home. Once you've cracked the seal, the beer is best consumed immediately; I find they go flat pretty quickly. Then, once you've emptied it, rinse it out and bring it back to the brewery where you bought it—or another brewery that fills growlers—for a refill. This time, you'll only pay for the fill, not for the growler itself. (It's not a deposit system; breweries will not accept the bottle for a refund.)

The name "growler" has an interesting origin. According to the *Oxford Companion to Beer*, back in the late 1800s and early 1900s, most beer was consumed on draft in American cities. If people wanted to bring beer home, the container most often used was a galvanized steel pail with a lid on it to prevent spillage. That lid would rumble or "growl" as carbonation escaped, and the name growler was born. There was even an expression for fetching the beer: "rushing the growler." It became such a common practice that many saloon keepers installed a special service window called the "family entrance" which allowed women and children to avoid walking through the saloon to the bar.

This trend died out during Prohibition and did not return until the craft beer craze brought it back into vogue. Over the past several years, growlers have arrived in British Columbia, big time. Happily, breweries will fill growlers from other breweries without complaint, though many growler enthusiasts still end up buying more than one—even going so far as to collect them. Okay, I'll admit I own a dozen.

When Tofino Brewing opened in 2011, part of their business plan was connected to marketing growlers as good environmental choices for locals, trying to tap into the green-minded citizenry. It turns out they were overwhelmed by demand and now base most of their business on filling growlers at the brewery. Townsite Brewing in Powell River and Hoyne Brewing in Victoria each followed Tofino's lead when they opened in 2012 and both now do brisk business with the big brown jugs. Then, a wave of growler-focused neighbourhood breweries opened in Vancouver in 2013 and 2014—places like Brassneck, 33 Acres and Main Street Brewing, where the model is to drop in and sample a few different beers before filling a couple growlers to take home. This new model, which makes the brewery itself a destination, has given Vancouver the most dynamic craft beer scene in the province.

Victoria is also a great place for growlers with so many different breweries and brewpubs to choose from. I can simply check the victoriabeers.com/growlers website to see what's on tap, and then it's simply a matter of tossing an empty growler in the back of my son's bike trailer—with him in his seat up front—and minutes later we're "rushing the growler."

spinnakers.com
250-386-2739
308 Catherine Street, Victoria
E-MAIL
  spinnakers@spinnakers.com
TWITTER @spinnakers

Spinnakers
Gastro Brewpub

Tap List

**MITCHELL'S EXTRA
SPECIAL BITTER**

5.2% ABV | 40 IBU

The original and still
perhaps the best ESB in
B.C. Michael Jackson, the
celebrated British beer
writer, called it "beautifully
balanced."

**LION'S HEAD
CASCADIA DARK ALE**

6.5% ABV | 55 IBU

A leader in the CDA style
category: dark, malty and
hoppy. Just delicious.

NORTHWEST ALE

6.2% ABV | 85 IBU

One of my favourite B.C.
beers, this hop bomb is
balanced with a strong
malt foundation.

**DRAGONFLY
RYE SAISON**

6% ABV | 25 IBU

A dark Saison with a
fruitiness from the yeast
and a rich, earthy quality
from the rye malt.

||||||||||||||||||||||||||||||||||||||||||||||

WHEN ARCHITECT PAUL HADFIELD and two of his
friends decided they wanted to open a brewpub on the shores of Victoria's Inner Harbour,
it was not legal to do so in Canada. It was 1982,
and although the opening of the Horseshoe
Bay Brewery that year had already marked
the advent of the microbrewing movement in
Canada, the brewpub concept, where beer is
produced and sold within the same premises,
was not allowed. The Horseshoe Bay Brewery
had to be physically separated from the Troller
Pub where its beer was sold.

But Hadfield and his partners went ahead
with their plans, lobbying the government hard,
and a year and a half later, in May 1984, just two
months after legislation was changed to allow
for brewpubs, Spinnakers opened its doors and
began pouring pints of hand-crafted, British-
style beer. What a revolutionary concept!*

John Mitchell, one of the co-founders of
Horseshoe Bay, came on board as a partner and
was Spinnakers' original brewmaster, creating three signature brews to open the pub that
are still regulars on the tap list today: Mitchell's Extra Special Bitter, Mt. Tolmie Dark and
Empress Stout. He stayed around to brew the

....

* Looking back at those archaic laws that had to be changed for
brewpubs to be allowed, maybe the politicians were right to be so
strict. After all, Spinnakers did cause a revolution.

first forty batches there before moving on to other pursuits.

Hadfield became Spinnakers' publican in 1986, and under his guidance the brewpub has expanded considerably. It now boasts a nine-room guest house and a harbourside restaurant with a top-notch West Coast menu featuring locally sourced produce, meat, cheese and seafood. They also bottle their own malt vinegars and mineral water (from an aquifer 225 feet below the building), make their own chocolate truffles by hand and bake artisan breads and desserts on site. In 2004, as part of its twentieth anniversary, it was re-branded Spinnakers Gastro Brewpub to reflect its diverse offerings. And in time for its thirtieth anniversary, Spinnakers opened its On the Fly outlet at the Victoria International Airport, giving Victoria residents a great reason to show up early for flight departures.

Most importantly, though, Spinnakers hasn't forgotten the original point: beer. You can still enjoy cask-conditioned beers pulled through classic English beer engines at the bar and served at cellar temperature in proper pint glasses—or several other colder styles on draft.

Paul Hadfield is still running the show at Spinnakers, but now a second generation is getting involved, too. Daughter Kala joined the brewer team a few years back, bringing her love of hoppy West Coast IPAs and sour Belgian styles into the mix. I can still taste the delicious Brett Saison she prepared for the brewpub's thirtieth anniversary party. Not to be outdone, her sister Carly serves up Spinnakers beer at the Lion's Head Pub in Robson (see "The Lion's Head" on page 217).

As Canada's first brewpub, still thriving today more than three decades later, Spinnakers should be at the top of every beer lover's list of places to visit.

....
Facts & Figures

OPENED ▸ *1984* ✪ **STYLES PRODUCED ▸** *10 + seasonals* ✪ **WHERE TO BUY ▸** *The brewpub and in liquor stores in Victoria and Vancouver* ✪ **ON TAP ▸** *The brewpub and the Lion's Head Pub in Robson* ✪ **GROWLERS ▸** *Yes*

swanshotel.com/brew-pub
250-361-3310
506 Pandora Avenue, Victoria
E-MAIL
  brewery@swanshotel.com
TWITTER @swansvictoria

Swans Brewpub

Tap List

**APPLETON
BROWN ALE**

5% ABV

My go-to beer during my
first year in Victoria twenty
years ago, this is as good
as ever.

BUCKERFIELD'S BITTER

5% ABV

A creamy, malty and
bitter ESB—in other words,
perfect.

**COCONUT
PORTER** (seasonal)

5.5% ABV

A gold medal winner at the
Canadian Brewing Awards.
Creamy with a light
coconut aftertaste.

EXTRA IPA

6.8% ABV

This West Coast IPA
is hoppy and strong,
somewhere between a
standard and imperial IPA,
hence an "extra."

||||||||||||||||||||||||||||||||||||||||||||||

IN THE FALL of 1991, I moved five thousand
kilometres from southern Ontario to Victoria, about as far as I could go and still stay in
Canada. I had no job lined up, and not much
money saved, but I was twenty-one and had
my entire life ahead of me. My brother Pete
and I rented a little house right across from
the terminus of a brand-new walkway along
the Inner Harbour that connected with
downtown Victoria. It became our regular
route—following the meandering path, we
could be downtown in fifteen minutes by
bike or forty-five minutes by foot.

We quickly discovered Spinnakers, conveniently located on the walkway midway
between our home and downtown. Not
surprisingly, Pete and I often stopped there
for a "halfway pint" or two. But it wasn't the
only stop on our own private ale trail—at
the downtown end sat Swans, a beautifully
renovated brewpub that became our default
evening spot because of the regular live
music on offer and the fact that Spinnakers
closes at 10:30 PM.

My brother and I were hooked instantly
by the big main bar room with its high
ceilings, bricks and beams, and original
artwork everywhere. Owner Michael Williams had renovated the building from the

feed warehouse it was when he bought it, transforming it into a gorgeous hotel with a brewery and pub on the bottom. An avid art collector, much of his collection resides in the pub and hotel rooms upstairs. When he died in 2000, he bequeathed the entire place to the University of Victoria, and happily those smart people have not changed a thing since then. I remember seeing Mr. Williams at the pub regularly in the early '90s. In 2006, a statue of him sitting on a bench, gazing at Swans, was erected on the little grassy boulevard across the street, in front of Market Square. Sometimes I visit it to say "hi."

Of course, the beer had to be good to keep me coming, and it still is. Its brewery was set up in 1989 by Frank Appleton, who, together with John Mitchell, helped kick-start the craft brewing movement in B.C. when they built the Horseshoe Bay Brewery in 1982. He got things started and then hired a young graduate student named Sean Hoyne to be the first full-time brewer. Since 2003, the brewer has been Andrew Tessier, who grew up in Victoria. Tessier worked on the mainland at Back-woods Brewing (now Dead Frog) and R&B Brewing before becoming the brewmaster at Propeller Brewing in Halifax in 2001. He jumped at the opportunity to come home to Victoria when the job came open at Swans two years later.

My brother and I only lived in that house for a year. He moved to Vancouver and then back to Toronto, poor guy. Recently, Pete brought his family out west for a visit, and he and I headed down to Swans one evening. When the waitress came by to take our order, the words just rolled off my tongue as if twenty years had never passed.

"An Appleton Brown Ale and a Buckerfield's Bitter, please."

Facts & Figures

OPENED › *1989* ✪ **STYLES PRODUCED ›** *9 + seasonals* ✪
WHERE TO BUY › *In bottles from their neighbouring store, or in private liquor stores in Victoria and Vancouver* ✪ **ON TAP ›** *The brewpub and select taphouses* ✪ **GROWLERS ›** *Yes*

VICTORIA'S
BEER MILE

• •

AS I WAS working on the first edition of this book, I moved back to Victoria after twelve years away, and some old friends threw me a great welcome back party—they took me on a tour of what one of them dubbed "the Beer Mile." This mile-long loop (1.6 kilometres just doesn't roll off the tongue so we'll put aside metric usage for now) features four distinct brewpubs whose origins span three decades of the craft brewing movement in B.C.

Begin this counter-clockwise route at the Canoe Brewpub (450 Swift Street), nestled in a beautiful spot right down on the water below the Johnson Street Bridge, making it the perfect place to debate the relative merits of replacing or refurbishing that historic structure over a pint.

There is a Victoria Harbour Ferry (www.victoriaharbour ferry.com) stop right outside the Canoe—a five-dollar ride will get you to your next stop on the Beer Mile and also give you a unique perspective on the industrial waterfront of Victoria where new housing and retail developments are blossoming among shipyards, cement factories and other traditional businesses. Call ahead of time (250-514-9794) to request a boat to take you one stop north to Point Ellice Historic House, just beyond the Point Ellice Bridge (which locals just call the Bay Street Bridge). From there it's a short walk to the newest member of Victoria's brewpub club, the Moon Under Water (350 Bay Street).

Heading west from the Moon Under Water across the Point Ellice Bridge you now have to complete the longest leg of this quest for beer: about half a mile following Bay Street to Catherine Street and then down to the shore of the Inner Harbour. There you will find Spinnakers (308 Catherine Street), which was Canada's first modern-day brewpub when it opened in 1984.

After Spinnakers, you're on the home stretch. The final leg of the Beer Mile is a ten-minute walk (hopefully not a stumble) back to downtown along the Songhees Walkway, which follows the shoreline of the Inner Harbour with camera-worthy views of the downtown waterfront, the Empress Hotel and the provincial Parliament Buildings. Across the Blue Bridge is Swans (506 Pandora Avenue), which opened in 1989 in a heritage building with comfortable hotel rooms upstairs. Swans is a great place to finish the Beer Mile since the pub offers live music every night of the week.

If you want to stretch the Beer Mile out over a couple of days, stay at Swans or Spinnakers and visit some of the other craft breweries nearby. Hoyne Brewing and the Driftwood Brewery are only a block away from the Moon Under Water at the corner of Hillside Avenue and Bridge Street, but neither offers official tours. Still, you might be able to arrange an informal visit at one or the other, and both do have growler stations. Phillips Brewing (2010 Government Street) and Vancouver Island Brewery (2330 Government Street) in the Design District just a few blocks from Swans and the Canoe offer tours (check their websites for tour dates), and both have storefronts with growler filling stations. Lighthouse Brewing, the furthest afield, but still just a twenty-minute detour from this loop, also opened a tasting room and growler station as part of their expanded brewery in early 2013.

vanislandbrewery.com
250-361-0005
2330 Government Street, Victoria
E-MAIL
info@vanislandbrewery.com
TWITTER @vanislebrewery

Vancouver Island Brewery

Tap List

PIPER'S PALE ALE

5% ABV | 38 IBU

Piper's has been an Island
favourite since 1984—
think of it as an older
generation's Blue Buck.

**HERMANN'S
DARK LAGER**

5.5% ABV | 30 IBU

Named for the brewery's
original Bavarian
brewmaster, this is an
excellent example of the
German Dunkel style.

SABOTAGE ISA
(seasonal)

5% ABV | 37 IBU

Big fruity, citrusy hops
burst out of this lighter
"session IPA."

**HERMANNATOR
ICE BOCK** (seasonal)

9.5% ABV | 35 IBU

Celebrating its twenty-fifth
anniversary in 2013, this
unusual German Eisbock
is cold-aged for over three
months.

VANCOUVER ISLAND BREWERY was founded in 1984 as Island Pacific Brewing, the same year as Spinnakers Brewpub and Granville Island Brewing in Vancouver, making it one of B.C.'s original microbreweries (the name was changed in 1991). As Victoria's first stand-alone craft brewery, it has long been one of the industry leaders in the beer-drenched provincial capital. VIB has remained popular and stable—as a respected elder of sorts—while several new young bucks, first Lighthouse, then Phillips, Driftwood and Hoyne, appeared on the scene.

The thing with being a grizzled old veteran in the beer industry is that many craft beer lovers, especially younger ones, are interested in finding new styles and brands, checking off beers on their lists and seeking out that next great hop bomb. VIB's beers have been fine forever, but apart from the Hermannator Ice Bock, an annual winter seasonal that goes back twenty-five years itself, there wasn't anything in their lineup that made the average beer geek's heart flutter. It had the respect of many B.C. beer lovers, but didn't inspire the sort of excited devotion reserved for the newer, edgier breweries.

But the brewery started to feel the love

after the release of its first specialty bomber, Flying Tanker White IPA, in 2012. It was a very interesting beer, and VIB followed it up in the autumn with a delicious Oktoberfest-style beer called Iron Plow Harvest Märzen. A couple other interesting seasonals were released in 2013, and Hermannator was named Beer of the Year at the B.C. Beer Awards. Then, in 2014, the brewery celebrated its thirtieth anniversary with a boozy imperial red ale called Thirty Years and a super aromatic ISA called Sabotage.

However, despite all these successes, the brewery's ownership group took a big step back early in 2014 by firing the general manager who had been leading this transition toward craftier beer styles and limited releases, replacing him with someone with no previous experience in the beer industry. Several staff members chose to leave the company in the weeks and months that followed, and it once again became unclear what direction the brewery was taking.

Vancouver Island Brewery has one of the largest brewing facilities among the microbreweries in B.C., definitely worth visiting on a tour (Friday and Saturday afternoons). A storefront tasting bar and growler station was another smart addition in 2012.

Facts & Figures

OPENED ‣ *1984* ✪ **STYLES PRODUCED** ‣ *6 + seasonals* ✪
WHERE TO BUY ‣ *Liquor stores throughout B.C.* ✪ **ON TAP** ‣ *Throughout Vancouver Island* ✪ **GROWLERS** ‣ *Yes*

VICTORIA BEER WEEK

Held in Victoria for a Week in Early March

•••••••••••••••••••••••

WHEN I MOVED to Victoria in 2012, I had two main beer-related goals: 1) finish writing this book; and 2) start up a Victoria Beer Week festival similar to Vancouver Craft Beer Week, which had launched a couple years earlier.

Well, the book came out in May 2013, and a few months later I began meeting with a small group of dedicated beer lovers who had already begun planning a week-long beer festival here to complement the long-running Great Canadian Beer Festival that takes place in September every year.

The first annual Victoria Beer Week launched on Saturday, March 9, 2014, with a cask night at the Victoria Public Market, featuring more than thirty unique cask-conditioned beers from craft breweries throughout B.C. It was a great night, and over the course of the rest of the week, we staged a wide variety of events, including Beer School, brewery crawls, a Women and Beer documentary film screening and panel, beer movie nights, and a Brewmaster's Brunch that closed off the nine-day festival in style.

Look for a similar range of events in coming years. Come celebrate craft beer in British Columbia's craft beer capital.

www.victoriabeerweek.com

HOP IN THE SADDLE

BeerCycle Tours in Victoria

•••••••••••••••••••••••

A FEW YEARS ago, on a visit to Portland, Oregon, I got to jump on a bike and tour around the city, visiting breweries with a local beer writer on a gorgeous summer afternoon. This easily counts as one of my favourite travel experiences: cycling in the great outdoors with short stops to taste craft beer and enjoy some snacks.

That writer, my friend Lucy Burningham, co-wrote a guidebook on that very subject called *Hop in the Saddle*, and a picture she took of me that afternoon even made it into the book, which makes me famous in Portland! Obviously, that's where I stole the title to this section.

You can do the same thing in Victoria, either self-guided or as part of a package tour offered by local bicycle rental companies. Both of the tours listed below include stops at a few different brewpubs, breweries and taphouses, with sampling included, and are not particularly strenuous. Best of all, you won't feel guilty about all the calories...

The Pedaler
Hoppy Hour Ride
719 Douglas Street
778-265-RIDE (7433)
www.thepedaler.ca

Cycle Treks
City Brewery Tour
1000 Wharf Street
250-386-3147
www.cycletreks.com

BOTTLE SHOPS
Victoria

. . . .

VICTORIA HAS A wide assortment of private liquor stores where you can find local favourites or interesting craft beer from elsewhere. Many government stores stock a good range of craft options, too.

Cascadia Liquor (Four locations)
4-2631 Quadra Street
101-3671 Uptown Boulevard
2244 Sooke Road (Colwood)
200-444 Lerwick Road
　(Courtenay)

Cook Street Village Liquor
109-230 Cook Street
　(around back)

Hillside Liquor Store
3201 Shelbourne Street

Liquor Express (Six locations)
12-1153 Esquimalt Road
3170 Tillicum Road
930 View Street
759 Yates Street
498 Island Highway
2134 Keating Cross
　(Saanichton)

Liquor Plus
2915 Douglas Street

Metro Liquor (Three locations)
101-1660 McKenzie Avenue
4-3960 Shelbourne Street
100-7143 West Saanich Road
　(Brentwood Bay)

Penny Farthing Liquor Store
2187 Oak Bay Avenue

Spinnakers Spirit Merchants
　(Two locations)
130-176 Wilson Street
425 Simcoe Street

The Strath
919 Douglas Street

Vintage Spirits
653 Pandora Avenue

BEST BEERS
Victoria

....

Driftwood Brewery Fat Tug IPA
One of the best IPAs *anywhere*, not just in B.C.; if you could drink just one beer in B.C., this should be it.

Hoyne Brewing Hoyner Pilsner
This is exactly what I remember drinking in Prague and Plzen on my trip to the Czech Republic ten years ago.

Lighthouse Brewing Siren Red Ale
Although this red bombshell of a beer caught my attention with its racy label, I was hooked by its even more enticing flavour.

Moon Under Water This Is Hefeweizen
Brewmaster Clay Potter specializes in German beers—his Hefeweizen tastes exactly like they do in Bavaria.

Spinnakers Dragonfly Rye Saison
This unusually dark Saison is a great example of some of the newer styles Spinnakers is producing in its fourth decade. The Brett-aged version served at the brewpub's thirtieth anniversary party was one of the best beers I tasted in 2014.

TAPHOUSES
Victoria

• •

HERE ARE MY top places to check out the local beer scene.

Beagle Pub
301 Cook Street
A great pub with a long tap list in Cook Street Village. The Beagle hosts cask nights and other beer events on a regular basis.

The Churchill
1140 Government Street
The "new" Churchill, named after an infamous and dingy pub that existed in the same building in the 1970s, opened in 2014 with fifty taps.

The Drake Eatery
517 Pandora Avenue
Right across from Swans Brewpub on the exterior of Market Square, the Drake "only" has about thirty taps, but it has the best curated beer list in Victoria.

Garrick's Head Pub
1140 Government Street
Victoria's best taphouse, this Bastion Square pub was renovated late in 2012 and now boasts a long bar with forty-four taps—twenty-two local brews and the rest from elsewhere.

THE ISLANDS & * THE SUNSHINE * COAST

AT THE BREWERY	DRAFT	FOOD	GROWLERS	BOTTLES	TOURS	BEDS
Craig Street Brew Pub	✪	✪	✪			
Cumberland Brewing	✪	✪	✪	✪		
Forbidden Brewing	✪		✪			✪
Gladstone Brewing	✪		✪	✪		
Longwood Brewery	✪		✪	✪		
Longwood Brewpub	✪	✪	✪	✪		
Persephone Brewing	✪	✪	✪	✪		
Red Arrow Brewing	✪		✪	✪	✪	
Salt Spring Island Ales			✪	✪		✪
Tofino Brewing	✪		✪	✪		
Townsite Brewing			✪	✪		
Wolf Brewing			✪			

ISLAND ALE TRAIL

••••••••••••••••••••••••

NOTORIOUSLY INDEPENDENT, WANTING as little as possible to do
with the mainland, Vancouver Islanders are a loyal breed when
it comes to beer. For the latter half of the twentieth century,
that loyalty was to Lucky Lager, a brand that was brewed in
Victoria by Labatt from 1958 to 1981. After Labatt demolished
its historic brewery in 1982 (see "From Swan Lake to Spring
Ridge" on page 43), Lucky was mainly brewed in Edmonton
and sometimes in the Kokanee plant in Creston, but it continued to be most Islanders' beer of choice even as the craft beer
revolution began bringing new and interesting brands to the
island. That devotion might have had something to do with the
beer's packaging which still describes it as "Vancouver Island's
Original," or maybe it was just stubbornness. Mass market beer
drinkers do tend to stick to one beer, kind of like long-suffering
sports fans. (Go Canucks go!)

Vancouver Island Brewery was founded in 1984 (originally
as Island Pacific Brewing) with the Vancouver Island market
as its target. That company has had some success in converting people away from Lucky, and currently they produce the
Islander lager brand as a direct attempt to woo residents. And
Phillips Brewing has also made inroads with their Blue Buck
Ale and Phoenix Lager brands.

When I wrote the first edition of this book, most towns
outside Victoria were still Lucky towns, with only a few excep-
tions. The arrival of Tofino Brewing has changed the vibe up on
the remote west coast of the island, as did Townsite Brewing

in Powell River. And Persephone Brewing has found similar success in Gibsons, while also courting the thirsty masses in Vancouver given that it is an easy day trip away from the big city.

It seems like the trick for these small, remote towns is "build it and the locals will come." Both Tofino and Powell River have large contingents of urban ex-pats who brought a love of craft beer with them, which definitely helped them develop a strong core of local support. Hopefully, the three breweries that recently opened in and around Courtenay in the Comox Valley will enjoy the same type of success.

Nanaimo has a longer history of brewing, but apart from the Longwood Brewpub, there hasn't been a big success story there yet, something Wolf Brewing hopes to change. A third brewery called White Sails was scheduled to open there late in 2015. Twin City Brewing aims to open in Port Alberni in 2016.

The Cowichan Valley, a popular food and wine lover's paradise, has a jewel of a brewpub in Duncan, which recently opened its own production brewery, Red Arrow, along with some cideries that might interest craft beer lovers. In nearby Chemainus, Riot Brewing is aiming to open in early 2016.

Down on the south coast of Vancouver Island, Sooke should see one or perhaps even two breweries open in 2016.

Add the always interesting Salt Spring Island Ales to the mix and it's clear that the Island Ale Trail offers beer lovers a wealth of options to explore.

STOP THE PRESSES!

Here's a quick update on the newest Vancouver Island brewery:

Forbidden Brewing
1590 Cliffe Ave, Courtenay
forbiddenbrewing.com | 250.702.7975

This Comox Valley nanobrewery is based in the Westerley Hotel.

craigstreet.ca
250-737-beer (2337)
25 Craig Street, Duncan
E-MAIL csbrewery@shaw.ca

Craig Street Brewpub

Tap List

||||||||||||||||||||||||||||||||||||||||||||

MT. PREVOST PORTER

5% ABV | 26 IBU

A smooth, dark porter
with a great roasted malt
character. Perfect on a
cold, rainy day.

**SUMMER
WHEAT BEER** (seasonal)

4.8% ABV | 22 IBU

An excellent Hefeweizen.
Only available as a summer
seasonal.

HALFWAY BETWEEN VICTORIA and Nanaimo,
Duncan is home to the stylish and comfortable Craig Street Brewpub, the Cowichan
Valley's first and only brewpub, with a regular
lineup of pale ale, lager, porter and Irish ale
on tap, along with occasional specialty brews.

After moving to Victoria from Saskatchewan in the early 1990s, Chris Gress learned
how to brew in his own backyard while he
worked as a server at a popular downtown
restaurant. A chance meeting with the
people who were building Craig Street led
him to become the brewer there. Now, he is
partnering with them to build his own production brewery, Red Arrow Brewing, also
in Duncan. Gress will train and oversee the
new brewer at the brewpub as he gets Red
Arrow up and running.

The beer at Craig Street is generally fine
but unadventurous, limited by the ownership's perception that the local crowd isn't
ready for more sophisticated styles. My hope
is that once Gress starts putting out more
interesting beer at Red Arrow, then the
brewpub will start taking more risks, too.

....

Facts & Figures

OPENED ‣ *2006* ❂ **STYLES PRODUCED** ‣ *4 + seasonals* ❂ **ON TAP** ‣
The brewpub ❂ **GROWLERS** ‣ *Yes*

SCRUMPY, CYSER, CIDER (& MEAD)

Apples Never Tasted So Good

••••••••••••••••••••••••

FOR AN IDEAL detour off the Island Ale Trail, I recommend visiting Vancouver Island's iconic cideries: Merridale Ciderworks, Sea Cider, and—a new addition in 2014—Tod Creek Craft Cider. Each one produces exceptional ciders from different varieties of apples that rival what the province's best craft brewers do with barley and hops, and some have also been experimenting with hopped ciders.

Merridale Ciderworks
1230 Merridale Road,
Cobble Hill
www.merridalecider.com
250-743-4293

Tod Creek Craft Cider
273 Prospect Lake Road,
Victoria
www.todcreekcider.com
250-882-1061

Sea Cider Farm & Ciderhouse
2487 Mt. St. Michael Road,
Saanichton
www.seacider.ca
250-544-4824

Tugwell Creek Meadery
8750 West Coast Road, Sooke
www.tugwellcreekfarm.com
250-642-1956

cumberlandbrewing.com
250-400-2739
2732 Dunsmuir Avenue, Cumberland
E-MAIL
  darren@cumberlandbrewing.com
TWITTER @cumberlandbeer

Cumberland Brewing

Tap List

FOREST FOG
AMERICAN WHEAT

4.3% ABV

This creamy, flavourful
and thirst-quenching beer
was my reward midway
through a 30-km bike ride
in 30-degree weather. I
can still taste it! Bonus:
partial proceeds go to the
Cumberland Community
Forest Society.

MORE COWBELL

4.5% ABV

The first beer Mike brewed
at Cumberland was this
delicious Dunkelweizen,
bursting with big banana
flavours thanks to the
German Weissbier yeast.

Facts & Figures

OPENED ▸ *2014*
STYLES PRODUCED ▸ *2 +*
  numerous seasonals.
WHERE TO BUY ▸
  The brewery
ON TAP ▸ *Cumberland*
  and the surrounding
  area
GROWLERS ▸ *Yes*

|||||||||||||||||||||||||||||||||||||||||||||

MIKE TYMCHUK WAS a chef and brewer at
Spinnakers back in the 1980s, learning the
craft from John Mitchell himself. Later, he
opened Wild Rose Brewing in Alberta, but
after twelve years there, he left the business
and moved to Cumberland where he opened
Rider's Pizza.

Late in 2013, Darren Adam, an old friend
from my days working at the Belfry Theatre,
emailed to say he was thinking of opening a brewery with Mike—and asked me to
talk him out of the idea. Obviously, I did the
opposite.

When the space next to Rider's came
available, they installed the brewery there
and punched a window through the cinder-
blocks so that the pizza (and beer) can go
back and forth.

The town of Cumberland is bursting with
young families who have embraced their new
brewery wholeheartedly. Expect to see cou-
ples with one parent pushing a stroller down
Dunsmuir Avenue and the other carrying a
growler or two.

The brewery's small tasting room and
patio out back are always full, prompt-
ing Darren and Mike to start planning an
expansion to another building across the
street within eight months of opening!

GET LOCAL

B.C.'s Craft Brewers use
Local Ingredients

••••••••••••••••••••••••

USING LOCAL INGREDIENTS in brewing has been part of the craft beer movement since long before the terms "locavore" and "100-mile diet" entered the foodie lexicon, but there is no doubt that interest in local beers has grown in recent years. No true estate brewery exists in B.C., unfortunately, mainly because the climate here is not well suited to growing barley, but Crannóg Ales comes the closest with its farm brewery concept, and they do use their own hops exclusively.

Several other B.C. breweries are growing their own hops to use in some specialty batches—usually fresh-hopped beers brewed right after the harvest in the fall—including Salt Spring Island Ales, which grows them on a nearby farm, and Spinnakers, which has a hop yard in Sooke, about an hour from the brewpub. But generally, B.C.'s craft breweries are leaving the production of hops to the hop farmers.

On the grain side of things, while it is difficult to grow barley effectively in the damp, coastal climate, one Saanich farmer named Mike Doehnel has been working at it for a while and has had some success. Driftwood Brewery has been his main customer—they have used his hand-malted barley in several seasonal specialties, including: Cuvée d'Hiver, a Saison it brewed in 2011; Spring Rite Abbey Ale, which was also brewed in 2011; and Pilsner Doehnel, which was released in 2014.

Phillips Brewing has produced the most local beer yet: their 24-Mile Blueberry Pail Ale used Doehnel's malted barley along with hops from another Saanich farm and local blueberries.

Over on the mainland, Mission Springs Brewpub's Fraser Valley IPA features hops and barley from B.C. exclusively.

Apart from hops and barley, some B.C. brewers source interesting local ingredients to add to their brews. Pumpkin beers, like fresh-hopped beers, are popular in the autumn, and most breweries try to find local sugar pumpkins for their brews. Berries are the most common local adjunct, including blueberries, blackberries, raspberries, strawberries and even huckleberries, which Fernie Brewing uses to produce its excellent What the Huck Huckleberry Wheat Ale all year round. Cherries, peaches and apricots also make an appearance in beers, especially from Okanagan breweries, which certainly makes sense given the stone-fruit orchards there.

Tofino Brewing caught some attention at the Central City Summer Cask Festival in 2011 with its cask of IPA flavoured with locally harvested spruce tips. Phillips also tried adding spruce tips to an ale in 2012 with not quite as much success. And in 2013, several Vancouver breweries in the Brewery Creek area collaborated on a Spruce Tip Stout, which also featured a unique sewn fabric patch for a label that could be removed and re-affixed to a jean jacket, satchel or even a Scout leader's uniform.

MALTING UPDATE

Phillips Brewing launched its own malting facility in 2015, using barley and wheat grown by farmers on the Saanich Peninsula, north of Victoria. Driftwood Brewery continues to use Mike Doehnel's malted barley in its one-and-only lager, Pilsner Doehnel. And Longwood Brewery in Nanaimo is also using barley malted by local farmer, Geremy White, in some of its beers.

Gladstone Brewing ←

gladstonebrewing.ca
250-871-1111
244 Fourth Street, Courtenay
E-MAIL
  daniel@gladstonebrewing.ca
TWITTER @gladstone_beer

||||||||||||||||||||||||||||||||||||||||||||

DANIEL SHARRAT AND his wife Alexandra Stephanson used to live on Gladstone Avenue in Victoria. Gladstone Brewing was what they called the home brewing system he kept in the garage—when they opened their own brewery, the name stuck.

Coincidentally, when I worked at the Belfry Theatre, also located on Gladstone Avenue, I lived above a mother and her young son. Well, that boy is now the head brewer at Gladstone Brewing, John Adair. #SmallWorld.

Adair learned to brew while working at Parallel 49 Brewing in Vancouver. He's a smart and creative brewer who is brewing great beer in Courtenay. And I get to say "I knew him when."

The brewery's building was originally a car dealership and mechanic's shop in the 1940s, which is echoed by the decor in the thirty-seat tasting room where you can sample beer by the glass or fill a growler. Gladstone added a patio on the sidewalk out front in time for its first summer, and welcomed a gourmet pizza restaurant next door.

Tap List

GLADSTONE PORTER
6% ABV | 35 IBU
Winner of a bronze medal at the Canadian Brewing Awards, this dark, dry porter is very drinkable.

STIRLING SINGLE
5% ABV | 30 IBU
A Patersbier, or Belgian Single, this style of beer was traditionally brewed at Trappist monasteries for the monks themselves to consume. It has all qualities of a big Belgian Tripel without all the booze.

....

Facts & Figures

OPENED ▸ *2015*
STYLES PRODUCED ▸ *Up to 8 at a time.*
WHERE TO BUY ▸ *The brewery*
ON TAP ▸ *Courtenay and the surrounding area*
GROWLERS ▸ *Yes*

Brewery
longwoodbeer.com
250-591-2739
2046 Boxwood Road, Nanaimo
E-MAIL
 brewery@longwoodbeer.com

Brewpub
longwoodbrewpub.com
250-729-8225
5775 Turner Road, Nanaimo
E-MAIL
 feedback@longwoodbrewpub.com

Longwood Brewpub & Brewery

|||||||||||||||||||||||||||||||||||||||||||||||||

THE LONGWOOD BREWPUB has been an oasis in the craft beer desert of central Vancouver Island since it opened in 1999. The main floor is a restaurant while downstairs is more of a pub with a big fieldstone fireplace and dark wood throughout. Although there are small TVs, it is decidedly not a sports bar, but rather, a place where you can enjoy a pint and a conversation with friends.

The brewpub has four English-style draught engines pulling cellar-conditioned beer—appropriate styles such as ESB, Irish red ale, Scotch ale and imperial stout. Continental styles are served at colder draft temperatures, including a very good Czech Pilsner and Dunkelweizen. The brewery uses locally grown hops whenever possible, often in cask-conditioned beers that are served from the bar on Firkin Fridays from 3:30 PM on.

Longwood opened a separate production brewery with a tasting room in 2013, which produces and packages several beers in tall cans.

Tap List

EXTRA SPECIAL BITTER (brewpub only)
6% ABV
John Mitchell's original Spinnakers recipe. Delicious.

THE BIG ONE IPA
6.8% ABV
A good English-style IPA.

STEAMPUNK DUNKELWEIZEN
5.5% ABV
A very nice, light-bodied, dark-coloured German wheat beer.

STOUTNIK RUSSIAN IMPERIAL STOUT
7.5% ABV
Winner of numerous awards for its label design, this is a rich, black stout of astronomic proportions.

Facts & Figures

OPENED ▸ *1999* STYLES PRODUCED ▸ *6 + seasonals*
WHERE TO BUY ▸ *Private liquor stores and at the brewery*
ON TAP ▸ *The brewpub and the brewery tasting room*
GROWLERS ▸ *Yes*

persephonebrewing.com
778-462-3007
1053 Stewart Road, Gibsons
E-MAIL dion@thebeerfarm.ca
TWITTER @Persephonebeer

Persephone Brewing ←

||||||||||||||||||||||||||||||||||||||||||||||

PERSEPHONE IS THE first brewery to open on the Lower Sunshine Coast, following the lead of Townsite Brewing up in Powell River on the Upper Sunshine Coast. Gibsons is much closer to Vancouver and more easily accessible with only one ferry involved—I've even heard of Vancouverites biking there and back in a day.

Located on an eleven-acre farm just off the main road that runs into Gibsons from the Langdale ferry terminal, Persephone calls itself "the Beer Farm." The property had been a flower farm when the owners bought it—they installed the brewery in the large barn-like building where the flowers had been processed, and then planted 0.85 acres of Cascade, Centennial and Goldings hops in the spring of 2013. This field already produced a lot of hops in its second year, which were picked by staff and volunteers and then used in a wet-hopped Harvest IPA in 2014.

As this book was about to be published, the brewery had plans to plant four more acres of hops in a lower field in early 2015. A new building was added in late 2014 to help with storage, packaging and, eventually, hop processing. Eventually, the brewery will be able to rely almost entirely on its own hops year-round, except for certain specialty

Tap List

GODDESS GOLDEN ALE
5% ABV | 35 IBU
Stylistically, this is a British-style summer ale; it is moderately bitter with a big biscuit grain character and a floral hoppiness. Delicious and very refreshing.

RUM RUNNER ALE
6% ABV | 45 IBU
This hop-forward West Coast red ale has a big caramel malt character balanced by citrusy hops.

DRY STOUT
4.5% ABV | 30 IBU
Winner of Best Stout at the B.C. Beer Awards in 2013 and 2014, this is a slightly sweet stout. If you can find it on nitro, as it is served at the brewery, even better.

DOUBLE IPA (seasonal)
9% ABV | 85 IBU
Boom! Persephone didn't bother brewing a regular IPA in its lineup—it just brought out the big guns with this powerful hop bomb.

varieties that will still have to be purchased.

Originally, as I reported in the first edition of this book, this brewery was supposed to be named Beachcomber Brewing as a link to Gibsons's history as the longtime location for the CBC television show. When the name changed to Persephone (which is the name of Nick's boat in the show), I assumed the CBC had blocked them from using the name, but apparently our national broadcaster had no problem with it—in fact, they even thought it might bring more attention to the show—but Vancouver Island Brewery had rights to the Beachcomber name for one of its beers and nixed the idea. Persephone makes good sense, anyway, as she was the Greek goddess of spring growth.

Brewer Anders McKinnon was working as an assistant brewer at Russell Brewing when Persephone's owners approached Russell's head brewer, Jack Bensley, for advice with the brewery. They offered Bensley the job of brewmaster, but he already had plans connected to Main Street Brewing, where he is the brewer now, so he recommended McKinnon in his place. Anders grew up in Ladner, but was happy to move to Gibsons. He has proven to be a great choice for the job, launching a strong lineup of beers right out of the gate, adding interesting seasonals over the next couple of years and winning awards along the way.

Whether as part of a day trip from Vancouver or a longer visit to the Sunshine Coast that includes Townsite Brewing, Persephone is a great place to visit with a family-friendly tasting room and a licenced picnic area. There is an outdoor pizza oven on site, and the brewery also hosts a fresh produce market in the summer months.

....
Facts & Figures

OPENED ▸ *2013* ○ **STYLES PRODUCED ▸** *3 + seasonals* ○
WHERE TO BUY ▸ *The brewery or at private liquor stores* ○ **ON TAP ▸**
Sunshine Coast, Greater Vancouver and Victoria ○ **GROWLERS ▸** *Yes*

redarrowbrewing.ca
250-597-0037
5255 Chaster Road, Duncan
E-MAIL info@redarrowbrewing.ca

Red Arrow Brewing ←

||||||||||||||||||||||||||||||||||||||||||||||||||

RED ARROW WAS founded by Chris Gress, the longtime brewer at Duncan's Craig Street Brewpub, who has been trying to get his own brewery started in the Victoria area for as long as I've known him. He came close to opening one in the Rock Bay "brewery district" before finally forming a partnership with Craig Street's owners to build Red Arrow in Duncan.

Based in an ivy-covered, brick building that was previously a custom motorcycle shop, Red Arrow has one of the most attractive tasting rooms around. The brewing facility is a reasonably large 20 hL brewhouse (built by Specific Mechanical in Saanichton) that will provide enough capacity to sell beer throughout Vancouver Island and, eventually, on the mainland as well.

Just as I expected, now that Chris Gress has free rein to brew more adventurous styles than he could at Craig Street, he is proving to be a talented brewer, with each new release more exciting than the last.

Tap List

MIDNITE UMBER
5.1% ABV | 33 IBU
This very drinkable ale is not quite brown but it's too dark to be red—that's right, it's umber! Very tasty, too.

SWEET LEAF IPA
6.3% ABV | 65 IBU
Maltier than many west coast IPAs, the big dose of pungent, aromatic hops makes it all work quite well.

Facts & Figures

OPENED ▸ *2015* ✪ **STYLES PRODUCED** ▸ *3 + seasonals* ✪
WHERE TO BUY ▸ *The brewery or private liquor stores* ✪ **ON TAP** ▸
Lower Vancouver Island ✪ **GROWLERS** ▸ *Yes*

gulfislandsbrewery.com
250-653-2383 · 1-866-353-2383
270 Furness Road,
  Salt Spring Island
E-MAIL
  info@gulfislandsbrewery.com
TWITTER @SaltSpringAles

Salt Spring Island Ales (Gulf Islands Brewery)

Tap List

EXTRA SPECIAL BITTER

5.5% ABV

A great, flavourful ESB made with whole-cone hops and organic malts.

DRY PORTER

5.5% ABV

A light-to-medium-bodied porter with a great chocolate and roasted malt character.

HEATHER ALE

5% ABV

Infused with heather flowers from the world-famous Butchart Gardens, this ancient style dates back to 2000 BC.

SPRING FEVER GRUIT (seasonal)

5% ABV

This ancient ale style is brewed entirely with a variety of wild herbs, roots and spices—and no hops at all.

|||||||||||||||||||||||||||||||||||||||||||||||

SALT SPRING ISLAND ALES was founded as Gulf Islands Brewery in 1998 by Bob Ellison and Murray Hunter, who had run an all-grain brew-on-premises operation called Murray's Brewplace on the island before that. In 2009, "Uncle Bob" sold his interest in the company to family friends, and Hunter stayed on as brewmaster.

Based in a converted barn at the base of Mount Bruce, the tallest peak on Salt Spring Island, the brewery uses water from a spring on the mountainside above, and produces and packages its beer entirely on the island. In 2009, they planted hops in a nearby farm field where they host a hop-picking festival each fall, using the hops in a fresh-hopped beer. The brewery also produces an ancient beer style called Gruit with no hops at all..

While you can find Salt Spring's beers on tap in Victoria, I highly recommend a visit to the brewery's tasting room on the idyllic island paradise itself. Be warned, though: you might never leave.

Facts & Figures

OPENED ▸ *1998* ○ **STYLES PRODUCED** ▸ *5 + seasonals* ○
WHERE TO BUY ▸ *The brewery, or in liquor stores in Vancouver and on Salt Spring and Vancouver Island* ○ **ON TAP** ▸ *Victoria and on Salt Spring Island* ○ **GROWLERS** ▸ *Yes*

tofinobrewingco.com
250-725-2899
681 Industrial Way, Tofino
E-MAIL
info@tofinobrewingco.com
TWITTER @tofinobrewco

Tofino Brewing ←

IIIIIIIIIIIIIIIIIIIIIIIIIIIIIIIIIIIIIIIIIIIIIII

WHEN TOFINO BREWING opened its doors in the spring of 2011, it was like a novice surfer trying to stand up on a longboard for the very first time. As any newbie will admit, you splash into the water much more often than you manage to stay on your feet, and the frigid Pacific Ocean waters off the west coast of Vancouver Island make the task even more challenging.

Similarly, the fledgling brewery's trio of owners—all locals themselves—figured they'd have to work at winning people over one by one, converting them from long-held connections to other brands. So, in step with the community's strong interest in environmentalism, they decided to start off by selling refillable growlers. The brewery's first batch of three hundred growlers, which they thought would last them a month, sold out within a week of opening. An emergency order of six hundred more was gone in another week so they quickly ordered another thousand. They even stopped selling the jugs to tourists, recognizing that the local community had to be their focus.

"We had a growler for every man, woman and child in Tofino," quipped brewer Dave Woodward, who moved there from Vancouver to craft the beer—true, considering the town's

Tap List

TUFF SESSION ALE
5% ABV | 25 IBU
A bright, copper-coloured pale ale with a toasty malt base balanced with West Coast hops.

HOPPIN' CRETIN IPA
7.5% ABV | 60 IBU
A tawny, heartily hopped, West Coast IPA that gives off an aromatic bouquet of citrus and mango.

FOGUST WHEAT ALE (seasonal)
4.5% ABV | 10 IBU
A German-style, unfiltered Hefeweizen that is light and hazy with subtle notes of banana and clove up front.

DAWN PATROL COFFEE PORTER (seasonal)
6.5% ABV | 20 IBU
The potent smoky bitterness of roasted coffee blends perfectly with the sweet malt flavours of this dark elixir.

year-round population is about 1,650. Co-owner Chris Neufeld added that they had to change their business plan, capping keg sales to allow for the unexpected popularity of the growlers, which accounted for more than half of their business within a few months of opening. Indeed, when I visited the brewery on a rainy Thursday evening in November shortly after it opened, there was a steady stream of customers stopping by to refill their growlers with some Tuff Session Ale, Hoppin' Cretin IPA or a special seasonal brew.

As much as possible, Tofino Brewing tries to access the local agricultural community for ingredients, including wild berries, hops from a Port Alberni farm and spruce tips harvested from the surrounding forest in the spring. They also work with local business partners, such as Shelter Restaurant, where all their beers are featured, and Tofino Roasting, a coffee company across the street that created a custom roast for the brewery's Dawn Patrol Coffee Porter. Other interesting beers include a Kelp Stout (you have to taste it to get it), Cosmic Wave Double IPA and The West Kölsch.

Since installing a bottling line in late 2012, the brewery has expanded its offerings in 650 mL bombers to government stores as well as private bottle shops. Another improvement was the addition of a tasting room at the brewery where you can sample the brews and soak in the vibe.

As B.C. destinations go, it doesn't get much better than Tofino, so Tofino Brewing is well worth a visit. While you're there, maybe you can try to catch a wave, dude.

....
Facts & Figures

OPENED ▸ *2011* ✪ **STYLES PRODUCED ▸** *5 + seasonals* ✪
WHERE TO BUY ▸ *The brewery and liquor stores in Vancouver and Victoria* ✪ **ON TAP ▸** *Vancouver Island and Greater Vancouver* ✪
GROWLERS ▸ *Yes*

Townsite Brewing

townsitebrewing.com
604-483-2111
5824 Ash Avenue, Powell River
E-MAIL
  info@townsitebrewing.com
TWITTER @townsitebrewing

||||||||||||||||||||||||||||||||||||||||||||

IN POWELL RIVER, the past, present and future are interwoven in the very geography. Born as a mill town a century ago, the original townsite was built between 1910 and 1930 by the Powell River Paper Company according to a utopian planning philosophy called the Garden City movement that respected the humanity of industrial workers and their families first and foremost. The resulting grid of houses around and above the paper mill was recognized as a National Historic Site in 1995.

The Townsite neighbourhood features a cluster of heritage houses built in the Arts and Crafts style that can be had for a song compared to anything in Vancouver or Victoria. As a result, it has become the destination for a wave of urban ex-pats trading the bustle and exorbitant real estate prices of Vancouver for Pow Town's affordability and artsy, outdoorsy vibe. One of those people was Karen Skadsheim, who arrived in 2007 after a year of travelling abroad, intending to stay with her brother for a while before returning to urban life in North Vancouver. Before too long, however, she realized her future lay right there. The only thing missing for her was craft beer.

"This brewery is all about me and my

Tap List

ZUNGA GOLDEN BLONDE ALE
5% ABV | 25 IBU
Zunga is Powell River-ese for "rope swing over water." Dive into this refreshing blonde ale.

TIN HAT IPA
6% ABV | 55 IBU
A solid West Coast IPA with an aromatic hop nose and a great malt foundation.

POW TOWN PORTER
6% ABV | 35 IBU
A rich, creamy porter with a great roasted malt character. Ideal for a rainy evening in front of the fireplace.

SHINY PENNY (seasonal)
8.5% ABV | 80 IBU
This complex Belgian IPA is a potent marriage of brewer Cédric Dauchot's Belgian heritage and North American brewing sensibilities.

needs," she explained with a laugh at the brewery's opening in April 2012. She and her friends had often talked about the perfect building for a brewery: an architectural treasure built by the federal government in 1939 to house the post and customs offices that had sat empty for a long time. One night, after a couple of beers, she e-mailed the address on the For Lease sign, saying she was looking into setting up a microbrewery in town and wondered what the rent would be. The owner loved the idea and formed a partnership with her to build the brewery.

Townsite Brewing opened in typically Powell River fashion: with an eclectic parade that featured decorated goats and a bride and groom riding in a bicycle rickshaw carrying the first keg of beer in their laps. The brewery's launch was very successful—its first order of 550 growlers sold out in a month, and demand for refills pushed the brewery to open seven days a week by early summer. Townsite donates one dollar from every growler fill to a local charity, and since it opened, nearly $20,000 has been raised.

Skadsheim decided to pursue a new career in local politics in 2014, but she left the brewery in good hands, especially when it comes to its brewmaster, Cédric Dauchot, who brings a Belgian brewing pedigree with him (see "From Belgium to B.C." on page 97). His wife, Chloe Smith, a brewer herself, took on the role of brewery manager when Skadsheim left, and the whole Townsite team includes some of the friendliest and welcoming folks you'll ever encounter.

Facts & Figures

OPENED ‣ 2012 ✪ STYLES PRODUCED ‣ 6 + seasonals ✪
WHERE TO BUY ‣ The brewery and bottle shops in Greater Vancouver, on Vancouver Island and on the Sunshine Coast ✪ ON TAP ‣ Sunshine Coast, Vancouver Island and Greater Vancouver ✪ GROWLERS ‣ Yes

FROM BELGIUM TO B.C.

Townsite Brewing's Cédric Dauchot

•••••••••••••••••••••••

A KEY PART of Townsite Brewing's story is its brewer, Cédric Dauchot, the only Belgian-born-and-trained brewer in B.C.

Dauchot grew up just south of Brussels, close to France. He graduated from L'institut Meurice in Brussels in 2004 as a chemistry-biochemistry engineer with an emphasis on fermentation and brewing. Most of his classmates ended up taking jobs with Belgian brewing empire Interbrew (now Anheuser Busch-InBev), the world's largest brewer with 25 per cent of the global market share. His own experience there as a lab technician for a few months was enough to make him realize he did not want to go that route with his brewing career. Little did he know he'd end up about as far from that as one can get, both figuratively and physically.

After graduating, he took a job with the French chain Les 3 Brasseurs, which sent him to Montreal to set up several brewpubs in Quebec. During his four years there, he met and married a Canadian woman named Chloe Smith, who is a brewer herself. After learning everything there is to know about setting up breweries, they moved to her hometown of Saskatoon to try to open their own, the Shiny Penny Brewery, which they intended to be the first "gastronomic brewpub" in Saskatchewan. But after "chasing our own tail for a year and a half," they saw an advertisement for a head brewer in Powell River and decided to apply.

Townsite's founder, Karen Skadsheim, says she definitely wanted to hire him, but admits she was nervous about bringing this couple—who were about to have their first baby—all the way to the remote northern end of the Sunshine Coast, far from family and friends. She needn't have worried. As Dauchot explains in his accented but perfect English, "Saskatoon to Powell River is less far than Belgium to Canada."

It turned out to be the perfect fit. Cédric and Chloe love the Townsite neighbourhood's laid back, artistic vibe. Most importantly, Dauchot says, "I had the freedom to put the brewery together the way I wanted." Chloe has since taken over for Skadsheim as brewery manager.

With the recent surge in interest in Belgian styles in the craft beer world, Townsite is lucky to have its own resident expert, as demonstrated by the delicious Tripel he brewed for the BierCraft Belgian Showcase event during Vancouver Craft Beer Week in 2012, just a few months after Townsite opened. I had the pleasure of hanging out with Dauchot that night—we sampled various Belgian beers and he shared his memories of them. ("This is the one I used to drink when I was sixteen and getting into trouble," or, "This brewery is five minutes from my father's house.")

Late in the evening, the restaurant owner walked over with a small, unlabelled bottle and offered us each a tiny glassful. It was the fabled Westvleteren 12, a Trappist beer that is brewed by monks in Belgium and is incredibly hard to find. The monastery only sells the beer on site, and it is not supposed to be resold.

I was thrilled to try it, but Dauchot's reaction to it was priceless. "This should not be here!" he sputtered in shock, staring at the small glass in his hands as if it were liquid gold. He demanded we find a quiet corner and insisted we warm the small glassful a little in our hands before sipping it. How was it? You'll have to try it yourself to find out. I want to keep that moment between Cédric and me.

wolfbrewingcompany.com
250-716-2739
2-940 Old Victoria Road, Nanaimo
E-MAIL
  info@wolfbrewingcompany.com

Wolf Brewing

||||||||||||||||||||||||||||||||||||||||||||||

NANAIMO DOES NOT have a great history with breweries. Only the Longwood Brewpub can be described as successful. One other operation, Fat Cat Brewery, struggled for more than a decade before it was sold and rebranded as Wolf Brewing in 2011. The new owners have been working at establishing new clients and developing new brews, but things have not progressed very quickly, certainly not in comparison with most of B.C.'s booming craft brewers.

At the end of 2014, however, Wolf announced it was expanding into the neighbouring space in its industrial complex, which means increased capacity and a tasting room that will hopefully be open around the time this book is published.

Positive changes, indeed. I look forward to checking it out on my next summer getaway to Rathtrevor Beach in Parksville. A growler of Wolf beer would be the perfect addition to my camping provisions list.

Tap List

RANNOCH SCOTCH ALE
6% ABV | 30 IBU
This "wee heavy" is rich and malty with big caramel flavours. Delicious.

RED BRICK IPA
6% ABV
On the maltier side but with a substantial offering of hops, this is an English IPA with a bit of West Coast flair.

....

Facts & Figures

OPENED ▸ *2011 (originally Fat Cat Brewery, which opened in 2000)* ✪
STYLES PRODUCED ▸ *5* ✪ **WHERE TO BUY ▸** *The brewery and in liquor stores on Vancouver Island* **ON TAP ▸** *Vancouver Island.* ✪
GROWLERS ▸ *Yes*

BEST BEERS

The Islands
and the Sunshine Coast

••••••••••••••••••••••••

Cumberland Brewing Forest Fog American Wheat
Creamy and refreshing: perfect for a summer afternoon patio
session.

Persephone Brewing American Pale Ale
Overflowing with much more hop flavour and aroma than you
might expect for its colour and body.

Salt Spring Island Ales ESB
Day trips to Salt Spring from Victoria are a whole lot easier to
justify now that the brewery's tasting room and growler station
are open.

Tofino Brewing Tuff Session Ale
If this book sells a million copies I think I will retire to Tofino
and spend my royalties on growler fills of this bitchin' beer.

Townsite Brewing Pow Town Porter
Or maybe I'll retire to Powell River so I can sip this creamy
porter gazing at the incredible sunset every night.

VANCOUVER

AT THE BREWERY	DRAFT	FOOD	GROWLERS	BOTTLES	TOURS	BEDS
33 Acres Brewing	✪	✪	✪	✪		
Bomber Brewing	✪	✪	✪	✪		
Brassneck Brewery	✪	✪	✪			
Callister Brewing	✪		✪			
Coal Harbour Brewing						
Doan's Craft Brewing	✪		✪	✪		
Dockside Brewing	✪	✪	✪		✪	
Dogwood Brewing	✪		✪	✪		
Granville Island Brewing	✪	✪		✪	✪	
Main Street Brewing	✪	✪	✪	✪		
Off the Rail Brewing	✪		✪	✪		
Parallel 49 Brewing			✪	✪		
Postmark Brewing	✪	✪	✪	✪		
Powell Street Craft Brewery	✪	✪	✪	✪		
R&B Brewing			✪	✪		
Red Truck Beer	✪	✪	✪	✪	✪	
Steel Toad Brewpub	✪	✪				
Steamworks Brew Pub	✪	✪	✪	✪		
Steamworks Brewery	✪	✪	✪	✪	✪	
Storm Brewing	✪		✪		✪	
Strange Fellows Brewing	✪	✪	✪	✪	✪	
Yaletown Brewing	✪	✪	✪	✪		

CRAFT BEER
CENTRAL

....

IN THE TWO short years since the first edition of this book was published, Vancouver has more than earned the title of "craft beer central." Nowhere in B.C. has craft beer culture taken hold of the general consciousness as it has there. Stretching back to 2012, thirteen new breweries and one brewpub have opened in the city limits, along with nearly as many in the immediate suburbs. Craft beer has gone from being a specialty product available in certain beer-focused restaurants and pubs to being embraced as part of Vancouver's lifestyle the same way as it is in Portland or Seattle.

Beer is so much a part of the Vancouver zeitgeist right now that one could be forgiven for thinking it always has been. In fact, B.C.'s largest city was rather slow to embrace craft beer, lagging behind Victoria for much of the first thirty years of the craft beer revolution. After Granville Island Brewing opened in 1984, only Shaftebury opened in the city in the next decade. Fogg n' Suds, a chain started there in the 1980s, was an oasis for a time because of the diversity of beers on its menu. In the mid-'90s there was a brewpub boom with the opening of Yaletown Brewing, Steamworks, Dockside and Dix, but the only production breweries that opened during that decade were R&B and Storm, both pretty small affairs. And after Dix opened in 1998, no new breweries or brewpubs opened in the city until 2011. Most of the growth occurred in the suburbs where the lower cost of rent or real estate made the business of brewing more viable. Granville Island's sale to Molson-Coors (via Creemore Springs) in 2009 seemed to mark a low point in the city's beer scene, but it is clear in retrospect that the scene was actually about to explode.

The Alibi Room's conversion to a craft beer focus in 2006 played a big role in waking up the city to craft beer (see "Nigel's Alibi" on page 110). There were other contributing factors, too. Private liquor stores like Brewery Creek and Firefly began increasing their craft beer sections, becoming full-fledged bottle shops, which encouraged distributors to expand their portfolios. Cask-conditioned beer could be found any night of the week, and seasonal multi-cask festivals became must-attend events. Other taphouses such as St. Augustine's followed, and the membership ranks of the Campaign for Real Ale (CAMRA) swelled. A younger generation of "foodies" turned to craft beer instead of wine, and food-pairing or brewmaster dinners followed. More and more women began showing up at craft beer events. And the brewers began to answer the demand for new and more challenging styles.

In the past eighteen months, two distinct brewery neigh-bourhoods have formed: around Powell–Victoria and along Main Street where the original Brewery Creek once flowed (see "Brewery Creek" on page 124). As this edition was being writ-ten, another beer-soaked neighbourhood around Clark and Adanac was also coming together (see "Neighbourhood Beer" on page 116). The geographical preference for East Van has more to do with the location of scarce industrial-zoned build-ings in the city than anything else, I'd argue—after all, there's no doubt that a storefront microbrewery like Brassneck or 33 Acres would do well in Kitsilano or nestled among South Cam-bie's restaurants and shops.

Vancouver has become the engine that drives craft beer in B.C.—its unique and diverse array of breweries, taphouses and bottle shops makes it now, without question, *the* craft beer des-tination in British Columbia, if not all of Canada.

33acresbrewing.com
604-620-4589
15 Eighth Avenue West,
  Vancouver
E-MAIL
  hello@33acresbrewing.com
TWITTER @33Acres

33 Acres Brewing

Tap List

IIIIIIIIIIIIIIIIIIIIIIIIIIIIIIIIIIIIIIIIIIIIIII

33 ACRES OF LIFE
4.8% ABV | 40 IBU
This California Common
beer (ale-lager hybrid) is
full-bodied with a distinct
hop character and a dry,
crisp finish.

33 ACRES OF OCEAN
5.3% ABV | 50 IBU
This fine example of the
West Coast pale ale style
showcases citrus and
pine hop flavours with a
caramel malt backbone.

33 ACRES OF MERCKX
7.6% ABV | 33 IBU
A strong, amber Saison
with some tartness and a
delicious peppery-citrus
yeast character.

33 ACRES OF SUNSHINE
(summer seasonal)
5% ABV | 14 IBU
A French-style Blanche,
this light and hazy wheat
beer has a subtle yeast
character with added
orange peel, coriander and
anise.

THE FIRST OF a trio of storefront brewer-ies that have opened along Main Street in Vancouver's aptly named Brewery Creek neighbourhood, 33 Acres sets itself apart with its clean white aesthetic, café feel, and just-off-Broadway location.

Founder Josh Michnik decided to open a brewery in 2011 after leaving his first career in film and television production behind and helping his wife open a hip clothing store in Chinatown. He searched for a year for the right location in a neighbourhood where he could focus on the locals primarily.

Just one block off busy Broadway on Eighth Avenue between Main and Cambie, the brewery's storefront has become very popular among local residents and workers at nearby businesses, including the thirsty digerati at Hootsuite, whose headquarters is one block away. Snacks, charcuterie, coffee and tea are available at the brewery, or you can buy something from one of the food trucks that park out front on a daily basis. The brewery's tasting room has even hosted a Morning-After Social Yoga class on Sunday mornings, with brunch and a beer included after the yoga session.

According to Michnik, the brewery's name refers to "success through hard work," with thirty-three being a numerologically powerful number and "Acres" acting as a reference to the honest human labour associated with farming. Each beer is named "33 Acres of…" something—Sunshine, Ocean, Life, Nirvana, etc.—with further details of the beer style added in a subtitle on the label.

Brewer Dave Varga was lured away from a longtime gig at Red Truck, and based on the subtlety and complexity of the beers he has brewed here, it seems his sensibility suits 33 Acres' neighbourhood focus more than Red Truck's province-wide approach. Right from the start, 33 Acres' beers have been interesting and well made across the board.

While it is possible to get some of 33 Acres' beer on tap in pubs and restaurants in Vancouver and Victoria or in 650 mL bombers at bottle shops, the majority of the brewery's offerings can only be obtained right at the source—either by the glass in the tasting room or in growlers to take away. It's the same approach you will find at Brassneck Brewery and Main Street Brewing, which are just a few blocks away, and the result is the most exciting brewing neighbourhood in all of B.C. (see "Neighbourhood Beer" on page 116).

As is the case with many of my favourite breweries in B.C., my opinion is based on more than just the beer in the glass—it's about the people behind the brewery and the type of community they help to create. Certainly, 33 Acres Brewing brings together all of those elements: delicious beer produced by great people as part of a diverse and inclusive community.

Facts & Figures

OPENED › *2013* ❂ **STYLES PRODUCED ›** *2 + seasonals* ❂
WHERE TO BUY › *The brewery or at private liquor stores* ❂ **ON TAP ›**
Vancouver and Victoria ❂ **GROWLERS ›** *Yes*

bomberbrewing.com
604-428-PILS (7457)
1488 Adanac Street, Vancouver
E-MAIL
  info@bomberbrewing.com
TWITTER @BomberBrewing

Bomber Brewing

Tap List

||||||||||||||||||||||||||||||||||||||||||||||

ESB

5.2% ABV | 40 IBU

Malt-forward with a bit of a West Coast hop character, this is a solid, drinkable ESB in the same category as Driftwood's Naughty Hildegard.

PILSNER

4.8% ABV | 35 IBU

This light-bodied Czech Pilsner has a grainy malt profile and a pronounced hop finish. Ideal hockey beer!

BIKE ROUTE BEST BITTER (seasonal)

3.9% ABV | 35 IBU

This delicious Mosaic hop–forward bitter proves that lower alcohol doesn't mean low flavour.

SHUTOUT STOUT

6% ABV | 45 IBU

A medium-bodied oatmeal stout with rich roasted chocolate and coffee notes.

THE STYLIZED BOMBER Brewing logo splashed across the side of the brewery on Adanac Street, a busy Vancouver bike route, is hard to miss. A painted sign by the bike lock-up out front also offers "Free ~~Beer~~ Air" with a convenient air pump for bike tires courtesy of the air compressor inside the brewery. That plus the delicious beers on tap in the tasting room inside provide the perfect excuse to stop on the cycle commute home.

The brewery's name comes from the Vancouver Bombers, a beer-league hockey team that co-founders Don Farion and Blair Calibaba have played on for years. Farion, a certified cicerone, is co-owner of the BierCraft and Incendio restaurants in Vancouver. Calibaba developed his brewing skills as a home brewer and also worked at a U-Brew shop and at Dan's Homebrewing Supplies.

Given BierCraft's Belgian beer focus, one might expect Bomber's lineup to feature Belgian beers prominently, but so far, at least, apart from a Belgian Blonde Ale brewed exclusively for BierCraft, that is not the case. The core lineup is a solid trio of ESB, IPA and Pilsner, available in government liquor stores and private bottle shops in six-packs of cans, as well as a mixed twelve-pack that includes four of each.

Seasonal releases on draft and in 650 mL "bomber" bottles so far have included Shutout Stout and Bike Route Best Bitter, a low-gravity English bitter featuring Mosaic hops, as well as a Märzen, Cascadian dark ale, double IPA, Oktoberfest lager and summer fruit beers.

Bomber's tasting room is a popular spot open seven days a week. The brewery has its regular and seasonal beers on tap, and also uses a "Randall" to infuse beers with different interesting flavours there on a daily basis. Tuesdays are $2 off growler fills, and Wednesdays feature one-off cask-conditioned beers.

Bomber's location just off Clark Drive, halfway between Vancouver's two prominent brewing neighbourhoods—Powell–Victoria and Main Street—has become the latest trendy spot to open a new brewery in the city. Off the Rail is on the same block of Adanac, across the street from Bomber; Strange Fellows is just a few blocks south on Clark; Powell Street Craft's new location is a few blocks north; and Callister Brewing is also nearby on Franklin.

Funny to think, then, that Bomber almost didn't open there. Apparently, Calibaba and Farion were about to sign a lease on a different location when their realtor called them and told them to wait until they had checked this building out. It had been a seafood processing factory, which meant it had floor drains and a cooler already in place. They switched to this location and as a result were able to get the brewery open far sooner than is usually the case.

....
Facts & Figures

OPENED ▸ *2014* ⚙ **STYLES PRODUCED** ▸ *4 + seasonals* ⚙
WHERE TO BUY ▸ *Throughout B.C.* ⚙ **ON TAP** ▸ *Greater Vancouver and Victoria* ⚙ **GROWLERS** ▸ *Yes*

brassneck.ca
2148 Main Street, Vancouver
E-MAIL info@brassneck.com
TWITTER @brassneckbrew

Brassneck Brewery

Tap List

||||||||||||||||||||||||||||||||||||||||||||||||

PASSIVE AGGRESSIVE

7% ABV | 75 IBU

This so-called dry-hopped pale ale could pass for an IPA elsewhere but Gmoser was leery about jumping into the IPA pool too quickly. In any case, it's delicious.

FREE RADICAL WHITE IPA (seasonal)

6.5% ABV

Spicy Belgian yeast with lemony Sorachi Ace and citrusy Citra hops. Boom!

STOCKHOLM SYNDROME FARMHOUSE SAISON (seasonal)

6.5% ABV

This Saison, aged for months with Brettanomyces, will take your taste buds hostage. Don't worry, you'll love it.

MULTIWEIZEN

5.5% ABV

An open-fermented Hefeweizen made with five grains: rye, wheat, barley, oats and corn. Delicious.

I FIRST STARTED hearing rumblings about this brewery more than two years before it opened. Most of what I heard came in the form of rants by Nigel Springthorpe, the co-owner and manager of the Alibi Room, which always began with "This is off the record, right?" The rants had to do with the seemingly never-ending challenges he and his then-unnamed partner were facing as they tried to open the kind of brewery they wanted to open in Vancouver. And once they finally secured the space they wanted, the rants continued as it took more than a year to get the brewery open, during which time money was pouring out of the building like water through a sieve.

Well, the wait was worth it because in the end, Brassneck is, according to Springthorpe, "absolutely the dream I had years ago when I first imagined the brewery," and, in my opinion, the best place to drink beer in B.C. The prototypical Vancouver storefront brewery, Brassneck is located right on busy Main Street at Sixth Avenue, around the corner from The Whip, a restaurant that was a leader in the early days of the city's cask-conditioned beer scene (see "Tapping the Cask" on page 134), and a short walk from both Main Street Brewing and 33 Acres (see "Neighbourhood Beer" on page 116).

If you want to taste Brassneck's beers you have to go there because none of its products are packaged for sale outside of the brewery—Nigel doesn't even serve it at the Alibi Room even though he could thanks to relaxed Tied Houses rules. Brassneck's tasting room has fifty seats, which have generally been full every night since the brewery opened in October 2013. But fear not: if you can't get a seat, you can still take home any of eight different beers in three different sizes of growlers. Apart from two constant beers, Brassneck Ale and Passive Aggressive, which became the brewery's first runaway hit soon after opening, the rest of the beer lineup is in constant motion. And that's what makes Brassneck so great, that and the fact that the beer is so good.

Responsible for the beer side of things is brewer Conrad Gmoser, who brewed at Steamworks Brew Pub for seventeen years before joining forces with Springthorpe. Gmoser brought a great reputation with him, as well as the collective sense among the city's beer geeks that if given more freedom to explore styles he would create wonderful beers. And that is exactly what has happened.

Utilizing three separate small-scale brewing systems for extreme flexibility, Gmoser keeps the tasting room's taps in flux with a mix of styles that runs the gamut through continental lagers, English ales, North American hop bombs, Belgian sours, barrel-aged behemoths and hybrids of all of the above. You will always find something surprising on tap, and on most nights, you'll see the tap list change right in front of you.

If you only have time to visit one brewery in Vancouver, go to Brassneck. It really doesn't get much better than this.

Facts & Figures

OPENED ‣ *2013* ✪ **STYLES PRODUCED** ‣ *2 + seasonals* ✪ **WHERE TO BUY** ‣ *Only at the brewery* ✪ **ON TAP** ‣ *Only at the brewery* ✪ **GROWLERS** ‣ *Yes*

NIGEL'S ALIBI
In Search of Craft Beer

• •

GASTOWN, VANCOUVER'S OLDEST neighbourhood, is named for John "Gassy Jack" Deighton, the first foreign settler of the community that would eventually become Vancouver. The story goes that he arrived in a rowboat on September 30, 1867, with his family, two chairs and a big barrel of whiskey. He told some local sawmill workers they could have all the whiskey they could drink in exchange for building his bar. Thus, his Globe Saloon was erected in one day and Gastown was born.

Today, the Globe Saloon is long gone, and Gastown has evolved into an eclectic hybrid of touristy souvenir stores, restaurants, dance clubs and local fashion boutiques—as well as another saloon that has played a seminal role in the development of Vancouver's craft beer culture: the Alibi Room.

The Alibi Room is Vancouver's craft beer headquarters. You'll find the best craft beer on tap there, both from B.C. and elsewhere, served by knowledgeable, beer-loving staff, along with excellent food and a comfortable, welcoming atmosphere. Behind the bar you might get to meet Nigel Springthorpe—decidedly less loquacious than the city's original saloon keeper, but a founding father of Vancouver's burgeoning craft beer scene nonetheless—though he is there a lot less since he opened his own brewery, Brassneck.

Springthorpe went from employee to co-owner and manager back in 2006. At that time, he was just starting to get interested in craft beer, but over the next few years he systematically sought out new and interesting beer wherever he could find it, first from B.C. craft brewers, then later from farther south down the Cascadian coast, and finally from European sources.

"It was never really the plan," he admits in his characteristic British accent, "but as my own tastes changed and I started to discover the wonderful world of craft beer, I decided to explore the possibility of putting all of the best breweries, near and far, side by side in one location."

As the Alibi Room's row of taps grew to a dozen, then two dozen, then up to the current fifty plus three cask engines, the city's beer lovers arrived in droves and brewers clamoured to get their beers served there. A healthy sense of competition among the beer makers pushed them to create better and better beer, to be accepted by both Nigel's increasingly discerning palate and the ever-growing ranks of craft beer lovers seeking new and more challenging styles.

Now, with Vancouver's craft beer boom in full swing, the city has many different taphouses to choose from, some of which have even more taps, though perhaps not quite the same aesthetic or ambiance. On top of the incredible beer selection, it's a great room in a century-old heritage brick building. It has wonderful old hardwood floors, solid beams and tall windows. There's pretty much no place I'd rather be on a rainy evening in the big city.

---

www.alibi.ca
157 Alexander Street (at Main Street)
604-623-3383

callisterbrewing.com
604-569-2739
1338 Franklin Street, Vancouver
E-MAIL
info@callisterbrewing.com
TWITTER @callisterbeer

Callister Brewing

||||||||||||||||||||||||||||||||||||||||||

Tap List

**REAL CASK BURNLEY
BASTARD MILD**

3% ABV
This authentic cask-conditioned mild is fantastic: so rich and flavourful despite its low ABV.

**CALLISTER RYE
PALE ALE**

5.2% ABV | 40 IBU
Moderately hoppy with a rich, spicy malt base thanks to the addition of rye malts.

....

Facts & Figures

OPENED ‣ *2015*
STYLES PRODUCED ‣
2 + seasonals
WHERE TO BUY ‣
The brewery
ON TAP ‣ *Select pubs
and restaurants in
Vancouver*
GROWLERS ‣ *Yes*

IN THE SEA of new breweries opening in Vancouver, Callister Brewing stands out as unique. Founders Chris Lay and Diana McKenzie have created a community hive for brewing, providing space and equipment under a revenue-sharing model. It is an incubator for new brewers who will ideally move on to open their own breweries.

Lay is Callister's main brewer, but three other partners also brew on the small four-barrel (about 6 hL) system. Adam Chatburn, past President of CAMRA's Vancouver chapter, launched "Canada's first cask-only brewery" under the Real Cask brand. His beers are pulled through proper English draught engines from casks in the temperature-controlled cellar. Chester Carey, Canada's original Certified Cicerone, is brewing Belgian-style table beers on behalf of Brewery Creek Brewing. Rounding out the group is Machine Ales from Adam Henderson and Matt Kohlen of Copper & Theory, a beer import agency.

The name of the brewery is inspired by Callister Park Stadium, an East Vancouver athletic venue (1942–70) where Lay's grandfather was the on-site caretaker, living in a suite beneath the stands.

Coal Harbour Brewing

coalharbourbrewing.com
604-215-7471
1967 Triumph Street, Vancouver
E-MAIL
info@coalharbourbrewing.com
TWITTER @CoalHarBrew

|||||||||||||||||||||||||||||||||||||||||||

COAL HARBOUR BREWING opened quietly in early 2012 with a big plan to brew two specialty lagers, 311 Helles and Vancouver Vienna Lager. They added a rye ale almost as an afterthought. Well, it turns out the Triumph Rye Ale was their most popular brew, and when brewer Kevin Emms added the Powell IPA to the lineup later in spring, he was promptly rewarded with a gold medal at the Canadian Brewing Awards in the English IPA category. Not bad for a brand new beer from a brand new brewery.

Emms has since moved on to work at Deep Cove Brewers and Distillers, replaced by Ethan Allured, previously of Turning Point Brewery. Most of Coal Harbour's original beers stayed pretty much the same, but the few additions have not been that memorable.

With Parallel 49 Brewing's popular tasting room right across the street, it's a pity Coal Harbour Brewing has not seen fit to open one of its own. I keep hearing rumours that one is in the works, but it never seems to happen.

Tap List

311 HELLES LAGER
5.25% ABV | 18 IBU
A genuine Munich-style lager. *Prosit!*

POWELL IPA
6.5% ABV | 66 IBU
A surprise gold medal winner at the 2012 Canadian Brewing Awards just weeks after it was first brewed.

Facts & Figures

OPENED ▸ *2012* ✪ STYLES PRODUCED ▸ *4 + seasonals* ✪
WHERE TO BUY ▸ *Liquor stores in the Lower Mainland and Greater Victoria* ✪ ON TAP ▸ *Restaurants and pubs in Greater Vancouver* ✪
GROWLERS ▸ *No*

doanscraftbrewing.com
604-559-0415
1830 Powell Street, Vancouver
E-MAIL
  mike@doanscraftbrewing.com
TWITTER @DoansCBC

Doan's Craft Brewing Co.

Tap List

RYE STOUT

6.2% ABV | 53 IBU

Rye pale ales and IPAs have become fairly common in the last year or two but a rye stout?! It's really good, brewed with three different kinds of rye resulting in a rich and satisfying chocolatey stout.

ALT

5% ABV | 25 IBU

A malt-forward ale that is complex yet very drinkable with a subtle German Noble hop presence.

|||||||||||||||||||||||||||||||||||||||||||||||||||

THIS BREWERY HAS been in the works for a long time. Nearly every conversation I've had with beer geeks in Vancouver about what new breweries were about to open has included a mention of the Doan brothers. But whenever I'd follow up with Mike and Evan Doan, it was always still a dream in the future. So with this brewery due to open just as this book goes to press, I am pleased to finally be able to write this profile.

Doan's Craft Brewing is based in the same building that previously housed Powell Street Craft Brewery, which moved to a bigger space in 2014. If the Doans manage to have the same sort of success as their predecessor, they will be very pleased indeed.

With a small building footprint, the brewery plans on selling most of its beer through a twenty-five-seat tasting lounge by the glass or in growler fills. The Doans will also be sending kegs to local pubs and 650 mL bombers to private liquor stores when capacity allows.

Facts & Figures

OPENED ▸ *2015* ✪ STYLES PRODUCED ▸ *3 + seasonals* ✪ WHERE TO BUY ▸ *The brewery and in select bottle shops* ✪ ON TAP ▸ *Vancouver* ✪ GROWLERS ▸ *Yes*

Dockside Brewing Company →

docksidevancouver.com/ brewery
604-685-7070
1253 Johnston Street (Granville
 Island), Vancouver
E-MAIL
 info@docksidevancouver.com

||||||||||||||||||||||||||||||||||||||||||||||||

ORIGINALLY BUILT IN 1997 as part of the Granville Island Hotel, this brewpub shares its prime location right on the edge of False Creek with the Dockside Restaurant. Both pub and restaurant offer the same incredible patio with an amazing view of the glass towers of downtown Vancouver—it was perhaps *the* best patio in Vancouver until the two-level Tap & Barrel opened in the Olympic Village. You can order the same beers in either the pub or restaurant, but the food menus are significantly different. The restaurant is excellent but on the pricier side of the scale, while the pub's fare is more than adequate—you can decide based on the size of your wallet.

As often is the case in brewpubs that cater to a wider tourist demographic, though, the beer is not particularly challenging, but it isn't bad either. It's a good, safe bet, and the brewpub puts the occasional cask-conditioned beer on as well.

Tap List

HAUPENTHAL HEFEWEIZEN

4.8% ABV
One of the more authentic German wheat beers in Vancouver.

RAILSPUR IPA

5.7% ABV
A well-balanced, hop-forward IPA.

....
Facts & Figures

OPENED ‣ *1997* ✪ **STYLES PRODUCED** ‣ *7 + seasonals* ✪ **ON TAP** ‣
The brewpub ✪ **GROWLERS** ‣ *Yes*

NEIGHBOURHOOD BEER

How Brewery Lounge Endorsements Helped
Create Vancouver's Unique Beer Culture

• •

THE WAVE OF new breweries that have opened in Vancouver in the past few years includes several neighbourhood-focused operations that represent a new model for craft breweries in B.C. This phenomenon is fresh and exciting, and what's amazing is that it came about because of government initiative. Well, sort of...

On February 8, 2013, B.C.'s Liquor Control and Licensing Branch (LCLB) announced that breweries could apply for lounge endorsements that would allow them to open on-site tasting rooms. Prior to this, breweries could serve samples to visitors, but only up to 375 mL (12 ounces) per person per day. While they were allowed to charge for those samples, many breweries just offered them for free as a tasting opportunity and an incentive to fill a growler or buy packaged product. The new lounge endorsement would allow breweries to sell beer by the glass, adding an entirely new retail option to their business plans.

However, when existing Vancouver breweries inquired about this at the City of Vancouver's Liquor License Department, they were told they would have to apply to open a "neighbourhood public house," which requires a liquor primary license. And breweries in industrial zones could not apply since liquor primary licences were not allowed in those zones. Well, since breweries pretty much have to be located in industrial zones, it appeared to be a Catch-22.

What happened next was surprising: the City of Vancouver actually changed its policy. It didn't happen overnight, and it had a lot to do with the hard work of Paddy Treavor, a past president of CAMRA Vancouver and an ardent beer blogger, who challenged the mayor and council to do something about it. After Councillor George Affleck took up the cause, Mayor Gregor Robertson, a craft beer fan himself, got on board. Just two months later, council unanimously approved zoning changes to allow for lounge endorsements at breweries. That's impressively fast for making a change of that sort.

One brewing neighbourhood had already developed in the Victoria Avenue-Powell Street area with Coal Harbour, Parallel 49 and Powell Street Craft there, and another was developing along Main Street in the Brewery Creek neighbourhood (see "Brewery Creek" on page 124), but the tasting lounge concept changed things radically for those operations that were just in the process of opening, such as 33 Acres and Brassneck. Instead of fronting their breweries with a growler station and maybe a fridge, they could now offer their clientele a chance to sit down and sample the beers, either by the flight or by the glass, along with some snacks or maybe something from a food truck parked out front. And for breweries that had already opened, like Parallel 49, it was a welcome and unexpected addition to what they already offered. P49's tasting lounge quickly became one of the most popular in the city. At a panel discussion I moderated just before Vancouver Craft Beer Week in 2014, co-owner Anthony Frustagli acknowledged that he expected their lounge would gross more than a million dollars for the brewery that year—despite it being something they never planned for.

From the consumer's perspective, the lounge endorsement is fundamental to Vancouver's unique beer experience. One of the reasons why growlers took off a few years ago was the personal connection they help create—the act of taking your jug into a brewery to fill it up with the freshest beer possible forges a link between the consumer and the brewer. And a brewery lounge takes that one step further, creating an even stronger bond.

If you live in Vancouver, you might take this sort of setup for granted by now. But it doesn't even exist in Victoria despite its strong beer culture. In fact, no brewery there has even applied for an endorsement (at least as of December 2014), maybe because very few of Victoria's five standalone breweries have facilities where a lounge would make sense. Category 12, which is just opening north of the city on the Saanich Peninsula as I write this, has plans to seek a lounge endorsement, which would make it the first in Greater Victoria.

It's also a great model for breweries in smaller towns and cities—rather than serving a specific neighbourhood, it's more about the whole community. You'll find brewery lounges in Tofino, Cumberland and Courtenay on Vancouver Island, and in Kamloops, Quesnel, Prince Rupert and Valemount.

But nowhere does it work better than in Vancouver where the idea was honed to perfection. The trio of breweries in the Main Street neighbourhood—33 Acres, Brassneck and Main Street Brewing—located within a few blocks of each other, makes for an ideal afternoon or evening of strolling, sipping and sampling. It doesn't get much better than that.

Dogwood Brewing ←

dogwoodbrew.com
778-863-9596
8284 Sherbrooke Street,
   Vancouver
E-MAIL
   dogwood@dogwoodbrew.com
TWITTER @DogwoodBrew

||||||||||||||||||||||||||||||||||||||||||||||

VANCOUVER'S FIRST ALL-ORGANIC brewery is owned and operated by one of the few female brewers in British Columbia, Claire Wilson (see "Sisters of the Hop" on page 189). Wilson previously brewed at Big River Brewpub before deciding to strike out on her own. Dogwood joins Nelson Brewing and Crannóg Ales as B.C.'s only organic breweries.

Dogwood is the first brewery to open in the South Vancouver area. Although its location right next to the Knight Street Bridge near the Burnaby border is a bit out of the central core of the city, it makes it an ideal stop on the way home for commuters to fill a growler or pick up a six-pack. Wilson also believes the organic focus garners special attention from restaurants and pubs that want to offer a good organic beer on their menu.

In terms of packaging, Wilson loves the idea of putting craft beer in cans, although she might add some "fancy white tablecloth beers" in bottles later.

Tap List

ORGANIC STOUT
4% ABV | 20 IBU
You gotta think that a brewmaster from Ireland knows how to brew a proper stout. She sure does!

ORGANIC HONEY ALE
4.5% ABV | 15 IBU
With added organic honey, this light, refreshing ale is just sweet enough.

Facts & Figures

OPENED ▸ 2015 ✪ **STYLES PRODUCED** ▸ *4 + seasonals* ✪
WHERE TO BUY ▸ *The brewery or at private liquor stores* ✪ **ON TAP** ▸
Greater Vancouver ✪ **GROWLERS** ▸ *Yes*

gib.ca
604-687-2739
1441 Cartwright Street,
 Vancouver
E-MAIL info@gib.ca
TWITTER @itsgoodtobehere

Granville Island Brewing

Tap List

HEY DAY HEFEWEIZEN

5% ABV

Previously named after
Robson Street, this was
the first Hefeweizen to hit
the patios in Vancouver
and it's still one of the best
ones in B.C.

**SWING SPAN
AMBER ALE**

5.6% ABV | 45 IBU

Part of the brewery's new
Under the Bridge series,
this is a hoppy American-
style red ale with a tasty
dose of Mosaic and
Cascade hops.

**SHIPLOAD OF HOPS
IMPERIAL IPA** (seasonal)

8.2% ABV | 100 IBU!

This is one of my favourite
B.C. beers: the complex,
citrus-pine hops are
perfectly balanced by a
solid malt base.

**BURLY GOAT
WEIZENBOCK** (seasonal)

7.9% ABV | 35 IBU

One of the best of Vern's
monthly releases, this is
a rich, full-bodied, cloudy
wheat beer with big
flavours of banana and
caramel.

|||||||||||||||||||||||||||||||||||||||||||||||||

ONE OF B.C.'s first microbreweries dating
back to 1984, Granville Island Brewing grew
from its small, original facility on Granville
Island to become the city's favourite local
brewer, with all of its beer styles named
after popular city sites (English Bay Pale
Ale, Kitsilano Maple Cream Ale, etc.) and
its marketing focused on living the good life
on the West Coast—"It's good to be here." As
such, shockwaves ripped through the craft
beer community in B.C. back in 2009 when
word came out that it had been purchased by
Molson-Coors via its subsidiary, Creemore
Springs.

But the truth of the matter was that
Granville Island had been owned by a large
commercial winery for a long time before
that, with most of the beer actually being
brewed at the winery's facility in Kelowna.
Molson shifted the main production of GIB's
core brands to its big Vancouver plant, but
the original facility on Granville Island,
which had long been used by brewmaster
Vern Lambourne for making special seasonal
beers, was not changed in any way—until it
was renovated in 2012 to improve the brewhouse, tasting room and kitchen facilities. A
skilled and respected brewer, Lambourne's
departure in 2015 had me concerned, but

when Kevin Emms, previously of Deep Cove Brewing, was announced as his replacement, I was relieved.

Since the first edition of this book came out, I had the opportunity to interview Mitch Taylor, one of the original founders of the brewery, who had been involved with the group that guided the revitalization of Granville Island in the 1970s. He told me that GIB was a big hit right off the bat. It launched with one beer, Island Lager, a high-quality German beer that outclassed the big breweries' products at the time and was priced to compete with import beers from Europe. It was available in tall-necked bottles only, differentiating it even more from the "stubbies" the macros used then. It also helped that the brewery's store was the only place in Vancouver to buy beer on Sundays—for the first few years, at least, Sundays were GIB's busiest days by far.

Finding distribution options in the city was a big problem early on, and the lager focus was also detrimental to the growth of the brewery because of how long it took to age the beer properly, so GIB often ran out of beer. Eventually, the brewery expanded its capacity, began kegging its beer, and introduced other styles, including a Bock and Märzen, as well as Island Light and Island Ale.

Financial troubles forced Taylor to seek investment elsewhere, which led to the brewery becoming part of International Potter Distilling Corp., which also owned Calona Wines and Pacific Western Breweries at the time. Through various transitions, Taylor found himself a vice president in charge of GIB and other aspects of business, which was not the sort of entrepreneurial role he enjoyed. In 1992, he left the company and got back into the marina business.

....

Facts & Figures

OPENED▸ *1984* ✪ STYLES PRODUCED▸ *7 + many seasonals* ✪
WHERE TO BUY▸ *Everywhere in B.C.* ✪ ON TAP▸ *Everywhere in Vancouver, and many spots elsewhere in B.C.* ✪ GROWLERS▸ *Yes*

mainstreetbeer.ca
604-336-7711
261 East Seventh Avenue,
  Vancouver
E-MAIL info@mainstreetbeer.ca
TWITTER @mainstreetbeer

Main Street Brewing

Tap List

PILSNER
5% ABV | 22 IBU
Main Street's original beer, this is clean and crisp, not very malty or hoppy.

SESSION IPA
4.8% ABV | 55 IBU
A delicious, hoppy India Session Ale that still offers a big, citrusy hop aroma and flavour without a lot of alcohol.

HARE AND THE DOG BEST BITTER (CASK-CONDITIONED)
4.5% ABV | 35 IBU
This British style is ideal for cask conditioning—and Main Street's is excellent.

WESTMINSTER BROWN
6% ABV | 30 IBU
A hoppy brown ale? Why not? It works quite well. Malty and rich with an unexpected hop finish.

|||||||||||||||||||||||||||||||||||||||||||||||

I REMEMBER MAIN Street Brewing's first community meeting back in February 2012. I was still living in Vancouver at the time, just a few blocks away in fact, and I was so excited by the prospect of this brewery opening in its historic location: a building known as the Brewery Garage that had originally been part of the Vancouver Breweries complex when it was built in 1913.

Unfortunately, various roadblocks delayed the brewery's construction, and in the meantime I moved to Victoria and began writing the first edition of this book. Still, I assumed Main Street Brewing would be open by the time the book came out in May 2013. Nope. Originally, the owners wanted to open a brewery and restaurant side by side in the space, but met resistance from local condo residents about the potential restaurant noise and traffic late at night. Then, as the new brewery lounge endorsement rules came into effect, they retooled their vision, which sent the designers back to the drawing board. As time went by, two other pedestrian-friendly storefront breweries opened in the area, first 33 Acres a few blocks west, and then Brassneck just a block away.

Main Street Brewing sets itself apart slightly with its strong focus on cask-conditioned beer. The brewery's tasting lounge (sixty seats) has four rotating casks on at all times in addition to the regular lineup of Pilsner, brown ale and sessional IPA, with other seasonal releases mixed in on draft. It also has a bit more of a kitchen than the other nearby breweries do, with a menu featuring locally sourced and organic foods, including sandwiches made in-house every day, chili, meat pies and charcuterie selections.

Like Brassneck, Main Street has a separate retail area with a growler filling station. The cask beers are not available for growlers but other seasonal beers are. Throughout the tasting room and retail store, the design embraces the "bones" of the building—old wood and bricks have been left uncovered in many places. Where there are newly painted walls, they end at ceiling height with the vaulted roof visible above and the brewery's tanks in sight beyond.

Main Street's founders also own a couple of nearby restaurants, the Cascade Room and Portland Craft, and had previously created the Main Street Pilsner brand, which was brewed on their behalf by Jack Bensley at Russell Brewing. Bensley came along with them to Main Street Brewing where he has definitely proven he can do more than just brew a darn good Pilsner.

Early on, Main Street's beer was just available at the brewery by the glass or in growlers, but toward the end of 2014, they began packaging in 650 mL bombers, too. Six-packs of cans or bottles will follow in 2015.

....
Facts & Figures

OPENED ▸ *2014*   ✪   **STYLES PRODUCED** ▸ *3 + 4 casks + seasonals*   ✪
WHERE TO BUY ▸ *The brewery and select bottle shops*   ✪   **ON TAP** ▸
The brewery   ✪   **GROWLERS** ▸ *Yes*

BREWERY CREEK
Vancouver's Earliest Breweries

••••••••••••••••••••••••

WHEN MY WIFE and I first moved to Vancouver in 2001, we ended up renting an apartment one block west of Main Street at Fifteenth and Quebec. I remember I had a naïve impression that Main Street was a rough "East Van" area, but as I got to know the neighbourhood, I really fell in love with it. Some people were starting to call that area South Main or SoMa at the time. New restaurants started showing up there, followed by local fashion boutiques and, later, new condos. Eventually, this gentrification process forced us to seek less expensive housing elsewhere, but I have very fond memories of our time there.

When I was first exploring the area, I discovered a few plinths with historical plaques close to the intersection of Main Street and Kingsway that referred to the neighbourhood as "Brewery Creek." I was intrigued. It turns out that a stream once ran roughly along present-day Main Street from Tea Swamp (east of Main between Twelfth and Sixteenth Avenues) down to False Creek, which used to extend much farther east, all the way to where Clark Drive is now. This area, which early city planners called Mount Pleasant, became Vancouver's first suburb as the city began to grow beyond the downtown peninsula. And it also became the home of many of Vancouver's original breweries, including the City and Mainland breweries (both founded in 1887) and the Columbia Brewery (1888), which chose to build along the stream—giving it the name, Brewery Creek.

For the next twenty years (before it was covered over by

streets and sewers), Brewery Creek provided the water for a succession of breweries, including the Alexander Brewery (Sixth Avenue and Scotia Street), Doering and Marstrand (Seventh Avenue and Scotia Street), the San Francisco Brewery (Eleventh Avenue and Main Street), and the Vancouver Brewery (Sixth Avenue and Scotia Street), a red-brick building built in 1903 that still stands today, now converted into artist live-work studios. There was even a giant waterwheel that powered the original Doering brewery.

Brewery Creek's time as the centre of the brewing industry in Vancouver was short-lived, no doubt partially because the creek itself disappeared along with many others that flowed down to False Creek. Today, however, there are some interesting connections to that history. One of the original buildings from the Vancouver Brewery complex, which was used for much of the twentieth century as an auto mechanic's shop, was renovated as part of a condo development in 2011, and Main Street Brewing set up shop there in 2014. Brassneck Brewery is right around the corner on Main Street at Sixth Avenue, and farther "downstream" on First Avenue, just off Great Northern Way, Red Truck's new production brewery sits almost exactly where Brewery Creek once drained into False Creek.

There are a few other interesting historical connections in the neighbourhood, too. Brewery Creek Liquor Store (Fifteenth Avenue and Main Street) is one of the best places to buy craft beer in the city today, and a popular local restaurant, the Cascade Room (Tenth Avenue and Main Street), is named after Vancouver Brewery's flagship Cascade Beer, "The Beer Without a Peer," as a 1907 advertisement claimed.

offtherailbrewing.com
604-802-2505
1351 Adanac Street, Vancouver
E-MAIL
  steve@offtherailbrewing.com
TWITTER @OffTheRailBeer

Off the Rail Brewing

||||||||||||||||||||||||||||||||||||||||||||||||

Tap List

KAMA CITRA

4.4% ABV | 32 IBU

This summery session
beer has a crisp, clean
bitterness with tropical
fruit aromas and flavours
courtesy of Magnum and
Citra hops.

OLD WINSTON
SMOKED PORTER

6.3% ABV | 54 IBU

The smoked porter seems
to have become a popular
style among breweries in
the Lower Mainland. This
one has a subtle smokiness
against a rich malt base
with chocolate and coffee
notes.

OFF THE RAIL Brewing is located on the same
block of Adanac Street as Bomber Brewing. The breweries are similar in size, with
their giant logos painted on the sides of their
buildings, each within sight of the other.

Off the Rail's owner, Steve Forsyth,
was previously the longtime manager and
co-owner of the Railway Club, a popular downtown music bar. After selling the
nightclub in 2008, Steve and his sister Janet
started their own hop farm near Mission; at
one point Phillips Brewing made a special
Boxcar Bitter for the Railway Club using
their hops. Steve is brewing with Mike Evans,
who has helped customers brew their own
beer for years at West Coast U-Brew, not too
far away on Clark Drive.

Off the Rail has a comfortable tasting
room with twelve taps, including two nitrogenated lines serving a Boddingtons-style
cream ale and a stout or ESB. The emphasis is
on traditional recipes, with experimentation
mixed in. As Forsyth described the way he
learned about beer: "Practice makes perfect!"

....
Facts & Figures

OPENED▶ 2015 ⊙ STYLES PRODUCED▶ 5 + seasonals ⊙
WHERE TO BUY ▶ The brewery or private liquor stores ⊙ ON TAP▶
Greater Vancouver ⊙ GROWLERS▶ Yes

Parallel 49 Brewing ←

parallel49brewing.com
604-558-brew (2739)
1950 Triumph Street, Vancouver
E-MAIL
  info@parallel49brewing.com
TWITTER @Parallel49beer

|||||||||||||||||||||||||||||||||||||||||||||

THIS BREWERY IS the baby of the business partners behind St. Augustine's, one of Vancouver's best taphouses that is second only to the Alibi Room in beer selection. Running that popular Commercial Drive eatery was ideal market research for Parallel 49, which hit the ground running hard when it opened in the spring of 2012 and hasn't looked back since. P49 has quickly become one of the most popular breweries in Vancouver—its beer can be found on tap everywhere, and the tasting room at the brewery is packed day and night despite a location that is not exactly central.

To set up and run this brewery, Parallel 49's owners hired Graham With, a local star home brewer with an engineering degree from UBC. They immediately flew to China with him to complete the purchase of their brewhouse equipment. With the boom in craft brewing across North America, it can take years to get new equipment from North American builders, and even with the distance and shipping costs, a brewhouse built in China costs far less than one built here.

The equipment arrived on With's thirtieth birthday, but unfortunately, the two Chinese engineers who were supposed to accompany it did not—they had not been granted visas

Tap List

FILTHY DIRTY IPA
7.2% ABV | 76 IBU
Once named Lord of the Hops, this big, bold IPA features an array of citrusy, floral and pine hop aromas.

OLD BOY
5% ABV | 27 IBU
A tribute to English pub beers, this is a well-balanced brown ale.

GYPSY TEARS RUBY ALE
6% ABV | 40 IBU
A ruby red ale with a solid malt base that showcases some aromatic West Coast hops.

HAY FEVER SPRING SAISON (seasonal)
6.5% ABV | 20 IBU
A beautiful Saison with a peppery, citrus character from the yeast and a gooseberry, Sauvignon Blanc finish courtesy of Nelson Sauvin hops.

by Canadian officials. After enlisting the aid of a local MP, the Parallel 49 partners finally got the help they needed and started brewing their first batches of beer on Easter weekend, 2012.

This brewery has grown significantly since then, expanding into neighbouring and nearby warehouses and adding employees at a rapid pace. One of the reasons for P49's popularity is its cartoony branding style and the highly creative, often punny beer names they come up with, as well as the sheer number of different beers they have released. Graham With's attitude seems to be that once they come up with a good name for a beer then he might as well brew a batch of it.

It took a while for P49 to produce a hoppy IPA—With said he was waiting to get the right hops before he finally released the cheekily named Lord of the Hops early in 2013. As it turns out, the name caught the attention of the Tolkien estate, so the name was changed to Filthy Dirty. Several other different styles of IPA have also been released in limited batches, including Toques of Hazzard Imperial White IPA (great name!), Hopnotist One Hop IPA, Robo Ruby Imperial Red IPA, and my personal favourite both for its name and its flavour: Snap, Crackle, Hop Imperial Rice IPA.

With also has some beers aging in barrels, including a Russian Imperial Stout and a Braggot, which is a blend of mead and honey. The N2 series features an ESB and milk stout that are nitrogenated to give them a velvety smoothness and attractive cascading quality in the glass.

I can't wait to see what Parallel 49 comes up with next.

....
Facts & Figures

OPENED ▸ *2012* ✿ **STYLES PRODUCED** ▸ *6 + numerous seasonals* ✿
WHERE TO BUY ▸ *The brewery and liquor stores throughout B.C.* ✿
ON TAP ▸ *Throughout B.C.* ✿ **GROWLERS** ▸ *Yes*

postmarkbrewing.com
604-699-1988
55 Dunlevy Avenue, Vancouver
E-MAIL
  info@postmarkbrewing.com
TWITTER @Postmarkbrewing

Postmark Brewing ←

||||||||||||||||||||||||||||||||||||||||||||

THE FIRST BREWERY in Vancouver's edgy Railtown neighbourhood, just a few blocks east of the Alibi Room, Postmark Brewing shares the Settlement Building with the Vancouver Urban Winery and a restaurant called Belgard Kitchen.

It is a unique and attractive setup with the brewery and winery sharing the restaurant: along with Postmark's beers, Belgard Kitchen has thirty-six different wines on tap to go with enticing and reasonably priced brunch, lunch and dinner options.

Postmark's first brewer, Craig Noble, is also a filmmaker who produced the feature documentary *CRAFT*, which chronicles his apprenticeship and development as a brewer. He spent two years researching and filming across North America.

Noble departed in the summer of 2015 to return to filmmaking. He was replaced by Dominic Giraldes who had previously brewed with Dave Varga at Taylor's Crossing Brewpub in North Van, and then under Gary Lohin at Central City—both the brewpub and the fancy new brewery.

Tap List

PILSNER
4.7% ABV | 24 IBU
I tasted this straight from the tank, which is always the freshest and best way to enjoy beer. It is a no-frills Czech Pilsner, clean, dry and very drinkable.

RASPBERRY LEMON ZEST HEFEWEIZEN
4.8% ABV | 14 IBU
An interesting twist on the Hefeweizen style. The lemon is quite subtle and the berries show up in the background.

....

Facts & Figures

OPENED ▸ *2014*
STYLES PRODUCED ▸
  3 + seasonals
WHERE TO BUY ▸ *The brewery.*
ON TAP ▸ *Vancouver*
GROWLERS ▸ *Yes*

powellbeer.com
604-558-2537
1357 Powell Street, Vancouver
(new location)
E-MAIL info@powellbeer.com
TWITTER @PowellBeer

Powell Street Craft Brewery

Tap List

DIVE BOMB PORTER

5% ABV | 33 IBU
Named for the iconic
East Vancouver crows
who are known to attack
unwary pedestrians, this
porter has a great roasted
character.

OLD JALOPY PALE ALE

5.5% ABV | 40 IBU
A rich and malty pale
ale with some peppy
Northwest hops. Winner of
Beer of the Year at the 2013
Canadian Brewing Awards.

HOPDEMONIUM IPA

8% ABV | 88 IBU
At 8% ABV, this veers into
the double IPA category. It
is big, bold and beautiful.

95 POUNDS OF WET HOP
GOODNESS (seasonal)

6% ABV | 30 IBU
This delicious pale ale is
brewed with 95 pounds
of "wet" Cascade and
Centennial hops fresh from
the harvest at Lillooet's
Harvesters of Organic
Hops.

||||||||||||||||||||||||||||||||||||||||||||||

IN JULY 2011, David Bowkett decided to turn
his love of craft beer into more than just
a home brewing hobby. The Powell Street
Craft Brewery opened a year and a half later.
Bowkett and his wife, Nicole, created an
inviting storefront atmosphere where traditional half-gallon growlers and one-litre
versions they call "Boston Rounds" could be
bought and filled, along with pre-filled 650
mL bottles. Powell Street began by focusing on three core brands—a pale ale, porter
and hoppy IPA. The limited capacity of the
small nanobrewery setup didn't give Bowkett
much flexibility for trying different styles
but he experimented whenever he could, all
while remaining at his full-time day job as
an architectural technician so that he didn't
have to draw a salary from the brewery.

Then, in April 2013, Bowkett's world was
rocked when his Old Jalopy Pale Ale was
awarded Beer of the Year at the Canadian
Brewing Awards, which were held in Victoria that year. I remember the stunned look
on his face as he walked up to the stage to
collect his award—I was just as surprised,
and I made sure the emmcee knew that
Powell Street Craft had only been open for
five months. The brewery had already been
popular, but the resulting publicity led to

lineups down the block. It also meant that the brewery ran out of beer often since the small system simply couldn't keep up with demand.

By 2014, Bowkett was ready to ditch his day job and expand his brewery. That meant a new location, somewhat limited by geography given the name of the brewery, but he managed to find an appropriate space still on Powell Street, but closer to downtown, right by Clark Drive. This actually moves the brewery halfway between the original "Yeast Van" neighbourhood cluster it shared with Parallel 49 and Coal Harbour Brewing and a new group close to Clark and Adanac that includes Bomber, Off the Rail and Strange Fellows.

The new location has a welcoming tasting room that always seems to be busy despite the location (good luck finding parking if the brewery's small lot is full) with food trucks regularly parked out front. Most importantly, it has a much bigger brewing space that will allow Bowkett to produce a lot more beer, and many more styles of beer, too. He is also adding barrel-aging and souring to his repertoire—great news, indeed, since I don't think I've ever tasted an average beer from Powell Street Craft, let alone a poor one. Maybe it's his background as lead vocalist for a hardcore punk band, but every one of Bowkett's beers I've enjoyed has been memorable for its boldness.

Powell Street Craft Brewery's success story is proof that, within Vancouver's craft beer boom, brewers of good, quality beer will be rewarded for their efforts.

....
Facts & Figures

OPENED ▸ *2012* ✪ **STYLES PRODUCED ▸** *4 + seasonals* ✪
WHERE TO BUY ▸ *The brewery or bottle shops in Vancouver* ✪ **ON TAP ▸**
Taphouses in Vancouver ✪ **GROWLERS ▸** *Yes*

r-and-b.com
604-874-ales (2537)
54 Fourth Avenue East,
  Vancouver
E-MAIL ales@r-and-b.com
TWITTER @RandBBrewing

R&B Brewing

Tap List

||||||||||||||||||||||||||||||||||||||||||||||

SUN GOD WHEAT ALE

4.2% ABV | 12 IBU

A light, flavourful wheat
beer ideal for summer
patio sipping.

RED DEVIL PALE ALE

5.2% ABV | 28 IBU

A rich, reddish pale ale
with a floral hop aroma and
malty sweetness.

RAVEN CREAM ALE

4.8% ABV | 18 IBU

A "Vancouver cream ale" (à
la Shaftebury and Russell)
that is unexpectedly dark
for the style, this is a tasty
beer with a nutty, roasted
character.

**BIRRA FRESCA
CUCUMBER MINT IPA**

6% ABV | 50 IBU

Based on R&B's
Hoppelganger IPA, the
addition of cucumber
and mint make this beer
uniquely delicious and
refreshing.

RICK DELLOW AND BARRY BENSON, the R and
B in R&B Brewing, became friends while
working at the Vancouver Molson plant in
the 1980s, and then worked together at New-
lands, an Abbotsford-based company that
makes brewing equipment. After several
years installing new brewhouses at places
like Steamworks, Russell and Granville
Island, as well as elsewhere around the world,
Benson and Dellow decided to start their
own brewery.

R&B Brewing was founded to "stand
in opposition to what the beer world had
become—big, nondescript, faceless and
corporate." Back in 1997, the Main Street
neighbourhood where it opened was definitely East Van edgy, even if the official
dividing line between east and west in the
city is Ontario Street, only half a block away.
An address in that area is now much more
desirable than it would have been in the '90s,
when I'm sure they picked it up for an attractive price tag.

One of the reasons for R&B's early success
was its specialization in cask-conditioned
beer. As the cask beer movement took hold in
Vancouver about twelve years ago at places
like The Whip restaurant, just a few blocks
away, R&B recognized this niche market and

became the go-to brewery for casks.

As the neighbourhood evolved in recent years, becoming more and more trendy, it became attractive to new upstart breweries like Brassneck, 33 Acres, Main Street Brewing and the Steel Toad Brewpub. Unfortunately, those flashy new operations with their tasting room-focused cultures had a negative effect on R&B. The brewery struggled to find new customers and keep the tap lines it had long held. Finally, in January 2015, it was forced to lay off its nine employees.

But that wasn't the end of R&B. In April, Squamish-based Howe Sound Brewing announced that it had acquired the brewery. It planned to use the facility to brew its Howe Sound Lager and would also keep the R&B brand alive.

On a separate note, one of the funniest experiences from my original book tour has an R&B connection. When I was invited to go on Shaw TV's The Rush to talk about my book with host Fiona Forbes, I asked R&B to put some Birra Frisca cucumber mint IPA in a growler so I could bring it along to the TV studio.

The cameras started rolling and we chatted about my book and the beers I had brought in to sample. I twisted the cap off the growler and was reaching for Fiona's glass when beer started gushing out of it like a geyser. I was stupefied. *Can we start the show over after we clean up the mess?* I thought, but then I remembered that we were live. Suddenly, guest host Grant Lawrence shoved me aside—and I should point out that I am the size of a football linebacker while he is, well, a scrawny CBC radio host—and wrapped his lips around the mouth of the growler, sucking up the fountain of beer. Hilarious and unforgettable, it lives on through the magic of YouTube.

....
Facts & Figures

OPENED ▸ *1997* ❂ **STYLES PRODUCED** ▸ *8 + seasonals* ❂
WHERE TO BUY ▸ *Liquor stores in Vancouver area and on Vancouver Island* ❂ **ON TAP** ▸ *Throughout Vancouver* ❂ **GROWLERS** ▸ *Yes*

TAPPING THE CASK

Vancouver's Cask Beer Scene

••••••••••••••••••••••••

CASK-CONDITIONED BEER UNDERGOES a secondary fermentation in a sealed vessel, often with special added ingredients such as hops or other flavouring agents, and then is served directly from the cask without being filtered or pasteurized. The yeast remains with the beer, gently carbonating and conditioning it. The beer is essentially "alive" right up until the moment you drink it.

The cask typically used is a metal barrel known as a firkin, which holds approximately forty litres or eighty pints. This is a size that allows it to be transported relatively easily. It is also reasonably possible to empty a firkin in just a few hours so pubs will often just prop the cask on top of a bar until it is empty. Bars that have regular casks on tap use a refrigeration system to keep the beer at a proper "cellar temperature" no matter when it is served.

Known as "real ale" in the UK, cask beer was long the traditional method of brewing in Britain, but as bigger breweries took over the market there, it began to disappear in favour of mass-market bottled beers. This led to the formation of the Campaign For Real Ale (CAMRA) in 1971, which has helped revitalize the brewing of traditional ales in the UK and around the world.

Cask conditioning allows the malt and hop flavours to deepen and expand so the resulting beer is usually richer and more complex than typical beer from a keg or bottle. Brewers love to experiment by either adding something special to the cask or by testing a new recipe they've never tried before. Either way, it's a chance to taste a unique and delicious brew you can't get anywhere else.

Dix BBQ & Brewery was the first place in Vancouver to hold a regular monthly cask event starting in July 2002. A year later, they began tapping casks weekly on Thursday evenings. But Barry Benson, the B in R&B Brewing, says that there were a few one-offs in the years before that. He remembers tapping a cask of their Auld Nick Winter Ale in 1998 at the old Fogg n' Suds restaurant on West Broadway, an early haven for beer lovers in Vancouver.

In late 2006, R&B Brewing put together a weekly event at The Whip restaurant called Real Ale Sundays. R&B played a major role in organizing the event for the first three years or so, talking to other brewers, encouraging them to supply casks, and filling in with their own casks when needed. Eventually, as cask events began catching on in other restaurants, more and more breweries got on board and started producing casks of their own. Main Street Brewing, which opened in 2014, features four cask beers along with several draft beers at its tasting lounge.

There are now casks tapped every night somewhere in Vancouver, and places like the Cascade Room, Irish Heather and Alibi Room keep casks on all the time. CAMRA Vancouver hosts a major cask event with each new season and Central City Brewing hosts a very popular cask festival each summer and winter at its brewpub in Surrey.

redtruckbeer.com
604-682-4733
295 First Avenue East, Vancouver
E-MAIL info@redtruckbeer.com
TWITTER @redtruckbeer

Red Truck Beer

IIIIIIIIIIIIIIIIIIIIIIIIIIIIIIIIIIIIIIIIIIIIIIII

Tap List

RED TRUCK ALE
5.2% ABV
A solid, dependable ale.
Nothing special, but very
drinkable.

RED TRUCK LAGER
5% ABV
A solid, dependable lager. If
this sounds repetitive, you
get the picture.

RED TRUCK IPA
6.3% ABV | 69 IBU
A solid, dependable IPA...
No, I'm kidding—this is a
fine IPA with a great body
and a citrus-floral hop
aroma.

RED TRUCK PORTER
6.6% ABV
This seasonal porter won
a silver medal at the 2014
Canadian Brewing Awards.

STARTED AS A draft-only brand by the Mark
James Group, which runs a chain of brewpubs in Vancouver, Surrey and Whistler, Red
Truck beer was brewed at the North Vancouver brewpub Taylor's Crossing even after
it was closed. When Mark James decided to
build a new brewery on First Avenue near
Main Street, construction was launched by
dropping a red truck from a crane.

In the first edition of this book, I
announced that the new brewery would be
open by the fall of 2013, but it took nearly a
year longer to finish construction, and even
by the fall of 2014, the promised truck stop–
themed restaurant and tasting room was not
open. But beer was coming out of the brewery,
which is the most important thing. It's a very
large brewery so you will likely see Red Truck
become a popular brand throughout B.C.—
except, perhaps, on Vancouver Island where
fans of Phillips Brewing will remember that
Red Truck's litigiousness is the reason why
Blue Truck Ale was changed to Blue Buck (see
"Phillips Brewing" on page 62).

....
Facts & Figures

OPENED ▸ *2005* ✪ **STYLES PRODUCED ▸** *3 + seasonals* ✪
WHERE TO BUY ▸ *Throughout B.C.* **ON TAP ▸** *Throughout B.C.* ✪
GROWLERS ▸ *Yes*

VANCOUVER CRAFT BEER WEEK

Held for Nine Days at the End of May Each Year

••••••••••••••••••••••••

SINCE ITS LAUNCH in 2010, Vancouver Craft Beer Week has grown into one of the biggest events in B.C.'s festival calendar. With signature and satellite events put on by the VCBW organizers and affiliated events put on by individual breweries, pubs and restaurants, the 2014 edition included twenty-one events attended by more than 9,000 people.

Some of the most popular events each year include the quick-to-sell-out Hoppapalooza, hosted by Nigel Springthorpe at the Alibi Room; the Cicerone vs. Sommelier beer- and wine-pairing contest; Sisters of the Tap (previously Women in Beer); and the two-day VCBW Beer Festival that closes out the week. Personally, I am a big fan of the Belgian Showcase held at the two BierCraft locations.

The major events go on sale in advance through the VCBW website, but many of the associated events are not ticketed so there are always plenty of opportunities to join in the fun.

www.vancouvercraftbeerweek.com

steeltoad.ca
604-709-8623
97 Second Avenue East,
  Vancouver
E-MAIL info@steeltoad.ca
TWITTER @SteelToadBeer

Steel Toad Brewpub & Dining Hall

Tap List

SAISON

5.5% ABV

Quite a nice Saison—fruity and dry. Reminiscent of Dupont's iconic original.

OATMEAL STOUT
(cask conditioned)

5.5% ABV | 14 IBU

Rich and creamy with big, roasty chocolate and coffee notes.

RYE IPA

6% ABV

Great West Coast hop character along with spicy, earthy rye tones.

||||||||||||||||||||||||||||||||||||||||||||||||

STEEL TOAD WAS the first new brewpub to open in Vancouver since Dix opened in 1998. The high cost of real estate made it too challenging for anyone without deep pockets to contemplate building a new one.

Steel Toad is part of a major development that included a heritage "resurrection" of the dilapidated Opsal Steel building, built in 1918. The construction company carefully dismantled the building, salvaged what it could and rebuilt the rest, before putting the new/old building back together. The result is gorgeous inside and out. The brewery fills the east end of the building and its two-level dining hall reminds me of a German beer hall.

The brewpub has eight regular serving tanks and two unpressurized, cellar-temperature tanks that flow into traditional British beer engines, emulating cask conditioning. When I visited shortly after opening, the place was packed and everything tasted good. The brewer's plans for future brews sounded very exciting, including a Brett Saison that should come out around the time this book is published.

Facts & Figures

OPENED ▸ 2014 ✪ **STYLES PRODUCED ▸** 4 + seasonals ✪ **ON TAP ▸** Only at the brewpub ✪ **GROWLERS ▸** No

Steamworks Brew Pub & Brewery

Brewpub
steamworks.com
604-689-2739
375 Water Street, Vancouver
E-MAIL info@steamworks.com
TWITTER @SteamworksPub

Brewery
steamworks.com/brewery
604-620-7250
3845 William Street, Burnaby

||||||||||||||||||||||||||||||||||||||||||||

THE REAL ESTATE mantra of "location, location, location" could certainly be applied to Steamworks, which occupies one of the best spots in downtown Vancouver—right next to Waterfront Station at the edge of Gastown, the city's oldest neighbourhood which is now one of its most tourist-friendly areas. Anyone could be successful there, and one might expect to find a big chain restaurant or a pseudo-brewpub with basic, boring beer there, but instead, Vancouverites and visitors to the city have been blessed with a top-notch brewpub that has been serving up excellent, interesting beers and great food since 1995.

My first visit to Steamworks was as a brewers' groupie (a brewpie?). My friend Ken, the first brewer at Kelowna's Tree Brewing in the mid-'90s, was serving beer at the Autumn Brewmasters' festival at the Plaza of Nations in Vancouver so I followed him around the event all day. The real highlight was when I got to tag along to the after-festival brewers' party at Steamworks.

The brewpub had just opened, and to my eye (and taste buds), it was incredible. The cellar where the brewhouse is situated seemed ancient already, like something you'd find in a centuries-old pub in London,

Tap List

PILSNER
5.2% ABV | 35 IBU
Winner of Beer of the Year at the 2011 and 2012 B.C. Beer Awards, this pitch-perfect Czech Pilsner is full-bodied and surprisingly hoppy.

SAISON
6.3% ABV | 30 IBU
This excellent Belgian farmhouse ale boasts some big orange–lemon zest notes with a dry finish.

IMPERIAL RED
8.5% ABV | 75 IBU
This potent red IPA is full-bodied and hopped within an inch of oblivion.

FRAMBOZEN (seasonal)
7% ABV | 16 IBU
Famous for the "Frambozen accidents" this used to cause when it was a surprisingly quaffable 9% ABV, this raspberry ale has been toned down a bit for the bottle.

and I've never grown tired of that room in all the intervening years. We were given a "backstage tour" of the operation where we were shown the steam pipe that is used to heat the brew kettle—the same steam line that powers the nearby clock that draws tourists to Gastown for its steam whistle chimes every quarter hour. The original name for the brewpub was actually Quarterdeck, but when they discovered the steam pipe running through their building and realized they could use it in the brewing process, the new name and concept were born. Since then, Steamworks has consistently brewed great beer in its magnificent setting, never sacrificing quality to increase profits or to cater to the ravening hordes, even while increasing seats in its various dining rooms from the original 60 up to its current 750 or so.

In 2012, Steamworks underwent a rebranding of its marketing image to launch a new line of bottled products, adopting a playful, illustrated "steampunk lite" style, and began construction of a new production brewery in Burnaby, which opened in 2014. Although long-time brewer Conrad Gmoser left to open his own place, Brassneck, Steamworks has been well represented first by Caolon Vaughan, who returned to his native Australia in 2015, and then by Julia Hanlon, who made the move from the Molson plant where she worked for 10 years after studying chemical and biological engineering at UBC.

You can taste the beer at the original brewpub or in the tasting room at the new brewery, where you can also fill growlers. You won't be disappointed either way.

Facts & Figures

OPENED▸ *1995* ❂ **STYLES PRODUCED**▸ *6 + seasonals* ❂
WHERE TO BUY▸ *Liquor stores throughout the province* ❂ **ON TAP**▸ *The brewpub* ❂ **GROWLERS**▸ *Yes*

Storm Brewing

stormbrewing.org
604-255-9119
310 Commercial Drive,
  Vancouver
E-MAIL james@stormbrewing.org
TWITTER @StormBrewingVan

||||||||||||||||||||||||||||||||||||||||||||||

"WELCOME TO MY underground lair," says James Walton, his sinister greeting defeated by the huge grin on his face. The ramshackle brewery at the gritty northern end of Commercial Drive is not exactly a shining example of cleanliness, but there's no doubting the quality of the beer that Walton has produced here for nearly twenty years.

Walton uses "Super Genius" as his e-mail tag line, but "Mad Scientist" would fit just as well. He looks and dresses like a punk rock star, and jokes that he got into the brewing business "for the fame."

Originally from Port Alberni, he studied at UBC, then tried running an exotic mushroom farm before deciding to open a brewery in 1994. He cobbled together equipment from scrapyards and began brewing in the roughest of circumstances. His first beer, Red Sky Alt, was a big hit in Vancouver, and he also brewed a porter for a time. He considered brewing an IPA back then, but says Tall Ship (a Squamish brewery that existed for a few years in the mid-1990s) was doing one well and he didn't want to step on their toes. After they went under, he "waited a suitable mourning period," and then introduced Hurricane IPA, which he still brews today.

Tap List

BLACK PLAGUE STOUT
8.5% ABV
Once a winter seasonal, Storm now brews this black behemoth year-round.

HIGHLAND SCOTTISH ALE
5% ABV
Vancouver beer writer and Scottish émigré Jan Zeschky says this is as close to the real thing as it gets. Creamy, nutty, malty and delicious.

HURRICANE IPA
7% ABV
Vancouver's original IPA and still going strong. Often available on cask with some extra goodie in the mix.

IMPERIAL FLANDERS RED ALE
11% ABV
This beer is surprising quaffable for its alcohol potency and wild yeast sourness.

Walton says that original "cloudy, bitter ale" was not well received, partially because he dry-hopped every keg, which sometimes left chunks of hops floating in pint glasses—"scary for the uninitiated." He remembers how the co-manager of the Railway Club, Steve Forsyth, balked at the sight, saying he couldn't sell it. It turns out that Forsyth is now opening his own brewery, Off the Rail, not too far from Storm.

Eventually, Walton swapped out the Red Sky Alt for Highland Scottish Ale, replaced the porter with the Black Plague Stout, and added an authentic Czech Pilsner, which are all still brewed. Each beer is an ideal example of its style. Storm's other specialty is sour beers, an experiment Walton began in 1997 after Yaletown Brewing brewmaster Iain Hill encouraged him to re-pitch some yeast cultures from leftover spoiled beer in old kegs. The last of this sour Lambic, aged for twelve years in oak casks, was released in 2010 and won accolades.

Still on the sour side, Walton is now focusing on the Flanders red ale style, which is not quite as mouth-puckeringly sour as a Lambic. Aged at least a year in the same oak casks, the result is a potent reddish-hued beer with a sourness that is refreshing and satisfying—and surprisingly drinkable for a beer with 11 per cent ABV.

Walton is well known for adding pretty much anything to a cask of beer just to see what the result will taste like. For example: Basil IPA brewed for Italian Days on the Drive (delicious, and made me crave pizza); and Echinacea Stout (much less successful although good for my immune system, presumably).

When I visited the quintessential East Vancouver brewery, I just missed tasting a special fresh-hopped cask he "grew, picked, brewed, casked, delivered and drank" himself. It was called 100% James. Maybe he is in it for the fame after all.

Facts & Figures

OPENED ▸ *1994* ✪ **STYLES PRODUCED ▸** *5 + seasonals for every crazy idea James has* ✪ **ON TAP ▸** *Throughout Greater Vancouver* ✪ **GROWLERS ▸** *Yes*

Strange Fellows Brewing

strangefellowsbrewing.com
604-215-0092
1345 Clark Drive, Vancouver
E-MAIL
  info@strangefellowsbrewing.com
TWITTER @Strange_Fellows

|||||||||||||||||||||||||||||||||||||||||

THE TWO "STRANGE fellows" behind this new brewery are Iain Hill, ex–head brewer of the Mark James Group's Yaletown Brewing and Red Truck Beer, and his business partner, Aaron Jonckheere, who documented the process thoroughly at his blog, called *I'm Starting a Craft Brewery*.

Hill is one of the premier brewers in B.C., so I am *very* excited to see what he comes up with at his own brewery. He has a great reputation from his long tenure at Yaletown, especially for his sour and barrel-aged beers. When I visited the brewery just before it opened he already had eighty barrels there, ready and waiting to be filled with sour goodness.

Strange Fellows has a forty-three-seat tasting room. The emphasis will be on Belgian beers, including a Saison, Wit, golden strong ale, and, of course, Hill's specialty, Oud Bruin, a sour brown beer that he brewed for years at Yaletown. Look for the core beers in 473 mL cans—a format I love—and specialty beers in 750 mL cork-topped bottles.

Tap List

JONGLEUR
4.5% ABV | 12 IBU
Picture two jugglers sharing several balls in the air at once—in this creamy and fruity Belgian Wit two separate yeast strains work together to create this spicy, aromatic and delicious beer.

NOCTURNUM
6.5% ABV | 65 IBU
This Dark IPA is rich and malty with a great hop character.

TALISMAN
4.2% ABV | 29 IBU
Big flavour abounds in this hoppy, light-bodied, extremely sessionable pale ale.

Facts & Figures

OPENED ▸ *2014* ✿ **STYLES PRODUCED** ▸ *4 + seasonals* ✿ **WHERE TO BUY** ▸ *The brewery or private liquor stores* ✿ **ON TAP** ▸ *Greater Vancouver* ✿ **GROWLERS** ▸ *Yes*

VANCOUVER BREWERY TOURS

· ·

A GUIDED TOUR is a great way to check out the burgeoning craft beer scene in Vancouver. Below are several options, including bicycle and walking tours, as well as package options involving a van or mini-bus.

Cycle City Tours
The Brewery Tour (bicycle)
www.cyclevancouver.com/craft-beer-bicycle-tour
604-618-8626

Vancouver Brewery Tours
Public & Private Tours (by van)
www.vancouverbrewerytours.com
604-318-2280

Vancouver Food Tour
Craft Beer 'n Bites Tour (walking)
www.vancouverfoodtour.com
778-228-7932

Wildside Vancouver
Vancouver Brew Tour (by minibus)
www.wildsidevancouver.com

604-879-1117

Yaletown Brewing Company

mjg.ca/yaletown
604-681-2739
1111 Mainland Street, Vancouver
E-MAIL ybc@mjg.ca
TWITTER @YBC_brewing

||||||||||||||||||||||||||||||||||||||||||||||||

YALETOWN BREWING IS the oldest brewpub in Vancouver, and was actually part of the movement that transformed the Yaletown neighbourhood from a rundown warehouse district into the popular area it is today.

YBC is the flagship in the Mark James Group chain, which includes the BrewHouse in Whistler, Big Ridge Brewing in Surrey, Red Truck Beer in Vancouver and the Yaletown Distillery, which opened next door in 2013.

Frank Appleton, one of the co-founders of the Horseshoe Bay Brewery, Canada's first microbrewery, helped design the brewhouse. He also trained Iain Hill, who was Yaletown's longtime brewer before leaving to open Strange Fellows Brewing in 2014. The current brewer, David Macanulty, says he "survived" working with James Walton at Storm Brewing in the late 1990s and then worked at breweries in Montreal before moving back to Vancouver in 2013.

The only negative about YBC is that despite it being a brewpub, the beer can get lost among cocktail events, stag and doe parties, and so on. But I'll keep going back—as long as they keep the deep-fried pickles on the menu.

Tap List

LOADING BAY IPA
6.3% ABV | 66 IBU
More of a West Coast IPA than its predecessor, Brick & Beam.

ROUNDHOUSE WHEAT
5% ABV | 12 IBU
An excellent and very authentic Hefeweizen.

Facts & Figures

OPENED › *1994*
STYLES PRODUCED ›
  6 + seasonals
WHERE TO BUY › *In growlers at the brewpub*
ON TAP › *The brewpub*
GROWLERS › *Yes*

TAPHOUSES

Vancouver

• •

VANCOUVER IS BLESSED with several excellent taphouses that serve a wide variety of craft beer from B.C. and elsewhere. Here are my favourites.

Alibi Room
157 Alexander Street

BierCraft (Two locations)
3305 Cambie Street
1191 Commercial Drive

Portland Craft
3835 Main Street

St. Augustine's
2360 Commercial Drive

Tap & Barrel
1 Athletes Way

12 Kings Pub
395 Kingsway

BOTTLE SHOPS

Vancouver

....

VANCOUVER HAS SEVERAL excellent private liquor stores that feature extensive craft beer collections. Here is the crème de la crème.

Brewery Creek
3045 Main Street

Cedar Cottage
3728 Clark Drive
(at Kingsway)

Crosstown Liquor Store
568 Abbott Street

Darby's
2001 MacDonald Street

Firefly
2857 Cambie Street

Granville Liquor Store
2658 Granville Street

Hastings Liquor Store
2769 East Hastings Street

Legacy
1633 Manitoba Street
(Olympic Village)

Libations
928 West King Edward
Avenue

Value On
1450 Southwest Marine
Drive (at Granville)

Viti
900 Seymour Street

West Coast Liquor (Two locations)
7651 Royal Oak Avenue
5503 West Boulevard

BEST BEERS
Vancouver

. . . .

33 Acres Brewing 33 Acres of Axel M.

Apparently, Axel Mercx is a former professional cyclist from Belgium who now lives in Kelowna. Dry-hopped with Amarillo hop—amazing aroma, very fruity, dry and simply delicious.

Bomber Brewing Bike Route Best Bitter

How can a beer this light in alcohol (3.8% ABV) carry so much flavour and body? Goes to show that the Brits were light-years ahead of the current session ale fad.

Brassneck Brewery Multiweizen

I was tempted to just write "anything at Brassneck" here. This is an excellent twist on the Hefeweizen style, made with five different grains (rye, wheat, barley, oats and corn), open fermented with a great Hef yeast. Delicious and creamy.

Parallel 49 Brewing Snap, Crackle, Hop

This is a weird beer—an imperial IPA made with flaked rice, which keeps the body very light despite the high 9.3% ABV level. This showcases the huge tropical fruit flavours of Motueka hops from New Zealand.

Powell Street Craft Brewery Old Jalopy Pale Ale

It's tough to pick a favourite among David Bowkett's excellent lineup, but I'll go with the one that won Beer of the Year at the 2013 Canadian Brewing Awards.

RICHMOND, SURREY & FRASER VALLEY

AT THE BREWERY	DRAFT	FOOD	GROWLERS	BOTTLES	TOURS	BEDS
Be Right Back Brewing (formerly Big River Brewpub)	✪	✪	✪		✪	
Big Ridge Brewing	✪	✪	✪			
Central City Brewpub	✪	✪	✪	✪		
Central City Brewery	✪		✪	✪	✪	
Dageraad Brewing	✪		✪	✪		
Dead Frog Brewery	✪			✪	✪	
Four Winds Brewing	✪		✪	✪		
Maple Meadows Brewing	✪		✪			
Mission Springs Brewpub	✪	✪	✪	✪		
Moody Ales	✪		✪	✪		
Old Abbey Ales	✪		✪	✪		
Old Yale Brewing			✪	✪		
Ravens Brewing	✪		✪	✪		
Ridge Brewing	✪		✪			
Russell Brewing						
Steel & Oak Brewing	✪	✪	✪	✪		
Twin Sails Brewing	✪		✪	✪		
White Rock Beach Beer			✪			
Yellow Dog Brewing	✪		✪	✪		

SIPPING
IN THE SUBURBS

....

Vancouver is expensive. Full stop. It costs a lot to live there, it costs a lot to eat and drink there, and it costs a lot to drive a car there. No wonder Vancouver's suburbs are growing at a phenomenal rate. Surrey, especially, is predicted to surpass Vancouver in population within twenty-five years. For many people who either grew up in Vancouver or who moved there in the past decade or two, it's often the same story: as you enter your professional life and then start looking at raising a family it becomes apparent very quickly that it is almost impossible to own a home within the city itself. So that leads to a move out to Burnaby, New Westminster, Richmond, Surrey, Port Moody, Pitt Meadows or Maple Ridge. And there's nothing wrong with that—there are lots of great benefits to living in the suburbs, including craft beer.

In the first edition of this book I wrote that Vancouver's suburbs already had a well-established craft beer culture with four breweries and three brewpubs. Fast forward two short years and the craft beer scene has exploded throughout the Lower Mainland, just as it has in Vancouver itself. Eight new breweries have opened in Abbotsford, Burnaby, Delta, New Westminster, Port Moody and White Rock. Some of these companies chose to open in the 'burbs because it is far cheaper to set up and run a business there than it is in Vancouver. But most are there because that's where they want to be: serving the local community's interest in craft beer—especially as more and more Vancouverites find themselves priced out of the real estate market in the city and choose to move to one of the satellite communities, bringing their enthusiasm for craft beer with them.

It is exciting to watch as some of the gaps in the regional map get filled in with new breweries. But there are still some blank spots, such as Coquitlam, Langley and Maple Ridge. Burnaby certainly has room for another brewery or two, especially one that could serve the university crowd. And what about Steveston? There must be a great old canning factory or something similar that would be perfect for a brewery.

And then there is the potential for hop farming. Hops were once a major agricultural crop in B.C., and the Fraser Valley was the epicentre of that industry, Chilliwack in particular. Hundreds, perhaps even thousands, of migrant workers would help harvest the crop each fall, many of them travelling up the coast picking hops in Oregon and Washington before joining the crowd here (see "Brewer's Gold" on page 166). Today, that industry is mostly gone, but there has been a renewed interest in growing hops there once more with at least one major producer focused on the craft beer market.

MORE NEW BREWERIES!

Following this book's publication in early 2015, several more new breweries have sprouted in this region, including two in Maple Ridge—Maple Meadows Brewing and Ridge Brewing—as well as Ravens Brewing in Abbotsford and Twin Sails Brewing in Port Moody (see "Stop the Presses!" on page 172). Look for more to open soon, including Trading Post Brewing in Langley, Field House Brewing in East Abbotsford, and Langley Brewing. Viva la Revolution in the Valley!

mjg.ca/big-ridge
604-574-2739
5580 152nd Street, Surrey
E-MAIL bigridge@mjg.ca
TWITTER @BigRidgeBrewing

Big Ridge Brewing Co.

|||||||||||||||||||||||||||||||||||||||||||||||||

Tap List

CHIMNEY HILL WHEAT
4.5% ABV | 12 IBU
An excellent and very authentic Hefeweizen even if the name doesn't say so.

CLOVER ALE
6.5% ABV | 65 IBU
Again, you wouldn't know it from the name, but this is a well-made IPA—with no clover anywhere near it.

AMARILLO ALE (seasonal)
5.5% ABV | 35 IBU
A delicious session IPA that highlights the fruity, Tang-like flavour profile of Amarillo hops.

BIG RIDGE IS the Mark James Group's outpost in Surrey. Unfortunately, it is not close to the SkyTrain so you need a car or a lot of patience with bus connections to visit if you don't live nearby. Still, it's a great brewpub with a relaxed, comfortable atmosphere.

The current brewer, Nick Bolton, who previously worked at Dead Frog Brewery and Yaletown Brewing, follows in the footsteps of Tariq Khan, who now heads Mark James's Yaletown Distillery in Vancouver. Bolton is somewhat limited in the styles of beer he can brew by the neighbourhood's traditional palate—the Harvest Lager is definitely the pub's biggest seller. Even the more challenging beers are given safe names to keep them from deterring customers who are not familiar with them. For instance, the Hefeweizen is just a "wheat beer" (though it's actually a great Hef), and the IPA is called Clover Ale, a twist on the nearby Cloverdale area.

Big Ridge hosts regular cask events in conjunction with the Surrey Beer Club and CAMRA's South Fraser chapter.

Facts & Figures

OPENED ▸ 1999 (moved across the street in 2010) ✪
STYLES PRODUCED ▸ 5 + seasonals ✪ **WHERE TO BUY** ▸ The brewpub ✪ **ON TAP** ▸ The brewpub ✪ **GROWLERS** ▸ Yes

Be Right Back Brewing Co.

(formerly Big River Brewpub)

brbco.ca
604-271-2739
180-14200 Entertainment
  Boulevard, Richmond
E-MAIL info@brbco.ca

||||||||||||||||||||||||||||||||||||||||||||||

OK, TRIVIA TIME, kids: what are the two B.C. brewpubs attached to bowling alleys? (Start whistling the Jeopardy! theme song now.) Give up? The answer: this one and Freddy's in Kelowna. Important fact: the beer here is far better than the other bowling alley brewpub's lineup for sure.

Originally named Big River, this brewpub rebranded as Be Right Back in September, 2015. Hopefully, the update will encourage folks to check it out again. Brewer Steve Pearce is being encouraged to experiment on a small-batch system, which is the right idea for sure.

The location is a little out of the way—it is part of a big-box complex off of Steveston Highway northeast of the Massey Tunnel, basically across the river from Four Winds Brewing.

Tap List

RED IPA
6.8% ABV | 65 IBU
This very interesting beer is brewed with crystal malted rye and fermented with fruity and earthy Brett B Trois yeast, then hopped up to big west coast standards.

ENGLISH MILD ALE
4.1 ABV | 21 IBU
A medium-bodied beer with caramel and toffee flavours in the best British tradition.

....
Facts & Figures

OPENED ▸ *1997* ✪ STYLES PRODUCED ▸ *7 + seasonals* ✪
WHERE TO BUY ▸ *The brewpub* ✪ ON TAP ▸ *The brewpub* ✪
GROWLERS ▸ *Yes*

A PASSION FOR BREWING

Central City's Gary Lohin

....

CENTRAL CITY BREWING'S Gary Lohin is one of the leaders of
B.C.'s craft beer revolution. He is an undisputed master of the
brewing arts who always has time for a chat with a beer lover—
especially if it's about Red Racer Beer, Central City's flagship
line. Lohin also believes the craft beer community should work
together to grow as an industry, and does his part by hosting
cask events that feature other craft brewers at his brewpub
in Surrey.

Lohin got his start brewing at home back in his twenties
before entering the brewing industry as a Vancouver-area sales
rep for Whistler Brewing in the late 1980s. He got involved on
the brewing side near the end of his time there and then found
work as a brewer with Okanagan Spring Brewery in Vernon in
the early '90s, back in that brewery's heyday when they were
still brewing some excellent beers.

However, Lohin really made a name for himself as brewmaster for Sailor Hagar's brewpub in his own hometown of
North Vancouver. After several years there, the pub's management decided to stop brewing their own beer, but Lohin was
ready to run his own place, so he and two partners opened the
Central City brewpub in Surrey, Vancouver's largest suburb, in
2003. Central City took some risks to get noticed in those early
days, and back in 2007 and 2008 when Red Racer beers began
showing up on liquor store shelves, the idea of craft beer *in
cans* was pretty revolutionary.

But it was what was in those cans that mattered, and that

excellent beer got the attention of B.C.'s beer lovers, especially those in Vancouver. Red Racer beer began flying off the shelves, and the brewpub could not keep up with the demand.

That all changed with the opening of Central City's big new brewery in the North Surrey Bridgeview industrial area. The facility is huge—65,000 square feet—and cost $35 million, but it will allow Lohin to brew up to 25,000 hL per year, up from 7,500 hL at the brewpub.

"We just want this to go back to being a brewpub," Lohin says of the original facility. "No packaging. Go back to brewing and moving beer through the serving tanks. It could really be an R&D [research and development] brewery for us, which would be great." The brewpub is also going to serve as the brewing laboratory for the new "Craft Beer and Brewing Essentials" certificate program being offered at SFU Surrey, which is conveniently located right next door.

The new brewery facility also includes a distillery, another of Lohin's passions—"That's a wave I want to catch, not follow"—and there is storage space for barrel aging and bottle conditioning. He has already laid down some whiskey and sour beers in barrels, with the first results expected to come out in 2016. He poured off a small, cask-strength taster for me when I visited late in 2014 and it already tasted incredible.

Lohin is proud of his accomplishments, but not arrogant. He takes his craft seriously and doesn't believe in resting on his laurels. Over the past couple of years, I have often heard him say that his goal was to make sure that the beer coming out of the new brewery wasn't just as good as the brewpub's: "It should be better." Indeed, Central City's clearly stated goal is to be the best brewery in B.C.

That's what I call a passion for brewing.

Brewpub
www.centralcitybrewpub.com
604-582-6620
13450-102 Avenue, Surrey
TWITTER @CentralCityPub

Brewery
www.centralcitybrewing.com
604-588-BEER (2337)
11411 Bridgeview Drive, Surrey
E-MAIL
  info@centralcitybrewing.com
TWITTER @CentralCityBrew

Tap List

**RED RACER
INDIA PALE ALE**
6.5% ABV | 80 IBU
Gary Lohin's signature
beer: one of the best IPAs
anywhere, this is a hop
bomb with glorious citrus-
pine aromas and flavours.

RED RACER ISA
4% ABV | 40 IBU
This is my favourite of
several India session ales
now available from B.C.
breweries.

IMPERIAL IPA
9% ABV | 90 IBU
Bursting with grapefruit,
tangerine and tropical fruit
flavours balanced with a
big malt foundation.

**THOR'S HAMMER
BARLEY WINE** (seasonal)
11% ABV
You can try a bottle-
conditioned or bourbon
barrel–aged version of this
award-winning brew.

Central City
Brewers & Distillers

||||||||||||||||||||||||||||||||||||||||||||||

I HAVE A distinct memory of the first time
I popped open a can of Central City's Red
Racer IPA. It was in the summer of 2008,
soon after the beer was released. I'd brought
a six-pack to a friend's house for a barbecue
and when I cracked the can my nose immediately caught a whiff of the pungent hop
aroma that is a trademark of this excellent
West Coast IPA.

"Holy —," I said to my buddy, Shawn, and
held the can out to him. "Take a whiff of
this." He waved it under his nose and smiled
back at me. My first sip led to another pro-
nouncement of excellence. And on that warm
summer evening, I became a full-fledged
hophead. Sure, I'd enjoyed hoppy beers
before that, but I'd never given myself over to
hops, body and soul, before that night.

I'm exaggerating, a little—it wasn't quite
a religious experience. But the arrival of Red
Racer IPA in its distinctive green can (and
the white ale in its yellow can) that "Red
Racer summer," as I think of it, marked a
turning point in B.C.'s craft beer revolution—
that was when Vancouver finally woke up to
craft beer, and a big part of that was the success of complex and challenging beers like
Central City's Red Racer lineup in attracting
new drinkers.

When Central City opened a brewpub next to the second-last SkyTrain stop, about thirty-five minutes from downtown Vancouver, the big city's beer drinkers barely noticed. But when the canned beer showed up on the market, beer lovers began converging on the brewpub to sample special brews that were only available there. The brewpub's regular summer and winter cask festivals are now must-attend events on Lower Mainland beer lovers' calendars, and brewmaster Gary Lohin is widely respected as one of B.C.'s best brewers, if not *the* best.

Lohin has won many awards, including top honours at the 2010 Canadian Brewing Awards, where he received gold medals for his Red Racer IPA, Imperial IPA and Barley Wine (which also won Beer of the Year), and took home the Brewery of the Year award. Central City was named Canadian Brewery of the Year again in 2012.

His biggest achievement, however, is the beautiful new brewery and distillery Central City opened in November 2013. The 65,000-square-foot, $35-million facility increases their brewing capacity by more than 400 per cent with plenty more expansion possible in coming years. The cooler alone is bigger than the brewhouse at the brewpub. Lohin is already barrel-aging both beer and whiskey, and new products have been added to the Red Racer lineup, including a copper ale, ISA and India-style red ale.

The brewpub remains as great as ever, and with the new brewery's increased capacity, Central City will be able to expand its reach beyond B.C., which means people across Canada will get to have their own "Red Racer summers."

....
Facts & Figures

OPENED ▸ *2003 (brewpub), 2013 (brewery)* ✪ STYLES PRODUCED ▸
8 + seasonals ✪ WHERE TO BUY ▸ *Liquor stores throughout B.C.* ✪
ON TAP ▸ *The brewpub, and throughout Greater Vancouver* ✪
GROWLERS ▸ *Yes*

dageraadbrewing.com
604-420-2050
114-3191 Thunderbird Crescent,
 Burnaby
E-MAIL
 ben@dageraadbrewing.com
TWITTER @DageraadBeer

Dageraad Brewing

||||||||||||||||||||||||||||||||||||||||||||||||

Tap List

AMBER
6% ABV
A solid pale ale with a slight
fruitiness and crisp finish.

BLONDE
7.5% ABV
This strong Belgian
golden ale is spicy and
effervescent thanks to
bottle conditioning. Maybe
it's because I'm blonde, but
I find myself returning to
this beer again and again.

RANDONNEUR
SAISON (seasonal)
6.4% ABV
This is a gorgeous Saison
with a fruity aroma,
peppery and hoppy flavour
and a dry finish.

....
Facts & Figures

OPENED ▸ *2014*
STYLES PRODUCED ▸
 2 + seasonals
WHERE TO BUY ▸ *The
 brewery or private
 liquor stores*
ON TAP ▸ *Greater
 Vancouver and Victoria*
GROWLERS ▸ *Yes*

NAMED FOR THE Dageraadplaats, a neighbourhood square in Antwerp, this is B.C.'s only
brewery that focuses exclusively on Belgian-
style beers. Founder Ben Coli fell in love with
Belgian beer culture over several visits there
and decided the time was right to bring it to
B.C.

Coli studied at Brewlab in the U.K. and
visited several Belgian brewers on a hands-
on brewing sabbatical. One of the things he
learned about Belgian beer is how much of
its character is derived from the yeast itself,
and that you can't push or rush the brewing
process.

"We're doing slow beer," he said when I
visited the brewery shortly after it opened.
"Belgian yeasts are lazy, inefficient... and
awesome!" he added with a grin.

Dageraad launched with just two beers,
simply called Amber and Blonde. Seasonals
have included an excellent Saison, an interesting sour Wit, and a wet-hopped version of
the Blonde. The brewery also has a *Tafelbier*
(table beer) called Burnabarian, which is
only available at the tasting room.

"Dageraad" means "daybreak" or "dawn" in
Flemish Dutch—indeed, it is a new dawn for
B.C. brewing.

deadfrog.ca
1-888-856-1055
1-27272 Gloucester Way,
  Aldergrove
E-MAIL info@deadfrog.ca
TWITTER @DeadFrogBrewery

Dead Frog Brewery ←

||||||||||||||||||||||||||||||||||||||||||||

DEAD FROG BREWERY has suffered from image problems forever, it seems. First, there is the name Dead Frog, which itself is a rebranding from their original name, Backwoods Brewing. Not that Backwoods was a better name. It wasn't. And then there was the marketing, epitomized by slogans like "Do it froggy style" and "Nothing goes down like a cold Dead Frog." They even used clear glass bottles for a while despite the fact that any self-respecting beer geek knows light degrades beer very quickly. Going on a reality TV show asking for money didn't help much either.

But things have been improving at Dead Frog. It has dropped the insipid marketing, mostly, switched to brown bottles and bombers, and most importantly, it has been putting out some really interesting beer for the past year or two. Beer enthusiasts are starting to come around, and more and more people are buying their products, though perhaps more slowly than the brewery might like. But it's tough to earn back a reputation after it's been tarnished—especially when there are so many exciting, new craft breweries to try.

Tap List

FEARLESS IPA
6.5% ABV | 77 IBU
Potent and bitter, but without the citrusy hop aroma it needs to truly be called a West Coast IPA.

ROCKETMAN INTERSTELLAR ESB
(summer seasonal)
5% ABV | 40 IBU
A delicious ESB with big Northwest hop flavours.

SUPER FEARLESS IMPERIAL IPA
(limited release)
9% ABV | 93 IBU
Hop bombs don't get much bigger than this. Keep it coming! I'm not scared...

....
Facts & Figures

OPENED ▸ *1998 (as Backwoods Brewing— renamed in 2006)*
STYLES PRODUCED ▸ *8 + seasonals*
WHERE TO BUY ▸ *Liquor stores throughout B.C.*
ON TAP ▸ *Throughout B.C.*
GROWLERS ▸ *Yes*

fourwindsbrewing.ca
604-640-9949
4-7355 72nd Street, Delta
E-MAIL
  info@fourwindsbrewing.ca
TWITTER @FourWindsBrewCo

Four Winds Brewing

||||||||||||||||||||||||||||||||||||||||||||||

Tap List

PILSNER

4.8% ABV | 38 IBU

My wife's favourite B.C. beer, and one of my favourites, too. This Czech Pilsner is dry-hopped with New Zealand Motueka hops for a zingy finish.

JUXTAPOSE BRETT IPA (seasonal)

6.5% ABV | 50 IBU

My vote for the most interesting B.C. beer to come out in 2014. Winner of a silver medal at the World Beer Cup. Juicy, tropical, funky and bitter.

PHAEDRA BELGIAN RYE IPA (seasonal)

7.2% ABV | 65 IBU

As one of the judges, I can say this was the clear winner of Best in Show at the 2014 Okanagan Fest-of-Ale. Complex with melon and citrus atop spice, pepper and lemon zest.

SAISON BRETT (seasonal)

7% ABV | 28 IBU

Take a delicious Saison and age it in red wine barrels with Brettanomyces yeast. The result is a wildly complex yet refined beer.

FOUR WINDS BREWING started selling beer on June 1, 2013, and very quickly became the darling of the B.C. craft beer scene. Before too long, it was being mentioned in the same breath as Driftwood as every beer geek's favourite brewery. The brewery's rapid ascent up the charts, so to speak, is all because of the excellent beers that its brewer, Brent Mills, has produced in rapid succession, including some very challenging and original styles rarely seen before in B.C.

Mills learned his craft at R&B Brewing with a stint at the Siebel Institute in Chicago, and then decided to go on his own with the help of his father Greg and brothers Adam and Sean. Greg handles the overall administration of the brewery, something he knows well from years of running Mills Paints, a family business he sold a few years ago. Adam ran his own business painting pubs and restaurants, which has set him up well with connections as he took on the sales role with Four Winds. Sean, a self-described "starving musician," will continue playing music on the side while he runs the tasting room and growler station at the brewery.

Brent describes his brewing as a hybrid of the Old World—German and Belgian styles— and contemporary craft beers. Four Winds' core beers reflect that mix well: a Saison, IPA, pale ale, Pilsner and oat porter. These beers are packaged in four-packs of 330 mL bottles, and each is a great example of its style.

Four Winds' seasonal and limited release beers are packaged in two larger formats. The Eurus series, named for the Greek god of the east winds, is a collection of bottle-conditioned beers of European heritage, packaged in 750 mL cork and cage bottles, including: Wildflower Saison, Saison Brett, Sovereign Super Saison and Triplicity Belgian Tripel. The Zephyrus series, named for the Greek god of the west winds, features cutting-edge beers such as Juxtapose Brett IPA, Phaedra Belgian Rye IPA and Apparition West Coast White Ale. These are also bottle-conditioned in 650 mL bombers.

Brent Mills is especially excited about his barrel aging program (mainly using Stag's Hollow red wine barrels). He has talked about a sour farmhouse ale blended with apricots and an American dark sour called Bistre that he plans on aging for at least a year.

Each new release seems to be better than the last, and with some experimental batches only on tap at the brewery, the tasting room always seems to be busy despite its location in a nondescript industrial park in Delta. Don't get me wrong: it's a very attractive tasting room, and the brewery is easy to get to, a short side trip off Highway 99 just south of the Massey Tunnel. If there weren't a ferry involved I'm sure I'd have a regular stool there myself.

....
Facts & Figures

OPENED ▸ *2013* ⚙ **STYLES PRODUCED ▸** *5 + seasonals* ⚙
WHERE TO BUY ▸ *The brewery or at private liquor stores* ⚙ **ON TAP ▸**
Greater Vancouver and Victoria ⚙ **GROWLERS ▸** *Yes*

missionsprings.ca
604-820-1009
7160 Oliver Street (at Lougheed
  Highway), Mission
E-MAIL info@missionsprings.ca
TWITTER @MSBCBREWERY

Mission Springs Brewing Company

Tap List

BIG CHIEF CREAM ALE
4.5% ABV | 17 IBU
A real cream ale, not the
Vancouver version—light,
creamy and easy-drinking.

BOMBSHELL BLONDE
4.5% ABV | 18 IBU
Not particularly
memorable as a beer, but it
has an incredible label.

**FAT GUY
OATMEAL STOUT**
4.5% ABV | 21 IBU
An excellent stout—thick
and creamy with a great
roasted malt character.

FRASER VALLEY IPA
6.6% ABV | 70 IBU
Definitely Mission Springs'
best beer, this IPA features
hops grown at the Sartori
Hop Farm in Chilliwack.

Facts & Figures

OPENED ▸ *1996*
STYLES PRODUCED ▸
  4 + seasonals
WHERE TO BUY ▸
  *Mission Springs private
  liquor store and select
  private stores in Greater
  Vancouver*
ON TAP ▸ *The brewpub*
GROWLERS ▸ *Yes*

|||||||||||||||||||||||||||||||||||||||||||||||

MISSION SPRINGS BREWING Company opened
in 1996 as an expansion to the existing pub
there, creating a real destination for beer
lovers with a 425-seat family restaurant and
a 120-seat adults-only pub. It is one of the
most interesting brewpubs in the province,
bursting with antiques and memorabilia. A
1949 Chevy truck is suspended from the ceiling, and all the walls are covered in tools,
mechanical equipment, hubcaps, musical
instruments and old signage of every kind
you can imagine: from soft drink producers,
gas stations and cigar and cigarette companies. The tabletops themselves contain
artifacts under transparent lacquer, including old spark plugs, license plates and bullet
shells.

Since taking over as brewer a couple years
ago, Kevin Winter has helped push Mission Springs' beer list up a notch. He has
also overseen an expansion in their brewing capacity, which means it is easier to find
their beer beyond the brewpub itself.

Mission Springs has even spread its
reach to South Korea where the company
has opened two separate Spring Tap Houses
in Seoul. Closer to home, the company also
recently opened Hearthstone Brewery in
North Vancouver.

moodyales.com
604-495-3911
2601 Murray Street, Port Moody
E-MAIL beer@moodyales.com
TWITTER @MoodyAles

Moody Ales ←

IIIIIIIIIIIIIIIIIIIIIIIIIIIIIIIIIIIIIIIIIIIIIIII

ONE OF TWO craft breweries that opened on Murray Street in Port Moody in 2014—with a third set to join them on the same block in 2015—Moody Ales was founded by two ex–IT consultants, Adam Crandall and Dan Helmer. The friends brewed together at home for a few years before opening their own brewery.

Initially, they looked at locations in Vancouver and Coquitlam (where they actually live), but Port Moody made the most sense when the building owner offered them a good deal on rent because he liked the idea of a craft brewery going into the space.

Much like Yellow Dog Brewing down the street, Moody Ales has a tasting room and growler station up front with a clear view of the brewing area. A giant mural describing the brewing process covers the tasting room wall, part of the brewery's mission to educate its customers about craft beer.

I really like the vibe at Moody Ales—the beer is good and the people working there are friendly, intelligent and funny. If I lived nearby, I'm sure I'd become a regular.

Tap List

HARDY BROWN ALE
5.1% ABV | 22 IBU
When I tasted this it was called "Release Candidate Brown," which apparently is software geek–speak for an early release. Tasted great at the time—a hoppy brown ale with a nice malt-hop balance.

AFFABLE IPA
6.8% ABV | 60 IBU
Moody Ales' early bestseller at the growler station, this well-balanced IPA is dry-hopped with three hop varieties: Amarillo, Cascade and Simcoe.

....

Facts & Figures

OPENED ▸ *2014*   ✪   **STYLES PRODUCED** ▸ *3 + seasonals*   ✪
WHERE TO BUY ▸ *The brewery or private liquor stores*   ✪   **ON TAP** ▸
Port Moody and Vancouver   ✪   **GROWLERS** ▸ *Yes*

oldabbeyales.com
604-607-5104
1A-30321 Fraser Highway,
  Abbotsford

Old Abbey Ales

Tap List

BELGIAN TRIPEL IPA

9% ABV | 50 IBU

Marrying American ingenuity and Belgian tradition, this delicious beer tops the charts in complexity: it's fruity, spicy, citrusy, and surprisingly quaffable.

BELGIAN QUAD

10.1% ABV | 27 IBU

This Belgian Quad is a huge malt bomb that tops out above 10% abv and is potentially great for cellaring.

Facts & Figures

OPENED ▸ *2015*

STYLES PRODUCED ▸
  4 + seasonals

WHERE TO BUY ▸ *The brewery or liquor stores*

ON TAP ▸ *Fraser Valley and Vancouver*

GROWLERS ▸ *Yes*

BEER IN THE heart of B.C.'s Bible Belt? Coming from a conservative Mennonite background myself, I understand all too well why it has taken this long for breweries to open in Abbotsford. It's why I left my hometown in Ontario and moved about as far away as I could without leaving Canada.

Truth be told, Old Abbey Ales has no interest in debating the place of beer in religion, although its name evokes a religious institution and some of its lineup of beers are Belgian styles associated with Trappist monks who have brewed beer for centuries: Dubbels, Tripels and Quadrupels.

Old Abbey was struggling to open as this book was going to press, first delayed by inspectors and then by health problems suffered by its owner. Brewer Tony Dewald, who made a name for himself at Dix BBQ & Brewery in Vancouver, plans to naturally carbonate all his beers through bottle conditioning and *can conditioning*—something I haven't encountered anywhere else in B.C. yet.

Plans also include a twenty-four-tap tasting room where Dewald wants to showcase "every kind of beer you've heard of and a few more I hope to invent."

Old Yale Brewing Company

oldyalebrewing.com
604-392-2011
4-7965 Venture Place, Chilliwack
E-MAIL info@oldyalebrewing.com
TWITTER @oldyalebrewing

||||||||||||||||||||||||||||||||||||||||||

EX–AIR FORCE PILOT Larry Caza got interested in beer when he was stationed in Goose Bay, Newfoundland, thanks to other international pilots who introduced him to beers like Czech Budwar and Sierra Nevada Pale Ale. Back home in Chilliwack after he retired from the military, Caza began home brewing and then made the leap to professional brewing when he opened Old Yale Brewing in 2000.

Although his beer was well respected, Caza says the business struggled because of a lack of interest in craft beer in the local community and because the original location had a limited capacity. By the fall of 2010, he had shut the doors and put it up for sale. Two ownership changes later, the brewery is in a new location just off the Trans-Canada Highway and Caza is still in charge of the brewing.

Old Yale added a hoppy West Coast IPA to put on tap at the brewery's new growler station for the summer of 2014, but Caza found himself brewing a lot more Sasquatch Stout than he expected after it was named Beer of the Year at the 2014 Canadian Brewing Awards.

Tap List

WEST COAST IPA
6% ABV | 55 IBU
This IPA featuring fruity Australian hops is a nice addition to Old Yale's lineup.

OLD YALE PALE ALE
5% ABV
A tasty pale ale with a solid malt base and some nice hop character.

SASQUATCH STOUT
5% ABV
This is a thick, robust stout that will keep you warm even if you aren't covered with hair. Winner of Beer of the Year at the 2014 Canadian Brewing Awards.

Facts & Figures

OPENED › *2000 (closed in 2010 and reopened in 2011)*
STYLES PRODUCED › *4 + seasonals*
WHERE TO BUY › *Liquor stores throughout B.C.*
ON TAP › *Chilliwack, Harrison Hot Springs, Hope and Vancouver*
GROWLERS › *Yes*

BREWER'S GOLD

The History of Hop Growing
in the Fraser Valley

••••••••••••••••••••••

ONCE UPON A TIME, hops were a major agricultural crop in British Columbia, attracting thousands of migrant workers during the harvest each August and September. The earliest cultivation of this vigorous plant in B.C. dates back to 1862 when farmers in Saanich, just north of Victoria, began growing hops to sell to local brewers. A shortage in other countries allowed Saanich hop farmers to make big profits in the 1880s, which created interest among farmers in other parts of the province, including Squamish, Kelowna, Vernon and around Chilliwack in the Fraser Valley.

The Saanich industry died out soon after because of a hop louse infestation, and farmers everywhere else except the Fraser Valley turned to other crops. But in the Chilliwack area, the industry grew and grew until the 1940s when nearly two thousand acres were under cultivation there, with four thousand people employed during the harvest each year. Temporary towns were struck among the hop fields, with stores, a dance hall and other amenities, and tents or cabins provided by the farmers. Among the pickers were First Nations people, as well as members of the Chinese, Japanese and Mennonite communities. Entire families would go to work in the hop fields: the men would take down the hop bines and the children and women would pick the hop flowers. Pickers were paid by weight—the best could harvest up to two hundred pounds in a day.

At its peak, the Fraser Valley represented the largest

hop-growing region in the entire British Commonwealth. But after World War II, the industry began shrinking, and in the 1950s, the farms began using mechanized pickers, which ended the need for such a large number of workers. Inexorably, fewer and fewer farmers chose to grow hops until the last of the great Fraser Valley hop farms closed down in 1997.

Thanks in part to the efforts of Crannóg Ales' co-founder Rebecca Kneen (see "Sisters of the Hop" on page 189), there has been a resurgence in hops cultivation in B.C., this time focused mainly on organic production. Now, it is estimated that there are at least six organic hop farms in B.C., along with other conventional (non-organic) farms, including the Sartori Hop Farm in Chilliwack, which supplies the fresh hops for Driftwood Brewery's famous Sartori Harvest IPA and also sells hops to several other B.C. breweries.

With so many new breweries opening in the Fraser Valley, there will be more and more incentive for local farmers to return to growing hops to supply them. I'm sure we will see a bigger hop farming industry once again, though not necessarily on the scale it once was.

For more information on this interesting part of B.C. history, check out the online exhibit, *Brewer's Gold*, at www.chilliwackmuseum.ca.

russellbeer.com
604-599-1190
202-13018 Eightieth Avenue,
  Surrey
E-MAIL cheers@russellbeer.com
TWITTER @Russell_Beer

Russell Brewing Company

Tap List

BLACK DEATH PORTER

6.5% ABV | 53 IBU

Thick and black as night with a strong roasted malt character and a deep bitterness.

BLOOD ALLEY BITTER

5.5% ABV | 50 IBU

Named for a notorious Gastown laneway, this is truly an extra bitter bitter. Exceptional.

EASTERN PROMISES CZECH PILSNER

5% ABV | 35 IBU

This delicious Pilsner wouldn't be out of place in a *Pivnica* (pub) in Prague.

WHITE RABBIT HOPPY HEFEWEIZEN

(summer seasonal)

6% ABV

Who knew Northwest hops and German wheat beer yeast could work together so well? I love this beer.

|||||||||||||||||||||||||||||||||||||||||||||||||

FOR A LONG time, Russell Brewing seemed to struggle with its identity. Was it a craft brewery, or was it trying to brew basic beer for the masses? It seems like the management finally has a clear focus on craft. Most of the insipid Lemon Ales and Rocky Mountain Pilsners have been banished (perhaps to Winnipeg where Russell owns Fort Garry Brewing or to China where the ownership also has ties), leaving a solid lineup across the board.

The Brewmaster Series is great: the IP'eh!, Black Death Porter, Blood Alley Bitter and Eastern Promises Czech Pilsner are excellent, the Hop Therapy ISA is a tasty, and A Wee Angry Scotch Ale is magnificently malty. Add to that limited releases like Truth Serum Wheat Wine, Summer Daze Saison, Märzen and White Rabbit Hoppy Hefeweizen, my personal favourite of their beers. Russell Cream Ale is an example of what I call the "Vancouver Cream Ale," a dark version of the style that was first brewed by Shaftebury in the late 1980s.

Facts & Figures

OPENED ▸ *1995 (new ownership as of 2004)* ✪ STYLES PRODUCED ▸ *10 + seasonals* ✪ WHERE TO BUY ▸ *Liquor stores throughout B.C.* ✪ ON TAP ▸ *Pubs and restaurants throughout the Lower Mainland* ✪ GROWLERS ▸ *No*

Steel & Oak Brewing

steelandoak.ca
604-540-6495
1319 Third Avenue,
  New Westminster
E-MAIL cheers@steelandoak.ca
TWITTER @SteelAndOak

||||||||||||||||||||||||||||||||||||||||||||||||||||

NEW WESTMINSTER HAS a long history of brewing thanks to the Sapperton Brewery, which opened in 1879. Although that company went through several ownership and name changes, the brewery operated for 126 years until Labatt closed the facility in 2006.

Beer finally returned to New West in 2014 with the opening of Steel & Oak Brewing, located a short distance from the popular Westminster Quay and Public Market. I wish it had been open back when I was teaching freelance writing at Douglas College—"OK class, it's field trip time: this is how you write a beer review."

Steel & Oak could easily fit in among the new neighbourhood breweries in Vancouver—its marketing aesthetic is very fresh and the tasting room is one of the most attractive around. It's a great option on a SkyTrain brewery crawl that could also include the Central City brewpub and Dageraad Brewing.

The beer is good, too. Brewmaster Peter Schulz grew up in White Rock but trained in Germany, and while he brings the strict adherence to technique associated with German brewing, he also injects lots of creativity into his beers.

Tap List

SMOKED HEFEWEIZEN
6.5% ABV | 15 IBU
A very interesting hybrid of two German styles—Hefeweizen and Rauchbier—this was Steel & Oak's most popular beer at its launch.

RED PILSNER
5% ABV | 35 IBU
A well-made Pilsner with a slightly darker and maltier body than what you'd typically expect.

....

Facts & Figures

OPENED ▸ *2014*
STYLES PRODUCED ▸
  3 + seasonals
WHERE TO BUY ▸ *The brewery or private liquor stores in Greater Vancouver*
ON TAP ▸ *Greater Vancouver and Victoria*
GROWLERS ▸ *Yes*

whiterockbeachbeer.com
604-319-4378
15181 Russell Avenue, White Rock
E-MAIL
bill@whiterockbeachbeer.com

White Rock Beach Beer

|||||||||||||||||||||||||||||||||||||||||||||

Tap List

WEST BEACH FRUIT

5% ABV | 36 IBU

This is not actually a fruit beer—the fruit in the title refers to the citrus fruit flavours featured in this American Pale Ale courtesy of Centennial hops.

EAST BEACH NUT

4.9% ABV | 32 IBU

A Canadian take on the traditional British-style Nut Brown Ale. It is mild and malty with a light dose of hops.

WHITE ROCK BEACH Beer makes most nano-breweries look large in comparison. I know home brewers who produce more beer than this tiny brewery does.

Owned and operated by three schoolteachers who definitely haven't left their day jobs, this brewery is only open on weekends and has trouble keeping up with demand. The founding trio is in the brewery most evenings and every weekend, brewing and kegging and doing whatever else needs to get done to ensure they have enough beer available.

Right now, every drop of beer produced is sold at the brewery itself in the form of growlers or 12 oz glasses. The brewery wants to be able to distribute kegs to local pubs and restaurants, but some expansion will have to occur first, both in terms of the brewing equipment and the tasting room.

White Rock Beach Beer is yet another prime example of how breweries can focus on their own communities, starting small and growing as demand warrants it.

Viva la craft beer revolution!

Facts & Figures

OPENED ▸ *2014* ✪ **STYLES PRODUCED** ▸ *2 + seasonals* ✪
WHERE TO BUY ▸ *The brewery* ✪ **ON TAP** ▸ *Select restaurants and pubs in White Rock.* ✪ **GROWLERS** ▸ *Yes*

yellowdogbeer.com
604-492-0191
1-2817 Murray Street, Port Moody
TWITTER @YellowDogBeer

Yellow Dog Brewing ←

|||||||||||||||||||||||||||||||||||||||||||||||

YELLOW DOG BREWING became Port Moody's first craft brewery in the summer of 2014, and then solidified that success with a big win at the B.C. Beer Awards a few months later when its Shake A Paw Smoked Brown Porter was named Beer of the Year.

Yellow Dog was founded by Mike and Melinda Coghill with Liam Murphy (ex–Parallel 49 Brewing) as the brewer. The Coghills looked at opening in East Vancouver first, but after they moved to Port Moody themselves, they decided it was the perfect spot.

The brewery has a growler station and tasting room with a view of the brewery beyond. A new "pilot" brew is put on tap every week. (It's going to get tough coming up with dog-themed names pretty quickly...)

Yellow Dog also has a licenced picnic area out back, which is very popular with locals on warm evenings—this sort of thing is fairly common at wineries, but few B.C. breweries have one. I love the concept.

Plans for 2015 include packaging in 650 mL bombers as well as cans.

Tap List

CHASE MY TAIL PALE ALE
5.2% ABV | 50 IBU

A great West Coast pale ale with a fresh, dry-hopped character—a "gateway IPA" as the folks at the brewery describe it.

PLAY DEAD IPA
7.2% ABV | 75 IBU

This IPA boasts a big fruity nose of Mosaic and Citra hops. Delicious.

SHAKE A PAW SMOKED BROWN PORTER (seasonal)
5% ABV | 24 IBU

Winner of Beer of the Year at the 2014 B.C. Beer Awards, this is a delicious, rich porter with a very palatable, background smokiness.

....

Facts & Figures

OPENED ▸ 2014 ✲ STYLES PRODUCED ▸ 3 + seasonals ✲ WHERE TO BUY ▸ The brewery or private liquor stores ✲ ON TAP ▸ Port Moody and Vancouver ✲ GROWLERS ▸ Yes

STOP THE PRESSES!

....

Since the original publication of this book, Surlie Brewing closed and several new breweries opened. Here's a quick update:

Maple Meadows Brewing
22775 Dewdney Trunk Rd, Maple Ridge
maplemeadowsbrewingco.com | 604-479-0999

This is a good introduction to craft beer for Maple Ridge residents who are interested in learning more.

Ravens Brewing
2485 Townline Rd, Abbotsford
ravensbrewing.com | 604-758-1557

Ravens has the Abbotsford beer lover squarely in its sights—something that both Surlie and Old Abbey seem to have overshot with their more eclectic beers.

Ridge Brewing
22826 Dewdney Trunk Rd, Maple Ridge
ridgebrewing.com | 604-380-0888

Across the street from Maple Meadows Brewing, Ridge is a little bit bigger with more potential for growth.

Twin Sails Brewing
2821 Murray Stret, Port Moody
twinsailsbrewing.com | 604-492-4234

Founded by twins Clay and Cody Allmin, Twin Sails is the third brewery to open on Murray Street in Port Moody in just over a year. This one is focusing on German-style beers, especially lagers.

BEST BEERS
Richmond,
Surrey & Fraser Valley

·························

Central City Brewing Red Racer IPA
Quite possibly the best IPA in Canada, certainly the best in a
can (and thus the best camping beer in history). It's still just as
good if not better from the new brewery, and now it's available
in bottles of various sizes, too.

Dageraad Brewing Blonde
This strong Belgian blonde is fruity, spicy, effervescent and dry.
I keep returning to it again and again because, as the saying
goes, we blondes *do* have more fun.

Four Winds Brewing Juxtapose Brett IPA
I could have picked so many of Four Winds' beers—Sovereign
Super Saison, Phaedra Belgian Rye IPA, even the regular IPA
or Pilsner—but I'll go with Juxtapose because it was such a
radically new and unusual beer when it first came out and continues to astonish me every time I try it.

Old Yale Brewing Sasquatch Stout
Winner of Beer of the Year at the 2014 Canadian Brewing
Awards, this thick, black, rich stout will put some hair on…
well, all over your body!

Russell Brewing Blood Alley Bitter
Just as a vampire's thirst for blood is never-ending, this excellent bitter will leave you craving more and more.

THOMPSON-OKANAGAN

AT THE BREWERY	DRAFT	FOOD	GROWLERS	BOTTLES	TOURS	BEDS
Bad Tattoo Brewing	✪	✪	✪	✪		
Barley Mill Brewpub	✪	✪		✪	✪	
Barley Station Brewpub	✪	✪	✪	✪		
BNA Brewing	✪	✪	✪			
Cannery Brewing	✪		✪	✪	✪	
Crannóg Ales			✪		✪	
Firehall Brewery			✪	✪		
Freddy's Brewpub	✪	✪	✪			
Marten Brewpub	✪	✪	✪	✪		
Noble Pig Brewhouse	✪	✪	✪			
Red Collar Brewing	✪	✪	✪	✪		
Tin Whistle Brewing				✪		
Tree Beer Institute	✪	✪	✪		✪	
Tree Brewing			✪	✪		

CRAFT BEER
IN WINE COUNTRY

· ·

WHEN YOU HEAR the word "Okanagan," you probably think of wine country. But the region also has a well-established and diverse craft beer community that keeps getting better and better. There are now nine breweries and five brewpubs spread among communities such as Oliver, Penticton, Vernon, Kelowna, Salmon Arm, Sorrento and Kamloops. The Okanagan is also home to a clutch of five small distilleries, which are part of the nascent craft distillery movement that is beginning to pick up steam here in British Columbia. The distilling industry in the Okanagan has a lot to do with the abundance of fruit grown alongside the grapes—and most of the craft brewers in the region also feature fruit prominently in their lineups.

Penticton's beer scene has grown even stronger in the past couple of years with the addition of a new brewery called Bad Tattoo Brewing to the already solid duo of Tin Whistle Brewing and Cannery Brewing, which has moved into a bigger facility downtown. Add in the Firehall Brewery in nearby Oliver and the region's beer scene is definitely worth checking out. Penticton also hosts the Okanagan Fest-of-Ale each April, a two-day event that showcases breweries from the region alongside their colleagues from elsewhere in Canada and the United States.

The arrival of the Marten Brewpub in Vernon is a cause worth celebrating. After all, Vernon was one of the early birthplaces of microbrewing in B.C. way back in 1985 when Okanagan Spring Brewery opened there, but nothing else has opened there since, and OK Spring ceased to be a craft brewery a long time ago.

The other place I am especially excited about is Kamloops. With the opening of Red Collar Brewing to go along with the Noble Pig Brewhouse and a local café with an amazing beer list, B.C.'s fifth largest city has something going on for sure.

Tree Brewing is growing its footprint in Kelowna with the addition of its Beer Institute there, and Crannóg Ales continues to do its own thing on its farm in Sorrento. The additions of a CAMRA Okanagan branch, which should be launched in March 2015, and a second beer festival—the Great Okanagan Beer Festival, to be held annually in Kelowna starting in May 2015—provide even more options for craft beer lovers.

All in all, there is definitely a case to be made for drinking craft beer in wine country.

STOP THE PRESSES!

Kelowna seems to be enjoying a mini boom with the arrival of one new brewery in 2015 and a couple more slated for 2016:

BNA Brewing Co.

1250 Ellis Street, Kelowna
bnabrewing.com | 236-420-0025

Located in the beautifully renovated BNA Tobacco factory, BNA Brewing has a great restaurant attached to a small brewery and growler station. The beer is supposed to be great, but it seems like they may have underestimated demand given how often they are selling out of it.

Coming in 2016:

Kettle River Brewing

731 Baillie Avenue, Kelowna
kettleriverbrewing.ca

Starkhund Brewing

816 Clement Avenue, Kelowna

badtattoobrewing.com
250-493-8686
169 Estabrook Avenue, Penticton
E-MAIL lagur12@hotmail.com
TWITTER @BTBrewing

Bad Tattoo Brewing

Tap List

ACP GOLDEN ALE

5% ABV | 35 IBU
The name stands
for "Achieve, Conquer,
Persevere." This golden
ale is very tasty and
sessionable.

FULL SLEEVE STOUT

5.5% ABV
The brewery really aimed
to keep this stout semi-
sweet with a silky smooth
mouth feel.

WEST COAST IPA

6.2% ABV | 65 IBU
Made with six different
hop varietals, including
the delicious Falconer's
Flight blend, this IPA has
a definite tropical passion
fruit character.

LOS MUERTOS
CERVEZA NEGRA

5% ABV
Reminiscent of a tasty
German Dunkel to my
palate, but I've never been
to Mexico to taste their
version at the source.

||||||||||||||||||||||||||||||||||||||||||||||

BAD TATTOO BREWING is a welcome addition
to the Penticton brewing scene. Founder
Martin Lewis has been an important part
of the city's craft beer culture for a while
already; he is active on the board of the
Okanagan Fest-of-Ale, the city's annual
beer festival, and he was the manager of the
Kettle Valley Station Pub at the Penticton
Ramada, which has been featuring diverse
craft beer from around the world for several
years.

The brewery has a prime location within
sight of Penticton's famous Peach on the
Beach, a refreshment stand that resembles a
giant peach. It is a brand new building, pur-
pose built for the brewery, with an on-site
rock oven pizzeria and a patio that is packed
throughout the summer. The brewery is
quite large, with a twenty-hectolitre kettle
and several twenty-, forty- and sixty-hecto-
litre tanks and room to grow, so I expect its
beer will eventually be available throughout
B.C., although as of late 2014, it was only
available at the source.

Bad Tattoo hired Robert Theroux to be
its head brewer. Previously, he had worked
at McAuslan Brewing and RJ Brewers in
Montreal. If you've met me, you know I'm a
pretty big guy, but I feel like a shrimp next to

Robbie, who played on the offensive line on his college football team.

Although Lewis does not have a brewing background himself, he definitely gets involved with the planning and execution of Bad Tattoo's beers. He and Theroux have a real connection when it comes to the beers they like—as Theroux put it, "We basically reverse engineer our beer recipes from our imagination."

As brewery names go, I wouldn't say Bad Tattoo is my personal favourite, but it is difficult to make a new operation stand out in such a busy and increasingly competitive market, and maybe the name will help. The most important thing is the beer being produced, and that is quite good across the board (if not necessarily up to the standards being set by some of the new breweries in and around Vancouver).

Bad Tattoo's most popular core beer is Los Muertos Cerveza Negra, a dark lager that is a popular style in Mexico but is pretty unusual in B.C. Continuing in the Mexican theme is Dia de los Muertos Cerveza Fuerte, a Belgian Quad–style beer the brewery released for a Day of the Dead celebration on November 1, 2014. Eight hundred litres were put into barrels to age—appropriately, it will be released as La Resurección one year later.

At the end of 2014, the brewery was packaging its core beers in 650 mL bombers, but plans were also in the works to package in six-packs of 330 mL aluminium bottles in 2015.

....
Facts & Figures

OPENED › *2014* ✪ **STYLES PRODUCED ›** *4+ seasonals* ✪
WHERE TO BUY › *The brewery or private liquor stores* ✪ **ON TAP ›** *The Okanagan* ✪ **GROWLERS ›** *Yes*

Barley Mill Brewpub

Tap List

MUSTANG PALE ALE

5% ABV

A basic pale ale, not very complex or challenging.

NITE MARE BROWN ALE

5% ABV

A brown ale with a bit of flavour, though not much body.

THE BARLEY MILL'S Tudor-style architecture stands out in downtown Penticton. Inside, the two-storey brewpub is very comfortable with a large restaurant downstairs and an upstairs bistro that features a large collection of sports memorabilia, including a Gordie Howe hockey jersey. While you're up there, ask for a tour of the tiny brewhouse, one of the smallest I've ever seen.

Unfortunately, the beer selection is not very inspiring. The standard menu has four very light, bland beers—two ales and two lagers that are virtually identical in flavour and appearance—and a slightly more flavourful brown ale. Hopefully, the rotating seasonal brew will be more interesting: it may be the only chance the brewer gets to experiment a little.

Facts & Figures

OPENED ▸ *1998* ✪ **STYLES PRODUCED ▸** *5 + seasonals* ✪ **WHERE TO BUY ▸** *In cans from the connected Barley Mill liquor store* ✪ **ON TAP ▸** *The brewpub* ✪ **GROWLERS ▸** *No*

OKANAGAN
FEST-OF-ALE

A Two-Day Festival Held
in Penticton Every April

••••••••••••••••••••••••

THE OKANAGAN FEST-OF-ALE is the biggest beer event held in central B.C. each year. Based in Penticton in the heart of wine country, it showcases all of the area's breweries as well as others from elsewhere in B.C. and the rest of Canada.

This is a popular Friday–Saturday event that is held in the local convention centre. It can be a bit of a drink-up for some attendees, but it's also a great way to check out the beer scene in the Okanagan. I recommend heading out a day or two early so you can visit some of the breweries and craft distilleries directly (or I guess you can check out a winery or two if you're into that). One local wine tour operator, Grape Friends, operates a "Barley Hops and Spirits" tour that is a great way to get a taste of the region. (Check out www.grapefriendsloungeand-tours.com for more information.)

And if you are in Penticton when the festival isn't on, drop by the Kettle Valley Station Pub. Connected to the Ramada Inn and Suites, it is a great place to enjoy all the best local beers, as well as interesting brands from around the world.

---

www.fest-of-ale.bc.ca

barleystation.com
250-832-0999
20 Shuswap Street SE
  Salmon Arm
E-MAIL bstation@telus.net

Barley Station Brew Pub

Tap List

BUSHWACKER BROWN ALE

4.7% ABV | 24 IBU

Even more robust than it looks with a chocolaty nuttiness and some roasted barley character.

ESB (seasonal)

5% ABV

An excellent ESB with a great balance of malt and hop bitterness.

SAM MCGUIRE'S PALE ALE

4.6% ABV | 45 IBU

A solid Northwest pale ale with some surprising hop bitterness, although with virtually no hop aroma.

TALKING DOG WIT

4.9% ABV | 12 IBU

An excellent Belgian Wit with subtle tones of coriander and orange peel.

||||||||||||||||||||||||||||||||||||||||||||||

MY FRIEND PEGGY drives back and forth between Victoria and Calgary a few times each year, and she always stops for lunch at the Barley Station. Situated right on the Trans-Canada Highway in Salmon Arm, this brewpub has one of the best locations you could ask for. The building, a replica of an old-fashioned train station, catches the eyes of many passing drivers. Once you've gone inside, consider yourself hooked. Just like Peggy, you'll plan on stopping there every time.

I'll admit that when I first dropped in I was not expecting to be impressed by the beer. I'd already visited two other disappointing brewpubs in the Okanagan, but here, at the Barley Station, my expectations were turned upside down. Brewer Damon Robson makes a solid range of five main beers along with some rotating seasonals.

The brewpub cans its beer for off-sales, and also has a growler program. The menu is diverse and even includes food-and-beer pairing suggestions, and the pub is very comfortable and spacious with a large patio.

Facts & Figures

OPENED ‣ *2006* ✪ **STYLES PRODUCED** ‣ *5 + seasonals* ✪ **WHERE TO BUY** ‣ *In cans and growlers at the brewpub* ✪ **ON TAP** ‣ *The brewpub* ✪ **GROWLERS** ‣ *Yes*

AN OKANAGAN ORIGINAL:
ONCE GREAT, NOW JUST BIG

Okanagan Spring Brewery

．．．．．．．．．．．．．．．．．．．．．．

BACK IN 1992, the first job I had after I moved to B.C. was as a box office clerk at the Belfry Theatre in Victoria. I worked evenings for the first couple years, putting the shows in and then tallying up the ticket sales before selling subscriptions or tickets for future events during intermission. After intermission, I'd close up the ticket window and, more often than not, head across the street to the George & Dragon Pub (now the Fernwood Inn) for a pint of Okanagan Spring Extra Special Pale Ale. Once the curtain was down, co-workers from the backstage side of the theatre would show up along with the actors, and more pints or pitchers of OK Spring would follow.

We served Okanagan Spring beer at the theatre, too, so I drank a lot of it in those days, and happily. Back in the late 1980s and 1990s, Okanagan Spring brewed some great beer. In addition to their standard pale ale and lager, they had a solid stout and some specialty styles, like Old Munich Wheat. And back then, they bottled their beer in stubbies, which were very cool.

The brewery was founded by Buko von Krosigk and Jakob Tobler in 1985. The story goes that they were disappointed with the mainstream beers in Canada after moving to the Okanagan from Germany. Even though they didn't have any brewing experience, they bought an old fruit-packing house in Vernon and turned it into a brewery, hiring a friend from Germany, Raimund Kalinowsky, to join them as their original brewmaster. Tobler's son Stefan mentored under Kalinowsky and then studied brewing in Germany before taking over as brewmaster himself in 1989.

Originally, OK Spring brewed German-style lagers, but they quickly found there was more of a market for ales so they switched their focus in that direction. They also realized that they needed to sell their beer outside of the Okanagan and aggressively marketed themselves in the Lower Mainland and on Vancouver Island. This pattern of growth continued until they had become B.C.'s largest "microbrewery" and were subsequently purchased by Sleeman Breweries in 1996, which itself was bought by Sapporo ten years later.

In the mid-'90s, I definitely noticed the quality of OK Spring's beer diminish. They were quickly surpassed by newer craft breweries arriving on the B.C. scene. It seems as if growth on the scale Okanagan Spring underwent resulted directly in a toning down of flavour in an attempt to make their beer more palatable to a wider audience. I've heard a story from someone who worked at Okanagan Spring back then about the day shortly after Sleeman bought the brewery when the "men in suits" arrived, gathered all the brewers together in the conference room, and told them what they would be brewing for the rest of the year. When accountants start brewing the beer, it's safe to say a brewery is no longer "craft."

Cannery Brewing ←

cannerybrewing.com
250-493-2723
198 Ellis Street, Penticton
  (new location)
E-MAIL
  info@cannerybrewing.com
TWITTER @CanneryBrewing

||||||||||||||||||||||||||||||||||||||||||||

RON AND PATT DYCK were well-established restaurateurs in 2000 with twenty-three years of experience operating the Country Squire restaurant in the town of Naramata just north of Penticton when their chef, an avid home brewer named Terry Schofer, told them about some brewing equipment he'd heard was for sale. Ron says he loved the idea of running a brewery right from the start, but he had to persuade a lot of people to agree with him: his wife, his banker, other business colleagues, and so on. He persisted and won out.

They decided to set up shop in the historic Aylmer fruit and vegetable cannery in Penticton, but it was a major challenge just getting the brewing equipment into this non-traditional space. And then there was a steep learning curve setting it up and making it operational. They finally brewed their first batch of beer, Naramata Nut Brown Ale, which is still one of their best sellers, on April 1, 2001 (no fooling). At first, Cannery only sold its beer in kegs to local restaurants and bars, but then it added an 8.5-litre "party pig" mini-keg which became very popular with the locals, especially in the summer months.

When they did start bottling, Cannery

Tap List

ANARCHIST AMBER ALE
5.5% ABV | 27 IBU
Named for nearby Anarchist Mountain, this is a nonconformist amber ale with a nice dose of West Coast hops.

NARAMATA NUT BROWN ALE
5.5% ABV | 25 IBU
This velvety smooth brown ale is named for the tiny town of Naramata, famous for its many wineries. And now for this great beer.

SQUIRE SCOTCH ALE
6% ABV | 20 IBU
Few brewers brew scotch ales. Fewer brew them this well. Deep caramel colour with a sweet, smoked malt flavour.

SKAHA SUMMER ALE (seasonal)
5% ABV | 20 IBU
This blonde ale celebrates summer with a different hop recipe each year. Perfect for a summer patio.

first used a clear-glass one-litre bottle with a resealable, Grolsch-style cap. Eventually they made the move to the industry standard 650 mL bomber bottle and when economics allowed it in 2006, they added a canning line to their operation. They were one of the first B.C. breweries to offer a mixed pack, the "Cannery Collection," which includes two cans each of Naramata Nut Brown, Lakeboat Lager and Anarchist Amber Ale.

Cannery has slowly been adding more adventurous beers to its lineup, including a Baltic Porter (8% ABV) nicknamed "Kiek in de Kök" and Red Dawn Saison. The brewery also puts out a special edition black IPA each year called Wildfire as a tribute to firefighters who help fight wildfires with partial proceeds going to the Canadian Fallen Firefighters Fund.

Early in 2015, Cannery moved into a brand new brewery located in downtown Penticton: a bigger 12,000-square-foot brewery as well as an expanded tasting room and growler station. The new facility was scheduled to open right around the time that this edition was published.

Facts & Figures

OPENED ‣ *2001* ✪ **STYLES PRODUCED** ‣ *11+ seasonals* ✪
WHERE TO BUY ‣ *The brewery and liquor stores throughout B.C.* ✪
ON TAP ‣ *Throughout the Okanagan* ✪ **GROWLERS** ‣ *Yes*

crannogales.com
250-675-6847
706 Elson Road, Sorrento
E-MAIL
  brewery@crannogales.com

Crannóg Ales ←

||||||||||||||||||||||||||||||||||||||||||||||

CANADA'S ONE AND ONLY certified organic farmhouse brewery, Crannóg Ales is a truly unique place that any B.C. beer lover should visit at least once. While Crannóg's exceptional beers are available on tap in much of southwestern and central B.C., it's another thing to go directly to the source and see what goes into it. But plan ahead: the brewery offers public tours by reservation only on Fridays and Saturdays in the summer.

Founders Brian MacIsaac and Rebecca Kneen left Vancouver to move to this ten-acre farm just above Shuswap Lake, halfway between Kamloops and Salmon Arm, in 2000. They built much of the brewery themselves, converting some of the farm buildings that were already there and using brewhouse equipment from B.C.'s original microbrewery, the Horseshoe Bay Brewery. Today, they brew ales in a traditional English/Irish style, including the very popular Back Hand of God Stout, Red Branch Irish Ale, Insurrection IPA, and Gael's Blood Potato Ale, which is brewed with organic potatoes.

The brewers planted their own organic hops in 2000 and began harvesting for production two years later. At that time, organic hops were only available from New Zealand, and apart from the costs and environmental

Tap List

BACK HAND OF GOD STOUT
5.2% ABV | 18 IBU
Crannóg's flagship beer—a dry stout that isn't heavy but has lots of flavour.

GAEL'S BLOOD POTATO ALE
5.2% ABV | 48 IBU
An Irish red ale with a smooth, rich body. Very tasty with quite a hop bite on top of a solid malt (and potato!) foundation.

INSURRECTION IPA
5.4% ABV | 54 IBU
A lightweight in terms of alcohol, this IPA holds its own against the big boys.

POOKA CHERRY ALE (seasonal)
5% ABV
A summer seasonal lightly hopped ale brewed with four hundred pounds of cherries from Crannóg's own trees or a local farm.

footprint of shipping over that distance, MacIsaac and Kneen were also concerned about relying on only one source. Hops were once a major crop in B.C., but the industry all but died out by the 1980s (see "Brewer's Gold" on page 166). Once Crannóg had a viable crop growing, the brewers found there was a lot of interest from other B.C. farmers and brewers, too. With government assistance, Kneen produced a manual on small-scale hop production and made it publicly available. They also began selling hop rhizomes (root stock for others to plant), single-handedly spearheading a revival in organic hop growing in Canada. Now, thanks in large part to Crannóg's efforts, there is a nascent renaissance in hop growing in British Columbia.

On only ten acres, the brewery doesn't have very much room to grow barley; besides, the climate isn't ideal for grains. However, Crannóg does use berries, plums and other fruit that grows on the property in its beers. And in the cycle of organic farming, the spent grains are fed to the pigs (who especially love the potatoes from the Gael's Blood brew). They also have sheep that keep the grass down in the hopyards and love to eat the leaves from the hop bines after they are picked.

Most aspects of this organic farm and brewery seem to go full-circle that way, including the brewery itself. After all, as John Mitchell, the founder of the Horseshoe Bay Brewery, pointed out when he visited Crannóg several years back: the equipment from Canada's first microbrewery is now being used by the country's first all-organic brewery.

Facts & Figures

OPENED ▸ *2000* ✪ **STYLES PRODUCED** ▸ *4 + seasonals* ✪
WHERE TO BUY ▸ *In growlers or party pigs from the brewery* ✪
ON TAP ▸ *The Shuswap, Okanagan, Greater Vancouver and Vancouver Island* ✪ **GROWLERS** ▸ *Yes*

SISTERS OF THE HOP

Leading Women of B.C.'s
Craft Beer Industry

••••••••••••••••••••••••

FOR MOST OF its history, beer was mainly the domain of women who brewed it for consumption by their families. Starting in the 1600s when beer began to be commercialized, however, brewing became a predominantly male occupation. And in the twentieth century, beer drinking came to be seen as a male pre-occupation, at least in North American popular culture. But as the craft beer revolution has overtaken North America, women have returned to the beer industry as brewers, managers and, of course, consumers.

Here in B.C., we have a small but strong contingent of female brewers, including Rebecca Kneen, the co-owner of Crannóg Ales. Claire (Connolly) Wilson was the brewer at Big River Brewpub for several years and is now striking out on her own with Dogwood Brewing. At Spinnakers, Kala Hadfield, daughter of founder Paul Hadfield, grew up in the brewpub and is now a brewer there. She is responsible for some of its hoppier beers, including the excellent Northwest Ale, as well as some very interesting Belgian styles, including a Brett-conditioned rye Saison she prepared for the brewpub's thirtieth anniversary in May 2014. Her sister Carly, though not a brewer, is evangelizing the message of craft beer in the heart of Kokanee country as co-owner of the Lion's Head Pub in Robson. Nelson Brewing and R&B Brewing also have female brewers.

There are also several B.C. breweries that are owned and run by husband-and-wife teams, including Salt Spring Island Ales, Mt. Begbie, Arrowhead, Wolf, Powell Street, the Moon

Under Water, Yellow Dog, Callister and Bridge Brewing. Howe Sound has a unique brother-and-sister management team, with Leslie Fenn as CEO. Townsite Brewing was the brainchild of Karen Skadsheim, and although she has since left the brewery, her replacement, Chloe Smith, works alongside her husband the brewmaster, Cédric Dauchot.

The Pink Boots Society is an international organization that aims to "empower women beer professionals to advance their careers in the beer industry through education." Pink Boots also has a consumer arm called Barley's Angels, and Vancouver is host to the Pink Pints chapter of that group, which is run by Lundy Dale, who is herself a leading female figure in the craft beer scene. She was one of the founding members of the CAMRA Vancouver branch, then its president, and also stood as president of CAMRA B.C. After working as a craft beer expert at one of the city's private liquor stores, she took a job in marketing at R&B Brewing in 2012. (Follow her on Twitter @PinkPints for information on events.)

Vancouver Craft Beer Week holds a Sisters of the Tap event each year, which features B.C. breweries with women in brewing or management roles. And there is a very active Sisters of the Tap group in Victoria, with regular events that include brewery tours, food-beer pairing seminars and beer style explorations. Victoria Beer Week hosted a special Women and Beer event on International Women's Day in 2014: a screening of the documentary *The Love of Beer* by Portland, Oregon, filmmaker Alison Grayson, followed by a panel discussion featuring Grayson and several women involved in B.C.'s craft beer industry. Plans for Victoria Beer Week's 2015 edition include a women-only bicycle tour to three Victoria breweries where women play prominent roles: Spinnakers, Driftwood Brewery and the Moon Under Water brewpub.

Check out sistersofthetap.tumblr.com for more information.

Firehall Brewery

firehallbrewery.com
778-439-2337
6077 Main Street, Oliver
E-MAIL
  firehallbrewery@gmail.com
TWITTER @FirehallBrewery

||||||||||||||||||||||||||||||||||||||||||||

THE TOWN OF OLIVER, halfway between Penticton and Osoyoos in the south Okanagan, calls itself the Wine Capital of Canada, but among all those vineyards and wineries you can also visit Firehall Brewery, which opened in April 2012. The tiny microbrewery is run by a young musician named Sid Ruhland who pours his enthusiasm and energy into every batch of craft beer.

Ruhland grew up in Oliver, then went away to school in Kelowna, where he says he was too young to buy beer, but not to brew it in his dorm room. Later, he spent a year abroad based in Austria where he travelled far and wide in search of beer. After graduating from business school, he decided to apply his brewing skills and business knowledge to opening this brewery.

The brewery is based in Oliver's original firehall, which was built in 1948 for the town's volunteer fire department. After a new firehall was built in 2003, the building was renovated to house a restaurant space upstairs, which is now called Pappa's Firehall Bistro, with the brewery in the basement. Sid's father, Jim Ruhland, who runs a local construction company, owns the building and is a partner in the brewery. Sid's brother Carson is the brewery's only other employee,

Tap List

BACKDRAFT BLONDE ALE
4.9% ABV | 24 IBU
Extinguish your thirst emergency with this crisp, quaffable light ale.

HOLY SMOKE STOUT
4.5% ABV | 24 IBU
This is a rather unique beer in B.C.: a dry stout melded with German Rauchbier (smoked beer), which uses barley malt smoked over a beechwood fire. You'll be pleasantly surprised by the smoky flavour.

STOKED EMBER ALE
4.8% ABV | 35 IBU
A traditional English-style bitter (amber ale) with a bit of an extra Northwest hop zing.

helping out as a "part-time brew hand."

As Ruhland showed me around the small brewhouse, I noticed that each of his pieces of equipment had an unusual name. The brew kettle was "BB King," and the hot liquor tank, "Hendrix." The fermenters were "Led" and "Zeppelin," another one read "Floyd." In the cold room, Ruhland saw me read the names on the two aging tanks, "Crosby" and "Stills," and with a wry smile between his thick muttonchop sideburns, he pointed to the empty half of the room. "Can you guess who we'll put in here one day?"

Music is a big part of life for Ruhland and his friends, many of whom help out at the brewery on a volunteer basis, no doubt in exchange for the occasional sample now and then. They believe music and beer go hand in hand—each summer they stage a Back Alley Concert Series behind the brewery.

Since opening, Firehall has expanded its capacity as much as possible given space limitations, but the brewery does not distribute its products beyond the Okanagan. Ruhland delivers the beer himself locally. That fits with his philosophy anyway: "the European model where every town needs a butcher, baker and brewer." The only time Firehall's products appear elsewhere is when those stores pick it up themselves. "It makes us exclusive so people have to come here," Ruhland explained, "and that supports our town, too."

So plan a visit and drop by the "hydration station" tasting room at the brewery for a chat and a sample—Sid is always ready with a smile and a story. Or visit on a summer night for what I'm sure would be a great concert.

Facts & Figures

OPENED ‣ *2012* ❂ **STYLES PRODUCED** ‣ *3* ❂ **WHERE TO BUY** ‣ *In growlers or bottles at the brewery* ❂ **ON TAP** ‣ *Oliver* ❂ **GROWLERS** ‣ *Yes*

Freddy's Brewpub

mccurdybowl.com
250-765-8956
948 McCurdy Road, Kelowna
TWITTER @McCurdyBowling

||||||||||||||||||||||||||||||||||||||||||||||

FREDDY'S IS A bit hard to find, part of a bowling alley on the edge of a suburban mall and, to be honest, its beer isn't that exciting. But if you can arrange a tour with brewer Jack Clark, it's definitely worth a visit. Clark is very entertaining and knowledgeable, bringing thirty years of anecdotes from his time working for Labatt in various capacities. He says he had no interest in microbrewing while he worked at Labatt, but since he took this part-time job to keep busy in his retirement, he has learned a lot—and developed a taste for darker, hoppier beers.

Unfortunately, you won't find many of those on tap here since the owners believe their customers aren't interested. Then again, Clark told me that the one time he brewed a hoppy IPA (at about 65 IBUS), "I was surprised how well it sold." Funny that. Good beer always sells.

Tap List

HONEY RIDGE ALE
5% ABV
Very light in body, this honey ale is tinged with coriander for a bit of a zesty kick.

LORD NELSON PALE ALE
5% ABV
The most hopped beer on tap, but still less than 20 IBUS—an easy-drinking pale ale.

....
Facts & Figures

OPENED ▸ 2001 ✪ STYLES PRODUCED ▸ 5 + seasonals ✪ WHERE TO BUY ▸ In growlers at the brewpub ✪ ON TAP ▸ The brewpub ✪ GROWLERS ▸ Yes

martenbrewpub.com
250-718-0996
2933 Thirtieth Avenue, Vernon
TWITTER @MartenBrewpub

Marten Brewpub

Tap List

No beers were quite ready for me to taste as this book went to press. The brewpub plans to have four regular, ongoing beers on tap at all times, along with four seasonal beers, casks and perhaps even some guest taps from time to time.

||||||||||||||||||||||||||||||||||||||||||||||||

VERNON FINALLY HAS a new craft brewery, the Marten Brewpub, located right downtown at Thirtieth and Thirtieth, thanks to local entrepreneurs Pearl and Stefan Marten. The couple brought in Stefan Buhl, ex-brewmaster of Kelowna's Tree Brewing, to install the equipment and get them started.

I visited before the brewpub was open, but the Martens had already opened the Naked Pig BBQ Smokehouse restaurant next door, and based on my experience there, I'm sure the brewpub will be a great spot. The building is large, with room for two hundred people on two levels, plus a separate convention room with space for another hundred. The basement has room for conditioning tanks and a cellar for cask conditioning.

The Martens plan on brewing a basic set of lagers and ales with more challenging seasonal styles to introduce craft beer to Vernonites, but through the Naked Pig they have already seen that there is a local appetite for IPAS and more daring styles. Welcome (back) to the craft beer revolution, Vernon!

Facts & Figures

OPENED ‣ *2015* ✪ **STYLES PRODUCED** ‣ *4 + seasonals* ✪
WHERE TO BUY ‣ *At the brewery* ✪ **ON TAP** ‣ *At the brewpub* ✪
GROWLERS ‣ *Yes*

The Noble Pig Brewhouse

thenoblepig.ca
778-471-5999
650 Victoria Street, Kamloops
E-MAIL
  meaghan@thenoblepig.ca
TWITTER @thenoblepigbrew

||||||||||||||||||||||||||||||||||||||||||

WHEN I VISITED Kamloops on my original Craft Beer Odyssey research trip in 2012, I had low expectations. After all, there had never been much of a craft beer scene there. So I didn't expect the Noble Pig to be very good. I figured I'd pop in, sample the beers and then return to my hotel and crash early.

Well, I couldn't have been more wrong. Based on how busy the pub was on a Sunday evening and the manager's anecdotes about beer geeks lining up with growlers outside the door when special beers went on tap, Kamloops had clearly become a craft beer hot spot while nobody outside the city had noticed. Most of the beer I tasted was excellent, as was the meal I enjoyed sitting outside on the sun-dappled patio under a spreading canopy of hops—which they would eventually pick to use in a special batch of beer.

I spent the evening chatting with founding brewer David Beardsell, who has since left to open Red Collar Brewing a few blocks away, and found myself really looking forward to my next visit to Kamloops. That turned out to be during the following summer as part of my promotional tour launching the first edition of this book, and I wasn't disappointed—the Pig put on a great event for me.

Tap List

BELGIUM PEPPERED ALE
5.5% ABV

A Belgian Saison or farmhouse ale using yeast from a Trappist brewery and added Sechuan peppers.

EMPRESS OF INDIA IMPERIAL RYE IPA (seasonal)
8.5% ABV | 100 IBU

Wow! Make the trip to Kamloops when this is on tap. It's incredible. With 20% rye in the mash.

KILT LIFTER SCOTCH ALE (seasonal)
11% ABV | 18 IBU

A strong Scottish ale released on Robbie Burns Day each year that is amplified with the addition of Highland Park scotch and cellar-conditioned for five months. Simply incredible.

TWIGS & BERRIES (seasonal)
4.8% ABV | 9 IBU

A Belgian fruit beer using blueberries, blackberries and raspberries, fermented with a Chimay yeast that dates back to 1989.

When I returned late in 2014 for Red Collar's opening, the new head brewer, Chris Stewart, who had been Beardsell's assistant, was maintaining his ex-boss's high standards, and the food and general vibe were just as good as always. I'm sure as time passes, Stewart will start branching out and exploring his own favourite styles more, too—and in a two-horse town (two breweries, that is) it will be interesting to compare his to Beardsell's over at Red Collar.

On-site demand is so high that there is not enough capacity to brew more beer to be packaged and sold elsewhere—that means you have to go directly to the source. And with the addition of Red Collar a short walk away, now there is even more incentive to plan a trip to Kamloops to taste these noble brews yourself.

Facts & Figures

OPENED › *2010* ✪ **STYLES PRODUCED ›** *6 + numerous seasonals* ✪ **WHERE TO BUY ›** *The brewpub* ✪ **ON TAP ›** *The brewpub* ✪ **GROWLERS ›** *Yes*

redcollar.ca
778-471-0174
355 Lansdowne Street, Kamloops
E-MAIL info@redcollar.ca
TWITTER @redcollarbrew

Red Collar Brewing ←

||||||||||||||||||||||||||||||||||||||||||||||

KAMLOOPS HAS DEVELOPED into one of B.C.'s craft beer hot spots almost singlehandedly because of one person. David Beardsell trained in Germany and the UK in the 1980s and then worked at Okanagan Spring Brewery in the early '90s before opening and running Bear Brewing in Kamloops for several years. He thought he'd retired from brewing when he sold Bear to Big Rock, and he took his family on the road in an old bus for two-and-a-half years.

But then the old itch returned and he joined some business partners in opening the Noble Pig in 2010. Then, he stepped away to help a friend open the Heid-Out BrewHouse in Cranbrook in 2013, and consulted with Bad Tattoo Brewing in Penticton. Finally, he and his wife, Anna-Marie, decided they should open their own brewery in Kamloops. The name Red Collar refers to their family dog, Goosie.

Red Collar is located in a big building that was originally a Chinese restaurant and then went through a series of reincarnations as bars or nightclubs that, according to the Beardsells, "just got seedier and seedier." So when they proposed turning it into a craft brewery, city council loved the idea because Kamloops really wants to revitalize the

Tap List

MÄRZEN
5.1% ABV | 32 IBU
This rich and flavourful lager reminded me of beer I enjoyed at Oktoberfest in Munich.

DUBBEL
6.3% ABV | 22 IBU
Brewed with Turbinado sugar, floor-malted Thomas Fawcett barley and two yeasts: Westmalle-Westvleteren's along with a unique mystery yeast Beardsell brought back from Belgium twenty-five years ago and has kept in a deep freeze ever since.

MILD
3.7% ABV | 32 IBU
This beer is proof that low-alcohol beers can still be flavourful. It's rich and creamy with an unexpected Amarillo hop aroma. Delicious.

TRIPEL (seasonal)
9% ABV
Beautiful with a big tropical fruitiness and creamy mouth feel.

downtown area and make it more attractive to tourists. The renovation was challenging, but the results show it was worth the hard work. The public tasting side is easily the largest brewery lounge I have encountered in B.C., with eighty seats inside and a patio outside that can seat another sixty in the summer. The on-site kitchen, managed by a local chef with aspirations to open his own taphouse, offers artisanal breads, sausages made in house, and grilled potato pancakes called Rösti. A smoker is also in the works, so rib nights will be another draw.

On the beer side, Beardsell began by exploring the European recipe book with a Märzen, British mild, Belgian Dubbel and English-style IPA to start. Each was excellent—the Märzen especially stood out to me—and the Belgian Tripel he poured directly from the fermentation tank was excellent. A few weeks later, I saw on social media that the Tripel had been released for Goosie's twelfth birthday, which was celebrated at the brewery in fine style.

Other brews since then have included an IPL (India Pale Lager), a couple different Bocks, and a winter ale featuring all Canadian ingredients. Early on, the beers were just available at the brewery—the tasting lounge has ten taps—but Red Collar plans on packaging in 650 mL bombers with some specialty beers going into 500 mL or 750 mL sizes depending on their styles. All the beers will be naturally carbonated, either in the fermentation tanks or through bottle conditioning.

Knowing David Beardsell, I'm sure Red Collar will brew a range of beers, most of which will only be available at the brewery. In other words, it's time to start planning a trip to the source. If you already live in Kamloops, consider yourself lucky to have one of B.C.'s best breweries right in your own backyard.

Facts & Figures

OPENED ▸ *2014* ✪ STYLES PRODUCED ▸ *4 + seasonals* ✪
WHERE TO BUY ▸ *The brewery and select private liquor stores* ✪
ON TAP ▸ *In Kamloops* ✪ GROWLERS ▸ *Yes*

Tin Whistle Brewing

250-770-1122
112-1475 Fairview Road, Penticton
TWITTER @TinWhistleBrew

|||||||||||||||||||||||||||||||||||||||||||||||

THE FIRST BREWERY to open in the Okanagan in 1995, Tin Whistle chugged along in its cramped space for a long time, constantly working to capacity, riding the wave of B.C.'s craft beer revolution while other Okanagan breweries opened and expanded around it.

But when Cannery Brewing moved into its new brewery in 2015, Tin Whistle took the opportunity to move into its old space at the old Cannery Trade Centre. While that space was too small for Cannery Brewing, it represented a big step up for Tin Whistle.

I think brewer Jeff Tod is one of the most underrated in BC. He is not given much leeway in creating new brews, but whenever he gets the chance, he knocks it out of the park. His Stag Apple Scotch Ale, which he first brewed on Robbie Burns Day in 2013, "wearing [his] kilt and blasting the Real McKenzies at volume 11," won Best in Show at the 2013 Okanagan Fest-of-Ale, a bronze at the Canadian Brewing Awards, and a gold at the B.C. Beer Awards.

I'm excited to see what the new space and expanded capacity will mean for Tin Whistle.

Tap List

HARVEST HONEY PALE ALE (fall seasonal)

5% ABV

A fresh-hopped pale ale brewed with organic hops from Harvesters of Organic Hops in Lillooet.

SCORPION DOUBLE IPA

8% ABV | 75 IBU

A big, malty IPA with a dash of citrusy West Coast hops.

Facts & Figures

OPENED ▸ *1995*

STYLES PRODUCED ▸ *4 + seasonals*

WHERE TO BUY ▸ *The brewery and at liquor stores throughout B.C.*

ON TAP ▸ *Restaurants and bars in Penticton*

GROWLERS ▸ *Yes*

Brewery
treebeer.com
250-717-1091
1083 Richter Street, Kelowna
E-MAIL info@treebeer.com
TWITTER @TreeBrewing

Beer Institute
treebrewingbeerinstitute.com
778-484-0306
1346 Water Street, Kelowna

Tree Brewing & Tree Beer Institute

|||||||||||||||||||||||||||||||||||||||||||||

Tap List

THIRSTY BEAVER AMBER ALE

5% ABV | 20 IBU
Available in both six-packs
and a budget-price single
tall can, this is a medium-
bodied amber ale.

HOP HEAD IPA
5.6% ABV | 65 IBU
One of the earliest IPAs in
B.C. to feature West Coast
hops prominently, Hop
Head is still solid although
it has been surpassed by
other hoppier IPAS.

JUMPIN JACK INDIA PUMPKIN ALE
6.5% ABV | 65 IBU
Tree's pumpkin beer has
always been one of the
better ones produced
in B.C. Turning it into a
Pumpkin IPA was genius.

CAPTIVATOR DOPPELBOCK
8% ABV | 45 IBU
This rich, malty
Doppelbock is a style not
commonly brewed in B.C.—
and rarely this well.

I FIRST VISITED Tree Brewing in the mid-1990s when my high school buddy, Ken Belau, became the first brewer there after graduating from a brewing university in Germany. I loved touring the facility and tasting fresh beer right at the source. In retrospect, I see now that it was one of the early experiences that pushed me down the road to writing this guidebook. Having such a personal connection to the beer meant a lot to me and got me more excited about searching out other beers and learning about the people and places behind them.

The brewery went through a few ownership changes in its early years and Ken moved on to other jobs in other places. I only managed one trip out to Kelowna while he was working there, but I've always kept an eye on the place. When it stabilized in the past decade I was happy to report the news to Ken. That success and stability had a lot to with the skills of brewmaster Stefan Buhl, who applied his distinctly German work ethic to the place. Buhl left Tree in 2013 to help set up the new Marten Brewpub in nearby Vernon, and was replaced by his longtime assistant Dave Gokiert, who has been with Tree as long as it has been around, including working with Ken right at the start.

Tree opened its Beer Institute in 2014. This is a separate showcase brewery located right in the heart of Kelowna's cultural district near Lake Okanagan. It has a tasting lounge downstairs and an educational space upstairs, as well as a constantly changing list of beers on the taps, with everything available for growler fills. There is also a great outdoor patio space upstairs with a trellis across the top, which should fill up with hop bines in the summer months.

Gokiert plans to brew each of the main Tree brands there once to test out the smaller 10 hL system, and then experiment with new styles that will only go on tap there. It will serve as research and development for him: he can try out new malts and hops, as well as ideas from the marketing team. And he will rotate his brewers through there "as a reward of sorts."

It sounds like a reward for the city's craft beer enthusiasts, who will be the beneficiaries of a wide range of new and interesting beers from Tree. I think it's great—while Tree's beers have always been solid, the brewery has not produced many cutting-edge styles, forcing locals to look to Vancouver or Victoria or beyond B.C. to satisfy their curiosity.

Facts & Figures

OPENED ▸ *1996* ✪ **STYLES PRODUCED** ▸ *5 + 5 seasonals* ✪
WHERE TO BUY ▸ *The brewery and liquor stores throughout B.C.* ✪
ON TAP ▸ *Throughout the Okanagan* ✪ **GROWLERS** ▸ *Yes (some beers only available in Tree-branded Braulers)*

BEST BEERS
Thompson-Okanagan

. . . .

Cannery Brewing Naramata Nut Brown Ale
Cannery's original beer and still one of the best in the region: a
creamy, malty brown ale.

Firehall Brewery Holy Smoke Stout
A blend of Rauchbier (smoked beer) and stout: this is a unique
and special beer.

Noble Pig Brewhouse Empress of India Imperial Rye IPA
A potent brew with a depth of malt and hop flavours that
has me planning annual trips to Kamloops around its brew
schedule.

Red Collar Brewing Märzen
One sip and you will be transported to a giant *Festhall* in
Munich. *Lederhosen und Dirndl* not included.

Tree Brewing Hop Head Black India Pale Ale
Call it a Cascadian Dark Ale or a Black IPA: either way, this is
a rich, dark beer with a great roasted malt character and a big
bite of hops.

THE
KOOTENAYS &
THE NORTH

AT THE BREWERY	DRAFT	FOOD	GROWLERS	BOTTLES	TOURS	BEDS
Arrowhead Brewing	✪		✪	✪		
Barkerville Brewing			✪	✪	✪	
Fernie Brewing			✪	✪		
Heid-Out Brewhouse	✪	✪	✪			
Mozart Inn & Brewpub	✪	✪	✪			✪
Mt. Begbie Brewing				✪		
Nelson Brewing						
Rossland Beer Co.			✪	✪		
Sherwood Mountain Brewhouse			✪	✪		
Three Ranges Brewing	✪	✪	✪	✪		
Torchlight Brewing	✪		✪	✪		
Wheelhouse Brewing	✪	✪	✪	✪		

MOUNTAINS
OF BEER

•••••••••••••••••••••••

ALTHOUGH I HAVE driven across B.C. many times over the past
two decades I never really took much time to explore the Kootenays region since I was usually in a rush to get somewhere
else. When I finally made it there on my Craft Beer Odyssey
I wished I had slowed down to explore the area long ago.
I loved the incredible natural scenery, of course, but more than
that I enjoyed getting to know some of the communities and
the people involved in the beer industry there. The common
refrain I heard from the craft breweries I visited in Revelstoke,
Fernie and Nelson was that before they opened there was virtually no interesting beer in the marketplace there. Everyone was
drinking Bud or Kokanee. And even when these small breweries took the risk and launched themselves, it was a long, uphill
struggle to get noticed and gain acceptance.

But the shared conclusions to their stories is that their hard
work paid off and now trailblazers like Mt. Begbie Brewing,
Fernie Brewing and Nelson Brewing are all successful enter-
prises that have earned respect and support, not only in their
own towns, but also in the surrounding area, and even across
the provincial border in Alberta. This sort of happy ending
must be inspiring to more recent start-ups like Arrowhead
Brewing, Rossland Beer Company, Three Ranges Brewing,
Torchlight Brewing, and Wheelhouse Brewing, all of which
hope to emulate their neighbours' business models.

In the first edition of this book, I had to delete "The North"
from the title of this section because the only northern craft

brewery, Plan B Brewing in Smithers, closed early in 2013. Happily, four new breweries have arrived in Prince Rupert, Quesnel, Terrace and Valemount to pick up the craft brewing torch in northern B.C., and I have heard rumours of more craft breweries in the works for Prince George and Golden. From what I've heard from these new brewers, they have had no trouble selling beer in their local communities. The biggest hurdle they face seems to be the high costs of shipping involved in both getting their raw materials and sending their packaged beer to the urban south to be sold in liquor stores or consumed in taphouses. There is definitely demand, but sometimes the economics just don't make sense.

There is a grand loop I hope to travel one day to visit B.C.'s more remote breweries. First, drive north from Victoria to Port Hardy near the top of Vancouver Island. There, board the ferry to Prince Rupert, which departs at 7:30 AM and arrives at 11:30 PM that night after stopping in Bella Coola or Klemtu and passing through the spectacular Inside Passage. After visiting Wheelhouse Brewing there, drive to Quesnel, perhaps stopping in Terrace and Prince George to see new breweries there. Check out Barkerville Brewing and the nearby Barkerville historic town before continuing on to Valemount, where one's thirst can be quenched in the tasting room at Three Ranges Brewing. From Valemount back to the coast via the Kootenays, where several breweries might be visited, it's another 1,600 kilometres, making for a grand total of 3,857 kilometres. Now that's a B.C. craft beer odyssey!

arrowheadbrewingcompany.ca
778-526-2739
481 Arrow Road, Invermere
E-MAIL info@arrowheadbrewing
company.com
TWITTER @ArrowheadBrew

Arrowhead Brewing

||||||||||||||||||||||||||||||||||||||||||||||

Tap List

**BLONDE
BOMBSHELL ALE**

5% ABV

Light and refreshing but
with far more depth and
flavour than you might
expect.

**DOC TEGART'S EXTRA
SPECIAL BITTER**

6.5% ABV

A delicious ESB with a
Northwest twist courtesy
of Galena and Mosaic
hops. Won Best Beer at the
2014 East Kootenay Beer
Festival.

**I'M SO FREAKIN'
HOPPY IPA**

7.3% ABV | 75 IBU

A big, brash IPA in the
tradition of the Oregon
breweries Tegart loved
while living there.

SHAWN AND LEANNE Tegart opened Invermere's one and only craft brewery in the fall of 2012. Shawn said that after he returned to B.C. following a stint living in Oregon, he found himself missing the quality and range of craft beer he'd enjoyed there. He home brewed for a time before making the leap to this full-scale operation.

Since then, Arrowhead has grown considerably. Its location across the street from Kicking Horse Coffee on the road into Invermere draws lots of visitors to its storefront tasting lounge and growler station. Since the brewery added a basic bottling and canning system in the spring of 2014, there are six-packs and 650 mL bombers available.

Beyond its local community, Arrowhead's main market is Alberta, but new fermentation tanks that will effectively double its capacity will allow the brewery to expand to the Okanagan, the Lower Mainland and Vancouver Island eventually. But that might take a while, so I suggest you plan a trip to Invermere. It's a beautiful spot and the beer is great.

....

Facts & Figures

OPENED ▸ 2012 ✪ **STYLES PRODUCED** ▸ *5 + limited releases* ✪
WHERE TO BUY ▸ *The brewery* ✪ **ON TAP** ▸ *Throughout the
Invermere area* ✪ **GROWLERS** ▸ *Yes*

EAST KOOTENAY
BEER FESTIVAL
Held on a Weekend in Mid-June Each Year

•••••••••••••••••••••••

A WELCOME ADDITION to the beer festival scene in B.C. in 2012, this event has contributed to the growth of interest in craft beer in the East Kootenays. While it includes a few brands that might not be considered "craft beer," the festival also showcases regional craft breweries like Mt. Begbie, Fernie and Nelson, as well the local favourite, Arrowhead Brewing.

The Fairmont Hot Springs Resort, which hosts this event, is a comfortable year-round destination with rejuvenating, odourless hot spring pools, restaurants, golf courses and many other outdoor activities.

---

www.fairmonthotsprings.com/beer

barkervillebeer.com
778-414-2739
185 Davie Street, Quesnel
E-MAIL
  sales@barkervillebeer.com
TWITTER @BarkervilleBeer

Barkerville Brewing

Tap List

|||||||||||||||||||||||||||||||||||||||||||||||||

18 KARAT ALE

5% ABV | 33 IBU

Barkerville's first release won a silver medal at the Canadian Brewing Awards in the North American Amber category. It's quite hoppy but lighter-bodied than an IPA.

52 FOOT STOUT

7% ABV | 52 IBU

A dark and roasty stout with the interesting addition of birch syrup, which is locally produced at Moose Meadow Farms in Quesnel.

WANDERING CAMEL IPA

6.5% ABV | 48 IBU

Not the hoppiest of IPAs, but there's plenty of flavour to go around. And did you know that camels were brought to Barkerville during the 1860s Gold Rush?

....

Facts & Figures

OPENED ‣ *2014*

STYLES PRODUCED ‣
  4 + seasonals

WHERE TO BUY ‣ *The brewery or liquor stores*

ON TAP ‣ *Quesnel, Vancouver and Victoria*

GROWLERS ‣ *Yes*

RUSS OVANS, a Victoria-based computer scientist who made a zillion dollars (OK, not quite a zillion) by selling a software company he had founded in Victoria, was enjoying his "retirement" in Scotland by attempting to visit 365 pubs in 365 days (as documented on his blog: www.365pubs.com) when he decided to open his own brewery. With family connections in Quesnel he thought the region was ready for its own craft brewery and decided to connect the name with Barkerville, the historical town located eighty kilometres away.

As his brewer, Ovans hired Troy Randolph, a longtime home brewer who had been working on the packaging side of things at Naramata's Township 7 winery. In the first year, Randolph already began experimenting with local ingredients, such as birch syrup, which he adds to the brew for Barkerville's 52 Foot Stout.

Barkerville's beers are available throughout B.C. in government liquor stores, making it a whole lot easier to sample them without having to drive all the way to Quesnel, although I can't wait to visit the brewery in person one day.

Fernie Brewing

ferniebrewing.com
250-423-7797
26 Manitou Road, Fernie
E-MAIL abi@ferniebrewing.com
TWITTER @FernieBrewingCo

||||||||||||||||||||||||||||||||||||||||||||||

WHEN FERNIE BREWING first opened in 2003, it was one of those rarest of breweries that was actually busier in the winter than in the summer. That's because during ski season there were generally more people (about nine thousand) on the slopes of the three ski hills situated around the town of Fernie than actually live there year-round (about five thousand). That meant the bars and restaurants on the slopes and the après-ski spots in town were packed whenever there was fresh powder. And since many of those skiers were coming from elsewhere, especially places like Europe, they were often more interested in craft beer styles than boring mass-market North American lagers.

That gave Fernie Brewing a good start in the business, but over the decade since then, the traditional brewer's model of just trying to keep up with the insatiable demand during the summer has definitely taken over, especially following the brewery's move from its original facility in a farm shed to its current setup just off Highway 3 in 2007.

While the small town of Fernie itself could not sustainably support a mid-sized craft brewery, the company has done a great job of finding other markets for its products. Being so close to the Alberta border, the

Tap List

KICKSTAND HONEY KOLSCH (summer seasonal)
4.8% ABV | 25 IBU
Light but flavourful in the best Kölsch tradition. Made with organic honey.

OL' WILLY WIT
5% ABV | 9 IBU
A seasonal beer that is now produced year-round due to popularity, this Belgian Wit is brewed with coriander and curacao orange peel.

WHAT THE HUCK HUCKLEBERRY WHEAT ALE
5% ABV | 15 IBU
A B.C. original: the huckleberry is native to the Rocky Mountain region. It works well in this purple-tinged wheat beer.

BLACK MAMMOTH WINTER ALE (winter seasonal)
8% ABV | 25 IBU
A decadent, strong winter ale, brewed with chocolate malt, dark organic cocoa, and curacao.

brewery enjoys a lot of popularity in the Calgary area, and its excellent, diverse range of beers is also available throughout B.C. in government liquor stores. It is one of a handful of B.C. breweries that offer a mixed sampler pack—both a summer and winter seasonal version. It's a great concept that responds to the craft beer consumer's innate desire for variety.

Fernie has also responded to the howls of consumer demand by adding the Lone Wolf IPA to its lineup, along with a series of seasonal beers in 650 mL-bomber bottles that definitely are directed at the craft beer drinker's palate: Ol' Willy Wit, Pumpkin Head Brown Ale, What the Huck Huckleberry Wheat Ale, and Sap Sucker Maple Porter.

Particularly exciting to me is Fernie's IPA Bucket List: over the course of a year, the brewery releases a different, special IPA each season: Rockpile Red IPA, Snowblind Belgian IPA, Quiet Rye'T Rye IPA, and Last Cast Summer IPA. Talk about hophead heaven! I honestly can't decide which one I like best; each has a certain quality that sets it apart from the others.

Fernie is a very welcoming community—a lovely place to visit. And when you do, be sure to ask a local about the legend of the Ghostrider. It's a great, spooky story to enjoy over a pint of beer.

Facts & Figures

OPENED ▸ *2003* ✪ **STYLES PRODUCED** ▸ *7 + numerous seasonals* ✪ **WHERE TO BUY** ▸ *Liquor stores throughout B.C.* ✪ **ON TAP** ▸ *Throughout B.C.* ✪ **GROWLERS** ▸ *Yes*

Fisher Peak Brewing at the Heid-Out BrewHouse

theheidout.ca
250-426-7922
821 Baker Street, Cranbrook
E-MAIL
theheidoutcranbrook@gmail.com

|||||||||||||||||||||||||||||||||||||||||||||||||

I REMEMBER THINKING that Cranbrook needed a craft brewery when I drove through on my Craft Beer Odyssey research trip back in 2012, so I was thrilled when I got to stop for lunch and a beer at the Heid-Out BrewHouse on my promotional book tour the following summer.

The unusual name reflects the history of the place—it was a popular local restaurant called Heidi's until owner Heidi Romich decided to turn it into a brewpub. Officially called Fisher Peak Brewing, the on-site brewery was put together by David Beardsell of the Noble Pig Brewhouse and Red Collar Brewing fame. He stuck around to train the staff before returning to Kamloops to open Red Collar.

The brewpub is now managed by Heidi's daughter Marlies, who brews the beer along with another business partner, Jordan Aasland. The food is upscale pub fare, and the beer is more than adequate, though definitely more safely described as approachable rather than cutting-edge. Certainly, it's a great lunch stop if you're making the long haul from Osoyoos to Fernie.

Tap List

HEFEWEIZEN
5.2% ABV | 21 IBU
A well-made German Weissbier. But really—there's no need for the orange slice any more.

ELEPHANT RUN IPA
6.3% ABV | 55 IBU
I agree with my friend Mike Garson's assessment: "Pretty good English IPA. Wish there were more hops."

Facts & Figures

OPENED ▸ 2013 ✪
STYLES PRODUCED ▸ 6 + seasonals ✪
ON TAP ▸ The brewpub ✪
GROWLERS ▸ Yes

mozartinnandbrewpub.com
250-427-7671
130 Spokane Street
Kimberley
E-MAIL oraniew@telus.net

Mozart Inn and Brewpub

Tap List

Unfortunately I have not had the chance to taste the Mozart brewpub's beers. If any readers stop there some time, drop me a line and let me know how they are.

||||||||||||||||||||||||||||||||||||||||||

FOLLOWING THE EAST Kootenay Beer Festival in June 2013, as I was on my way to Nelson, I distinctly remember seeing the sign for Kimberley and thinking about taking the turnoff so I could visit the town. But I was on a tight schedule and since there wasn't a brewery there, I couldn't really take the time.

It turns out there was a brewery there, but I just didn't know about it yet: Kimberley's Mozart Inn pub added its own brewing facilities in September 2012.

Owner and brewer John Oraniewicz came to Canada from Poland in 1982, first living in Winnipeg before moving to Kimberley to open this European-style inn and pub there. He brews a small range of basic styles—lager, Pilsner, ale and stout—with a few seasonal varieties mixed in, but nothing too trendy or unusual. The Pils is the most popular, he says, but like a parent asked to select a favourite child, he says, "I have to like them all."

I will definitely take the turnoff for Kimberley the next time I am in the area.

Facts & Figures

OPENED ➤ *2012* ✪ STYLES PRODUCED ➤ *4 + seasonals* ✪
ON TAP ➤ *The brewpub* ✪ WHERE TO BUY ➤ *The brewpub* ✪
GROWLERS ➤ *Yes*

Mt. Begbie Brewing ←

mt-begbie.com
250-837-2756
521 First Street West, Revelstoke
E-MAIL tlarson@mtbegbie.com
TWITTER @Begbiebeer

|||||||||||||||||||||||||||||||||||||||||||||

HOW MANY BREWERIES do you know that are run by a nuclear physicist?

There is probably only one: Mt. Begbie Brewing, where the founding brewer, Bart Larson, has a PhD in nuclear physics. His wife and business partner, Tracey, is no academic slouch either, with a background in zoology and biology. So how did they end up running a brewery in Revelstoke? Love, of course: for each other and for beer. Tracey says it was a honeymoon conversation: "Hey, maybe we should start a brewery." And even though neither of them had any experience brewing beer, they knew people involved with the original Shaftebury brewery in Vancouver, and the dream grew and grew until they found themselves setting up shop in Bart's hometown of Revelstoke.

Tracey remembers arriving there on New Year's Eve after there had been a huge dump of snow and wondering, "What have I gotten myself into?" But then she felt so welcomed by neighbours who invited them over for a New Year's Eve hot tub party that she knew it was the right decision.

Initially, Bart and Tracey were the brewery's sole employees. Bart focused on the brewing while Tracey handled administration and marketing, as well as all the

Tap List

HIGH COUNTRY KÖLSCH
4.5% ABV
An excellent Kölsch: a light, mildly hopped wheat ale.

BOB'S YOUR DUNKEL
8% ABV
A rich Dunkelweizen: sweet and malty with roasted barley and chocolate flavours.

NASTY HABIT IPA
6% ABV
A very popular English IPA with a good bitterness and solid malt backbone.

ATILLA THE HONEY (seasonal)
5% ABV
An amber ale with the distinctive taste of clover honey.

deliveries, including innumerable drives across Rogers Pass during the brutal winters the region is famous for. At first, they thought they could just focus on selling their beer in Revelstoke, but they quickly realized they had to expand beyond the small city's borders to sustain the business.

And expand is exactly what they have done. Mt. Begbie Brewing now has three brewers on staff; Bart mainly oversees things, but he keeps busy fixing and automating the brewing systems himself. Tracey runs the administrative side, and says she doesn't miss delivering the beer, although she "probably could still drive the forklift."

Mt. Begbie Brewing has worked hard to build a customer base in the Revelstoke area. When they started, everyone seemed to drink Bud and Kokanee, and Tracey says it took a while; but suddenly, in the last few years, it's become easier. She thinks it might have to do with the new ski hill that opened there a few years ago, since it attracts out-of-town visitors and seasonal employees who might already be used to more complex and challenging styles. It says something that the Nasty Habit IPA is now their biggest seller in bottles, when, according to Tracey, "six years ago that wouldn't have been possible." It was wonderful to see local restaurants proudly pouring their beers, especially an unusual and complex seasonal such as Hillaswilla Wit, which was on tap all over town.

Facts & Figures

OPENED › *1996* ○ **STYLES PRODUCED ›** *5 + 2 seasonals* ○
WHERE TO BUY › *Liquor stores throughout B.C.* ○ **ON TAP ›** *Throughout the Revelstoke area and select places in the Okanagan and Greater Vancouver* ○ **GROWLERS ›** *No*

nelsonbrewing.com
250-352-3582
512 Latimer Street, Nelson
E-MAIL nbc@netidea.com

Nelson Brewing ←

||||||||||||||||||||||||||||||||||||||||||||||||

AFTER I MOVED to B.C. from Ontario in 1991, Nelson soon reached the top of my list of places I wanted to visit here. Everything I heard about this West Kootenay community made it sound better and better: fine heritage architecture (with some buildings designed by Francis Rattenbury, the same architect who was responsible for the provincial legislature and the Empress Hotel in Victoria); many artists and craftspeople; a strong focus on local and organic food production; the hippie, draft dodger culture that helped drive its revitalization in the 1970s and '80s; and the beer, of course. I finally made it to Nelson as part of my Craft Beer Odyssey road trip and I can't believe I waited twenty-one years to do so. Maybe it was my ponytail-length hair, but everywhere I went I felt so comfortable and welcome.

But what about the beer? Nelson has a brewing history that goes back to 1897 and includes a spell as home to one of the Columbia Brewing chain of breweries. That all ended by the 1960s, but then the contemporary incarnation of Nelson Brewing opened in 1991 in the same building that housed the original Columbia brewery. The company has evolved considerably over its two decades plus, but the biggest transition

Tap List

HOOLIGAN ORGANIC PILSNER
5% ABV

A light but flavourful Pilsner, beautifully made in the best Central European tradition.

NELSON AFTER DARK
5% ABV

A British-style dark mild ale, this is delicious and surprisingly quaffable despite its dark colour. "Everyone looks better after dark."

PADDYWHACK IPA
6.5% ABV

One of the great original B.C. IPAs, Paddywhack is still one of the tastiest and most well balanced around.

FACEPLANT WINTER ALE (seasonal)
6.5% ABV

This might be my favourite B.C. winter seasonal beer. No mulling spices or vanilla, but some great body and flavour from added molasses and brown sugar.

occurred in 2006 when it decided to go all-organic, reflecting the healthy, organic lifestyle embraced by many Nelsonites.

The organic focus severely limits the choice of ingredients available to the brewery. Hops, especially, can be hard to get since certain varieties of the trendy, newer West Coast styles are simply not available from organic farms. Happily, that situation is changing with the growth of organic hop production in the U.S. and Canada, as well as abroad. Perhaps surprisingly, no hops are produced locally in Nelson, although it might have something to do with another significant local crop taking priority (wink wink, nudge nudge).

In the last few years, Nelson has added some great new beers to its lineup. My favourite is Full Nelson Imperial IPA, which is made with organic Nelson Sauvin hops imported from Nelson, New Zealand, that have a prominent Sauvignon grape character. Because of those unique hops, it stands apart from the rest of the crop of imperial IPAs in B.C. The cask-conditioned version that brewer Mike Kelly prepared for my book launch there was impossibly drinkable for its higher ABV level.

Other newer brews include the HopGood Organic Session Ale, which took first place at the 2013 B.C. Beer Awards, and the Hooligan Organic Pilsner.

Facts & Figures

OPENED › *1991* ✪ **STYLES PRODUCED ›** *6 + seasonals and limited releases* ✪ **WHERE TO BUY ›** *Liquor stores throughout B.C.* ✪ **ON TAP ›** *Throughout the Kootenays and at select places in the Okanagan and Greater Vancouver.* ✪ **GROWLERS ›** *No*

THE LION'S HEAD

An Oasis of
Craft Beer in Bud Country

••••••••••••••••••••••

IN ROBSON, JUST across the Columbia River from Castlegar, about forty-five minutes west of Nelson, the Lion's Head Smoke and Brew Pub is an oasis of craft beer in the West Kootenay region. They do not brew their own beer, but instead offer twelve craft taps featuring a cross-section of great beer from all across the province. This is "Bud country," a lesson the owners, Troy Pyett and Carly Hadfield, learned the hard way when they opened in June 2009. Carly, daughter of Spinnakers' publican Paul Hadfield, says they sold out of their small stock of Budweiser bottles in the first hour without selling any of the craft beer they had on tap.

"It was touch and go at first," she admits. "People thought we were crazy." They even faced a boycott from the local community who wanted them to drop the craft beer entirely. But they stuck to their cheeky motto: "Converting Bud drinkers and vegetarians since 2009," and it has paid off. "People began coming out of the woodwork," Carly says. Now, the place is busy all the time. They have added outdoor patio sections, hold an Oktoberfest pig roast each fall, and have live music as well. The pub has an excellent menu, featuring a variety of meats that are smoked right on site. I can vouch for the incredible brisket sandwich.

Their dozen taps usually feature six Spinnakers brews along with rotating taps from local breweries such as Tree Brewing, Nelson Brewing, Fernie Brewing, Mt. Begbie Brewing, Crannóg Ales and Cannery Brewing. It was great to get a taste of home, in my case a Spinnakers Northwest Ale, which became one of my favourite beers after I moved back to Victoria in 2012.

Carly and Troy have been renovating and improving the pub, including a new bar they call "the oldest bar in the world" because it is faced with rock slabs featuring ancient fossils. One day they hope to add their own brewing facilities and turn it into a brewpub of its own, but that is still a long-term dream.

Carly says the sold-out cask festival they held three years to the day they took possession of the pub was her proudest moment. And on a daily basis, it's incredible to see the variety of beer people are drinking there: "Just to walk around and see six different colours of beer on one table."

---

www.lionsheadpub.ca
250-365-brew (2739)
2629 Broadwater Road
Robson
TWITTER @lionsheadpubbc

Rossland Beer Co. ←

rosslandbeer.com
250-362-2122
1990 Columbia Avenue, Rossland
E-MAIL drink@rosslandbeer.com
TWITTER @RosslandBeer

||||||||||||||||||||||||||||||||||||||||||||||

THE FOUNDERS OF Rossland Beer, Petri Raito and Ryan Arnaud, started working together as the owner-operators of a U-Brew called Trail Brewing. As they developed their recipes and interest grew among their customers, they realized it made sense to grow the business into an actual brewery. The result of that decision was Rossland Beer Company.

The brewery purchased Bridge Brewing's original nanobrewery system when that company expanded. It's on the small side, but perfect for a start-up operation like this. Although the tasting room has five taps, the brewery rarely has that many beers on at once, given the limitations of the brewhouse. The tasting room has proven to be popular with locals, though, who enjoy the "view" overlooking the brewing area downstairs.

Rossland Beer is available on tap in local establishments, and one beer, the Paydirt Pale Ale, is also getting bottled in 650 mL bombers. Otherwise, all the beer is available through growler fills at the brewery.

I think it's great news any time a small community like Rossland gets its own brewery. I love watching the craft beer revolution spread across B.C.

Tap List

PAYDIRT PALE ALE
5.2% ABV | 37 IBU
This is a solid pale ale with a distinct grapefruit aroma and flavour from the Citra and Cascade hops.

7 SUMMITS MILK STOUT
5.1% ABV
A very creamy milk stout with a nice balance between sweetness and bitter roasted barley character.

....

Facts & Figures

OPENED ▸ *2014*
STYLES PRODUCED ▸
4 + seasonals
WHERE TO BUY ▸
The brewery
ON TAP ▸ *Rossland*
GROWLERS ▸ *Yes*

sherwoodmountain.beer

250-635-0080

101-4816 Highway 16 West, Terrace

E-MAIL

   hello@sherwoodmountain.beer

TWITTER @SherwoodMtn

Sherwood Mountain Brewhouse

Tap List

SKEENA WEST PALE ALE

5.5% ABV | 40 IBU

This is the brewery's flagship beer, which pours golden with hints of caramel, toasted bread and a nice range of hops.

SILENT NIGHT WINTER ALE

8% ABV

The story goes that a Belgian tourist, who visits Terrace every year to go fishing, stopped by the brewery shortly after it opened and suggested the recipe for this beer.

||||||||||||||||||||||||||||||||||||||||||||||||

FOUNDED BY DARRYL Tucker, a former airline marketing director, and Linda Parker, the Sherwood Mountain Brewhouse features a six-hundred-square-foot tasting room and a fifteen-barrel (18 hL) brewery.

Tucker studied to become a certified brewmaster at a six-month program in Berlin where there were thirty-nine students from nineteen different countries. He hopes to invite some of the friends he made there to visit him in Terrace and brew batches of beer.

He also worked at Ontario's Lake of Bays Brewing to get some experience, and brought a German brewmaster to Terrace to set up the equipment and help brew the first few batches.

That brewmaster gave him some invaluable advice: "Make sure you drink beer people want to drink or you'll have a lot of beer to drink and no job." Indeed!

There is no Sherwood Mountain in Terrace (or anywhere in B.C. for that matter) so what is the name all about? Ask Tucker when you visit the brewery. It's a personal story—perfect to be told over a beer.

Facts & Figures

OPENED ▸ 2014 ✪ STYLES PRODUCED ▸ 2 + seasonals. ✪
WHERE TO BUY ▸ The brewery ✪ ON TAP ▸ Terrace ✪
GROWLERS ▸ Yes

threeranges.com
250-566-0024
1160 Fifth Avenue, Valemount
E-MAIL info@threeranges.com
TWITTER @threeranges

Three Ranges Brewing

||||||||||||||||||||||||||||||||||||||||||||

I HAVE TO admit I didn't even know where Valemount was when I first heard of this brewery—turns out it's near the B.C.-Alberta border on the Yellowhead Highway, about an hour and a half east of Jasper. And, second admission, I have never been to this brewery, but I have tasted its beers and talked to its founder, Michael Lewis.

A retired U.S. Army pilot, Lewis was living in Victoria with his Canadian wife when he began home brewing. They chose Valemount to open the brewery partially because his wife's parents live there, but also because of its natural beauty and strong sense of community.

As the only craft brewery in the region (Kamloops is four hours south), Three Ranges has quickly become the local favourite. Even though Valemount only has about a thousand residents, the brewery has had trouble keeping up with demand pretty much from day one. The tasting room and growler station are always busy.

I definitely think it's time for a road trip!

Tap List

UP SWIFT CREEK PILSNER
4.7% ABV

As a home brewer, Lewis's Pilsner was good enough to win Phillips Brewing's Showcase Showdown contest in 2011. As a professional brewer, this is even better.

SWAMP DONKEY BROWN ALE
4.8% ABV

This is a solid brown ale with a great malt character and some hoppiness.

....

Facts & Figures

OPENED ▸ *2013* ✪ STYLES PRODUCED ▸ *4 + seasonals* ✪
WHERE TO BUY ▸ *The brewery* ✪ ON TAP ▸ *Valemount* ✪
GROWLERS ▸ *Yes*

torchlightbrewing.com
250-352-0094
511 Front Street, Nelson
E-MAIL
  sales@torchlightbrewing.com
TWITTER @Brew_Torchlight

Torchlight Brewing

Tap List

LED SLED PORTER
4.3% ABV | 25 IBU
Named for a classic hot
rod, this English porter has
a big flavour despite its
relative low ABV.

WARP 8.5 CDA
8.5% ABV | 100 IBU
This Black IPA has one of
my favourite names for a
beer in BC. Big, bold and
hoppy... yes, I'm going
there: it boldly goes where
no beer has gone before!

ORIGINALLY NAMED BEACON Brewing, this
nanobrewery opened in June 2014, joining
longtime local favourite Nelson Brewing in
the beautiful East Kootenay city of the same
name. Before the end of the year, however,
the brewery was relaunched as Torchlight
Brewing to avoid some legal issues.

Founded by two home brewers, Torchlight
has a small 4 hL system that uses plastic fermenters that can be moved in and out of the
their small cooler as needed, giving the brewers greater flexibility in their small space.

Torchlight sells its beer through growler
fills at the brewery only. Brewer Craig Swens-
don has been exploring the wide range of ale
styles in the brewery's first year, including
a pale ale, blonde ale, IPA, porter and raspberry wheat ale to start.

Although it is just a small start-up operation, I'm happy to see another brewery join
the scene in Nelson. The food and culture
scene there is excellent so I'm sure locals are
excited about having another option to try.

Facts & Figures

OPENED ▸ *2014* ✪ STYLES PRODUCED ▸ *3 + seasonals* ✪
WHERE TO BUY ▸ *The brewery* ✪ ON TAP ▸ *Nelson.* ✪
GROWLERS ▸ *Yes*

wheelhousebrewing.com
250-624-2739
217 First Avenue East,
 Prince Rupert
TWITTER @wheelhousebeer

Wheelhouse Brewing ←

||||||||||||||||||||||||||||||||||||||||||

WE ARE A *little brewery at the end of the road on the left side of British Columbia.*

Kent Orton, Craig Outhet and James Witzke, the co-founders of Wheelhouse Brewing, definitely travelled the farthest to participate in the Great Canadian Beer Festival in 2014—Victoria is more than twenty hours from Prince Rupert.

The trio of ex–home brewers—a biologist, a planner and a traditional Chinese doctor—were each drawn to Prince Rupert for different reasons and brought together by their common passion for beer. They were also inspired by another northern B.C. beer pioneer, Smithers's Plan B Brewing, which opened in 2008 but closed right around the time Wheelhouse opened. Indeed, some of Plan B's equipment has been put into use at Wheelhouse.

Year one went very well for Wheelhouse. The brewery's tasting room has proven to be a popular spot for locals, and its beers have been popping up on tap in other northern communities as well. And to honour Mark Gillis of Plan B Brewing, Wheelhouse relaunched one of his beers, McHugh's Oatmeal Stout, late in 2014.

Tap List

**GILLNETTER
GOLDEN ALE**

4.8% ABV

Described as a Kölsch, this is a solid, if basic, light ale, ideal for folks who haven't discovered the wide world of craft beer yet.

**BLACKSMITH
BROWN ALE**

6.3% ABV

This strong brown ale has a great malty character.

....

Facts & Figures

OPENED › *2013*
STYLES PRODUCED ›
 3 + seasonals
WHERE TO BUY › *At the
 brewery.*
ON TAP › *In Prince
 Rupert and Terrace.*
GROWLERS › *Yes*

BEST BEERS
The Kootenays
& The North

•••••••••••••••••••••••••

Arrowhead Brewing Doc Tegart's Extra Special Bitter
This is a tasty ESB with a West Coast twist courtesy of Galena and Mosaic hops.

Fernie Brewing What the Huck Huckleberry Wheat Ale
A standout among B.C. berry beers, this huckleberry-infused wheat ale is a delicious year-round brew.

Nelson Brewing Full Nelson Imperial IPA
Brewed with Nelson Sauvin hops from New Zealand, so-named because they smell distinctly of Sauvignon grapes, this IPA has a unique aroma and flavour.

Rossland Beer Paydirt Pale Ale
This small brewery really surprised me with this very well-made pale ale with a distinct grapefruit aroma and flavour courtesy of Citra and Cascade hops.

Three Ranges Brewing Tail Slap IPA
Here's the perfect beer to keep you warm while after snowmobiling, heli-skiing or snowshoeing. Bold, malty and hoppy.

CAPS,
CORKS &
COASTERS

B.C.'S CRAFT BEER
HISTORY & FUTURE

....

1982
- The Horseshoe Bay Brewery starts brewing beer for the Troller Pub, kick-starting B.C.'s Craft Beer Revolution.

1984
- Spinnakers, Canada's first true brewpub, opens in Victoria.
- Canada's first microbrewery, Granville Island Brewing, opens in Vancouver.
- Island Pacific Brewing opens in Victoria. It changes its name to Vancouver Island Brewery in 1989.

1985
- CAMRA B.C. launches in Victoria, and Okanagan Spring Brewery opens in Vernon.

1987
- Shaftebury Brewing opens in Vancouver.

1989
- Swans Brewpub/Buckerfields Brewery opens in Victoria with some help from craft beer godfather Frank Appleton.
- Whistler Brewing opens.

1991
- Nelson Brewing opens. Fifteen years later, it goes all-organic.

1993

> Great Canadian Beer Festival begins in Victoria. Although it starts small, it is now B.C.'s biggest and most important annual beer festival.

1994

> Bowen Island Brewing opens.
> Sailor Hagar's begins brewing its own beer. Its brewmaster, Gary Lohin, would later open craft beer powerhouse Central City Brewing.
> Tall Ship Ale Company opens in Squamish.
> Yaletown Brewing, Vancouver's first brewpub, opens.

1995

> Bastion City Brewing opens in Nanaimo, but closes its doors two years later.
> Bear Brewing opens in Kamloops. Six years later it acquires the Whistler and Bowen Island brands, then sells to Big Rock Brewery in 2003.
> Okanagan Fest-of-Ale launches in Penticton.
> Russell Brewing opens in Surrey.
> Steamworks Brew Pub opens in Vancouver.
> Storm Brewing opens in Vancouver.
> Tin Whistle Brewing opens in Penticton.

1996

> Canoe Brewpub opens in Victoria.
> Hopscotch Festival launches in Vancouver.
> Howe Sound Brewing and Inn opens with the help of John Mitchell, one half of the original Horseshoe Bay Brewery team.
> Mission Springs Brewing opens in Mission.
> Mt. Begbie Brewing opens in Revelstoke.
> Tree Brewing opens in Kelowna with my buddy Ken Belau as its first brewmaster.

1997

- Big River Brewpub opens in Richmond.
- BrewHouse High Mountain Brewing opens in Whistler.
- Dockside Brewing and R&B Brewing open in Vancouver.
- Wild Horse Brewing opens in Penticton and Windermere Brewing opens in Invermere, but each brews for only two years before closing its doors. Kimberley Brewing opens, but closes a year later.

1998

- Autumn Brewmasters' Festival launches in Vancouver and runs annually until 2006.
- Backwoods Brewing opens in Aldergrove. Eight years later it changes its name to Dead Frog Brewery.
- The Barley Mill Brewpub opens in Penticton.
- Dix BBQ & Brewery opens in Vancouver and operates for twelve years before closing its doors.
- Gulf Islands Brewery opens on Salt Spring Island. In 2011, it rebrands as Salt Spring Island Ales.
- Lighthouse Brewing opens in Victoria.

1999

- Big Ridge Brewing opens in Surrey and Longwood Brewpub opens in Nanaimo.

2000

- Crannóg Ales, the first certified organic brewery in Canada, opens in Sorrento.
- Fat Cat Brewery opens in Nanaimo. Eleven years later, it changes ownership, becoming Wolf Brewing.
- Old Yale Brewing opens in Chilliwack.

2001

- Cannery Brewing opens in Penticton.
- Freddy's Brewpub opens in Kelowna.
- Phillips Brewing opens in Victoria.

2003

> Central City Brewing opens in Surrey and Fernie Brewing opens.

2004

> Avalon Brewing opens in North Vancouver, and later becomes Taylor's Crossing Restaurant & Brewery. Unfortunately, it closes in 2011.

2005

> The Mark James Group begins brewing Red Truck beer.

2006

> Barley Station Brew Pub opens in Salmon Arm.
> Canada Cup of Beer launches in Vancouver.
> Craig Street Brewpub opens in Duncan.

2008

> Plan B Brewing opens in Smithers, brewing for five years before closing in 2013.
> Driftwood Brewery opens in Victoria.
> Surgenor Brewing opens in Comox, but closes three year later.

2010

> Noble Pig Brewhouse opens in Kamloops.
> Turning Point Brewery (Stanley Park Brewery) opens in Delta.
> Vancouver Craft Beer Week is launched.

2011

> Barley's Angels—Pink Pints Chapter, B.C.'s first women's beer group, and B.C. Craft Beer Month are launched.
> Hoyne Brewing and Moon Under Water Brew Pub open in Victoria.
> Tofino Brewing opens in Tofino.

2012

> Arrowhead Brewing opens in Invermere.
> Bridge Brewing opens in North Vancouver.
> Coal Harbour Brewing, Parallel 49 Brewing and Powell Street Craft Brewery open within a few blocks of each other in East Vancouver.
> East Kootenay Beer Festival launches in Fairmont Hot Springs.
> Firehall Brewery opens in Oliver.
> Mozart Brewpub opens in Kimberley.
> Whistler Village Beer Festival launches in September.
> Townsite Brewing opens in Powell River.

2013

> 33 Acres Brewing and Brassneck Brewery open in Vancouver.
> Central City Brewers & Distillers opens its production brewery in Surrey.
> Deep Cove Brewers & Distillers and Green Leaf Brewing open in North Vancouver.
> Four Winds Brewing opens in Delta, becoming B.C.'s fiftieth craft brewery.
> Longwood opens its production brewery in Nanaimo.
> Persephone Brewing opens in Gibsons on the Lower Sunshine Coast.
> Steamworks Brewing opens its production brewery in Burnaby.
> The Heid-Out BrewHouse opens in Cranbrook.
> Three Ranges Brewing opens in Valemount.
> Victoria Beer Week launches in March.
> Wheelhouse Brewing opens in Prince Rupert.

2014

> Bad Tattoo Brewing opens in Penticton.
> Barkerville Brewing opens in Quesnel.
> Black Kettle Brewing opens in North Vancouver.
> Bomber Brewing, Main Street Brewing, Postmark Brewing, the Steel Toad Brewpub and Strange Fellows Brewing open in Vancouver.

- Category 12 Brewing opens in Saanichton, just north of Victoria.
- Cumberland Brewing and Gladstone Brewing open in Courtenay.
- Dageraad Brewing opens in Burnaby.
- Four Mile Brewpub opens in View Royal, Victoria.
- Moody Ales and Yellow Dog Brewing open in Port Moody.
- Red Collar Brewing opens in Kamloops.
- Rossland Beer opens.
- Sherwood Mountain BrewHouse opens in Terrace, becoming B.C.'s northernmost brewer… for now.
- Steel & Oak Brewing opens in New Westminster.
- Surlie Brewing opens in Abbotsford, but closes in 2015.
- Torchlight Brewing opens in Nelson.
- White Rock Beach Beer opens.

2015
- Callister Brewing, Doan's Craft Brewing, Dogwood Brewing and Off the Rail Brewing open in Vancouver.
- Hearthstone Brewing opens in North Vancouver.
- Axe and Barrel Brewing opens in Langford.
- Marten Brewpub opens in Vernon.
- Red Arrow Brewing opens in Duncan.
- Forbidden Brewing opens in Courtenay.
- Twin Sails Brewing opens in Port Moody.
- Fuggles & Warlock Craftworks opens in Richmond.
- White Sails Brewing opens in Nanaimo.

JUST AROUND
THE CORNER

New Craft Breweries
in the Works in B.C.

....

TWENTY-ONE NEW BREWERIES opened in 2014, making it by far
the biggest year in B.C. craft beer history. Another ten were
close to opening at the start of 2015 with several more in the
works for later in the year.

Will 2015 match this growth? I doubt it. But it should still
be quite a big year for new breweries. My investigations indi-
cate that there are at least another dozen in the works, and I'm
sure there are more that I just haven't heard of yet. Some pro-
spective brewers trumpet their plans from the mountaintops as
soon as they begin the process of opening their brewery, while
others prefer to keep it quiet until the beer is actually flowing.

Here's what I know for sure. Adding to the two breweries
that just opened in Port Moody this year will be a third, Twin
Sails Brewing, which will join Yellow Dog and Moody Ales on
Murray Street, making for one heck of a good brewery crawl
once the Evergreen SkyTrain line opens. Abbotsford, as well,
will get its third brewery in less than a year with Ravens Brewing joining Surlie and Old Abbey Ales.

Staying in the Lower Mainland, look for Maple Meadows
Brewing and Ridge Brewing to open in Maple Ridge, and for
Langley Brewing to open in Langley.

On the Island, Courtenay will get its second brewery just
a few months after the launch of Gladstone Brewing there: a
nanobrewery called Forbidden Brewing, named for the Forbidden Plateau region of central Vancouver Island, will open
there early in 2015. If all goes well, Riot Brewing will open in

Chemainus, and Twin City Brewing of Port Alberni hopes to join the craft beer revolution in 2015 or 2016. A brewery is also in the works for the Roundhouse redevelopment in Victoria, and Sooke Oceanfront Brewery intends to open in Sooke.

Elsewhere in B.C., Whitetooth Brewing hopes to open in Golden before the end of 2015, and Starkhund Brewing is in the works for Kelowna.

Given the huge boom that occurred in Vancouver over the past couple of years, it is interesting to note that I haven't heard of any other new breweries in the works there. Maybe that market has been saturated—after all, there are now twenty craft breweries or brewpubs in the city itself and another dozen or so in the immediate suburbs. Or maybe the new ones starting up there are flying under the radar.

I would love to see more breweries or brewpubs in other smaller communities, such as Campbell River, Castlegar, Hope and Creston (watch out Kokanee!). I also think there is potential for growth in some larger markets like Kamloops, Kelowna and Richmond.

Given the wild ride of the past few years, who honestly knows what the future holds? Maybe I'll be updating this book with another shwack of new breweries in 2016? Or maybe things will settle down for a bit so we can all catch our breath—and take a sip.

YOU'RE SOAKING IN IT

Why some so-called craft breweries don't
make the cut to be included in this book and
one owned by Molson does

• •

As I WAS researching and writing this book, I had to make
some difficult decisions about whether or not certain breweries
qualified as "craft breweries." In some cases, it was easy: obviously, the so-called "macrobreweries," the big national brands,
Molson and Labatt, don't count as craft breweries, and neither
do their imitation craft lines, Rickard's and Alexander Keith's.
Astute readers will note, however, that I did include Granville
Island Brewing, which was purchased in 2009 by Molson-
Coors through their Ontario micro brand, Creemore Springs.
Molson seems to have been fairly hands-off with GIB, and I
consider the specialty beers brewed by Vern Lambourne in the
original brewhouse on Granville Island to be craft beer for sure.
So Granville Island makes the cut.

One step down from those breweries is a level often
described as "regional breweries." This includes some breweries that started as microbreweries but then grew into larger
entities that eventually got swallowed up by bigger breweries.
Okanagan Spring Brewery is the best example of that in B.C.
In order to achieve a certain size, regional breweries like OK
Spring often end up sacrificing the quality of their ingredients
and pulling back on flavours in order to make their beers more
palatable to a wider audience. Well, that ain't craft.

Likewise, I did not include Turning Point Brewery, makers of the Stanley Park line of beers. I considered including a
profile of the brewery in this edition because it has (finally)
started to brew some fairly good beer, but I still find it difficult

to call it a craft brewery, because it is all about marketing first and beer second. Take a look at the website (www.stanleypark-brewery.ca) and try to figure out where the brewery is located. It doesn't actually say Stanley Park, but it certainly implies it. It also claims to be connected to the original "Stanley Park Brewery, est. 1897." Turning Point has no actual connection to the park, which is managed by the City of Vancouver, nor the Stanley Park Brewery, which was one of Vancouver's early breweries, and its physical brewery is located on Annacis Island in Delta, nowhere near downtown Vancouver. The brewery does not have a tasting room nor does it offer public tours. Even the big Molson plant in Vancouver offers tours and tastings. Then there is the spurious claim that its single wind turbine somehow generates enough power to run the whole "sustainable" brewery. I believe British Columbians are a pretty savvy bunch, though, and have become fairly adept at spotting blatant greenwashing like that so I doubt anyone buys the beer because of that claim.

Speaking of the actual beer, Turning Point claims its "1897 Amber is a Belgian style Amber, regarded by brewers to be the most complex and distinctive, but also the most difficult to craft." That's all hogwash. What they brew certainly isn't distinctive or difficult to make. Taste it next to any real Belgian beer and you will certainly notice the difference. The brewery also produces Hell's Gate lager and pale ale, which might best be described as "gateway beers," aimed at appealing to traditional Kokanee, Lucky or Bud drinkers. In other words, Turning Point is closer to being a marketing company that brews beer than an actual craft brewery. That said, more recently, Turning Point has begun to produce some beers that could arguably be described as craft, such as the Windstorm West Coast Pale Ale. So perhaps there is some reason for optimism.

Here are some other breweries that didn't make the cut:
Pacific Western is a large, independent brewery based in Prince George that sometimes brews beer that craft beer drinkers

might enjoy. I've happily sipped their Canterbury Dark Mild, a brand that goes way back in B.C., or their Pacific Schwarzbock, on occasion, and they have an organic line called NatureLand that features a lager and an amber ale. They also brew the Cariboo line, which is an entry-level lineup. The Festbier they produced in 2014 was fairly good as well. In the end, it comes down to my interpretation of "craft beer" (see "What is Craft Beer Anyway?" on page 7): although independent, PW's focus isn't on brewing high-quality beer across the board, and it is also on the large size to be considered craft.

Including Whistler Brewing is this book was debatable. If they didn't have an actual brewery in Whistler, I probably wouldn't have done so. And despite the fact that Whistler celebrated its twenty-fifth anniversary in 2014, a brick-and-mortar brewery in Whistler has not existed for twenty-five years straight, far from it. Between 1999 and 2009, the beer was brewed elsewhere, first in Delta and then in Kamloops, including a stretch when Big Rock owned the brand and didn't brew it at all. Whistler's parent company, NorthAm Group, also produces the Bowen Island brand of budget craft imitators, but the actual Bowen Island brewery disappeared long ago. Thus, Whistler makes the cut because it has an actual brewery, but Bowen Island doesn't.

Similarly, Shaftebury has a great history in B.C., but in 1999 it was purchased by Okanagan Spring, which dismantled the brewery and used the brand as a budget line, brewing it at the plant in Vernon. Tree Brewing bought it in 2014,and continues to brew it as a budget craft brand, similar to Bowen Island. So it doesn't make the cut, either. That said, if Shaftebury Cream Ale is the only thing in the cooler at a barbecue, I certainly won't turn it down.

Prohibition Brewing and Scandal Brewing are both pseudo-craft lines or so-called "shadow brands" created by bigger, non-craft breweries to try to attract sales in the craft market, similar to Anheuser-Busch InBev's controversial Shocktop line. Prohibition is brewed by the same company as Big Surf Lager, which I have never included in this book because producing one generic lager doesn't qualify a brewery as craft in my opinion. Interestingly, if Prohibition had been the first line of beers produced then it might qualify, although the heavy focus on marketing (similar to Turning Point) might have disqualified it, too. What makes it even more complicated is that Prohibition actually opened a tasting room in Yaletown in 2014.

Similarly, Scandal is a brand created by Pacific Western. As with Stanley Park, there is no reference to where the brewery is on the Scandal website. Apparently, it is owned by a Hugh Hefeweisen and the brewmaster is named Suddly Brew Right (I'm not making this up), each depicted as a cartoon character. There are several other cartoon characters, some of whom are large-breasted women who are included for no appropriate reason, and... really, I don't know why I'm bothering writing about this. It ain't craft.

What about Big Rock? Why haven't I included its new Big Rock Urban Brewery that opened on Alberta Street (seriously) in the heart of Vancouver's Brewery Creek neighbourhood? Simply put: because it's from Alberta, not B.C.

Finally, if you are looking for Canuck Empire or Fuggles & Warlock, you will find them in "Contract Breweries" on page 238.

CONTRACT
BREWERIES

••••••••••••••••••••••••

ALTHOUGH CONTRACT BREWING is a relatively common practice in the craft beer industry throughout North America, it does not happen in British Columbia very much. The idea is that a business (Company A) pays an existing brewery (Brewery B) to produce beer, which it then markets and sells as its own product. It can be beneficial for both parties since Company A does not need to build an actual facility to make its beer, while Brewery B can earn some money while using up excess capacity.

The most famous example of this practice is Mikkeller, a so-called "gypsy" or "phantom" brewery founded by Mikkel Borg Bjergsø in Copenhagen in 2006. Mikkeller has no brewery of its own, but its founder has brewed more than two hundred different beers by collaborating with breweries all around the world. His brother, Jeppe Jarnit-Bjergsø, began his own phantom brewery called Evil Twin Brewing in 2010.

While those breweries are generally accepted as craft operations, less credible companies sometimes use contract brewers to capitalize on the popularity of craft beer without putting the effort and investment into building their own facilities. There is a lot of controversy around this practice in the United States for this very reason—so many new U.S. breweries are opening there that it is difficult to recognize "real" breweries from contract operations.

In Ontario, contract brewing is very common and generally quite widely accepted. At the end of 2014, the Ontario Craft Brewers association identified approximately seventy-five operating breweries and another twenty-five contract brewers operating in Ontario. In other words, one-quarter of the licenced breweries in that province do not actually have their own bricks-and-mortar facilities!

In British Columbia, by comparison, there are only a few examples of contract brewing. In 2013–14, while Steamworks was setting up its new brewery in Burnaby, Dead Frog Brewery acted as a stand-in, producing the Steamworks line of bottled and canned products.

As of the end of 2014, there were two "phantom" breweries operating in B.C.: Canuck Empire Brewing and Fuggles & Warlock Craftworks. Both companies say they are working towards building their own facilities, but in the meantime, both are being brewed by Dead Frog (although Fuggles & Warlock acted as resident brewers at the Big River Brewpub for a time).

Look for a few more contract breweries to join the craft beer scene in B.C. with the opening of Callister Brewing (see "Callister Brewing" on page 112). That operation's business model includes sharing its equipment with aspiring brewers who don't yet have facilities of their own. The first to sign on was Adam Chatburn, CAMRA Vancouver's ex-president, who plans to launch his Real Cask brewery there.

Links

canuckempirebrewing.com
fuggleswarlock.com

FURTHER
TASTING
Award-Winning Brews

●●●●●●●●●●●●●●●●●●●●●●

HERE ARE SOME of the B.C. craft breweries and individual beers that have won awards in recent years.

CANADIAN BREWING AWARDS
2014 **Beer of the Year**—Old Yale Brewing Sasquatch Stout
2013 **Beer of the Year**—Powell Street Craft Brewery Old Jalopy
    Pale Ale
2012 **Brewery of the Year**—Central City Brewing
2014 **Gold Medals**
    Coal Harbour Brewing 311 Helles Lager
    Mission Springs Brewpub Trailblazer Pilsner
    Cannery Brewing Kiek in de Kök Baltic Porter
    Parallel 49 Brewing Old Boy Brown Ale
    Russell Brewing Wee Angry Scotch Ale
    Old Yale Brewing Sasquatch Stout
    Cannery Brewing Maple Stout
    Parallel 49 Brewing Russian Imperial Stout
    Yaletown Brewing Oud Bruin

B.C. BEER AWARDS
2014 **Best in Show**—Yellow Dog Brewing Shake A Paw Smoked
    Porter
2013 **Best in Show**—Vancouver Island Brewery Hermannator Ice
    Bock

Turning Point Brewing Stanley Park Noble Pilsner

Steamworks Brewing Pilsner

Tree Brewing Captivator Doppelbock

Steamworks Brewing Kölsch

Moon Under Water Brewpub This Is Hefeweizen

Tin Whistle Brewing Stag Apple Scotch Ale

Main Street Brewing Sessional IPA

Yellow Dog Brewing Shake A Paw Smoked Brown Porter

Driftwood Brewing White Bark Witbier

Parallel 49 Brewing Lost Souls Chocolate Pumpkin Porter

Persephone Brewing Dry Irish Stout

Whistler BrewHouse 5 Rings IPA

Brassneck Brewery One Trick Pony

Driftwood Brewery Bird Of Prey Flanders Red

Steamworks Brewing Blitzen

Granville Island Brewing Lost In The Barrels

Central City Brewers Thor's Hammer Barrel Aged

CBC People's Choice Award—Four Winds Brewing Sovereign Super Saison

CAMRA VANCOUVER AWARDS—2014

Best Local Brewpub—Central City Brewing

Best B.C. Brewpub—Howe Sound Brewing

Best B.C. Brewery (non-brewpub)—Driftwood Brewery

Best Local Beer Establishment—Alibi Room

Best Local Beer Server/Bartender—Nigel Springthorpe

Best Local Private Liquor Store—Brewery Creek

Best Local Cask Night—The Whip

Best Local Beer Event—Vancouver Craft Beer Week

Best B.C. Beer—Driftwood Brewery Fat Tug IPA

Best B.C. Seasonal Beer—Driftwood Brewery Sartori Harvest IPA

Best Local Beer Blogger or Writer—Barley Mowat

Best Beer Name—Parallel 49 Brewing Toques of Hazzard

Best Beer Label Artwork—BC Craft Beer Month Collaboration Spruce Tip Stout

HOPHEADS
UNITE
B.C.'s Biggest Hop Bombs

• •

BACK IN THE Jazz Age, the term "hophead" referred to a drug user, but these days it is used more commonly (in beer circles at least) as a slightly self-deprecating label for those who prefer hoppy styles of beer above all others, especially West Coast IPAS. You know you are a hophead when everything you buy at the bottle shop has 60-plus IBUS and a name like "Palate Wrecker." Likely, you start your night off with an 80-IBU IPA and then switch to another IPA and finish off with a third one—and can discern the different hops used in each.

For those who dedicate your taste buds to the almighty hop, I salute you. Here is a list of B.C.'s best IPAS, divided into two levels of hop explosiveness starting with the hoppiest (and ordered alphabetically to avoid arguments).

THERMONUCLEAR ICBMS
"Why is my tongue glowing in the dark?"

Bomber Superpest Imperial IPA
Brassneck Passive Aggressive
Brassneck One Trick Pony Imperial IPA
Central City Red Racer IPA
Central City Imperial IPA
Driftwood Fat Tug IPA
Driftwood Sartori Harvest IPA
Driftwood Twenty Pounder Double IPA
Four Winds IPA

Granville Island Shipload of Hops Imperial IPA
Howe Sound Total Eclipse of the Hop Imperial IPA
Lighthouse Shipwreck IPA
Lighthouse Numbskull Imperial IPA
Parallel 49 Filthy Dirty IPA
Parallel 49 Hopnotist
Parallel 49 Snap, Crackle, Hop Imperial Rice IPA
Persephone Double IPA
Phillips Amnesiac Double IPA
Powell Street Craft Hopdemonium Double IPA
Russell Hop Therapy Double IPA

BUNKER BUSTERS
"Will my taste buds still love me in the morning?"

33 Acres of Nirvana
Arrowhead I'm So Freakin' Hoppy IPA
Bomber IPA
Bridge Deep Cove IPA
Fernie Bucket List series
Four Winds Phaedra White Rye IPA
Nelson Full Nelson Imperial IPA
Old Yale West Coast IPA
Phillips Hop Circle IPA
Russell IP'eh!
Spinnakers Hoptoria
Storm Hurricane IPA
Swans Extra IPA
Tofino Hoppin' Cretin IPA
Tree Hop Head Double IPA
Whistler BrewHouse 5 Rings IPA
Yellow Dog Play Dead IPA

GETTING INVOLVED

CAMRA BC

● ●

THE CAMPAIGN FOR REAL ALE was founded in the UK in 1971 in response to the near extinction of traditional, cask-conditioned beer and local pub culture there. It has since grown into Britain's largest consumer group with more than 144,000 members. Over its four-plus decades, CAMRA UK has affected real positive change in the beer scene there, and hosts the Great British Beer Festival each summer.

CAMRA BC was first incorporated in Victoria in 1985 with similar aims: it is dedicated to the promotion and responsible consumption of natural, craft beers. It supports "the brewing of traditional styles of beer in the traditional manner, using traditional ingredients." Its mission is to act as champion of the consumer in relation to the B.C. and Canadian beer industry.

There are branches in Victoria, Vancouver, Powell River (covering the Sunshine Coast) and the South Fraser Valley (including Delta, Ladner, Langley, Richmond, Surrey, Tsawwassen and White Rock). A new Okanagan branch should be up and running by the spring of 2015.

If you are interested in craft beer in B.C., I highly recommend joining CAMRA. If you live in a place without a branch, the provincial body produces a bimonthly magazine called *What's Brewing* that will help keep you informed.

---

www.camrabc.ca

STUDY UP

....

IF YOU WANT to learn more about beer or brewing, there are several good options available to you in B.C., including certification programs, tasting courses and full-fledged brewer training programs.

CICERONE CERTIFICATION

A cicerone (pronounced *sis-uh-rohn*) is to beer what a sommelier is to wine; in other words, a knowledgeable expert who has proven through a certification process that she or he knows a lot about beer selection, sales and service. Canada's first cicerone was Vancouver's own Chester Carey, who works at the Brewery Creek liquor store, is a co-founder of the B.C. Beer Awards festival and teaches the Serious Beer course (see below).

There are three levels of certification: Certified Beer Server in the Cicerone Program, Certified Cicerone and Master Cicerone (of which there is only one so far in Canada, Toronto's Mirella Amato, the author of *Beerology*).

Visit www.cicerone.org for more information.

SERIOUS BEER

This course is taught by Chester Carey, Canada's first certified cicerone, at the Pacific Institute of Culinary Arts by the entrance to Granville Island. Carey is a knowledgeable and entertaining teacher whose enthusiasm for craft beer is definitely infectious.

For more information, visit www.picachef.com/classes/beer-school.

KWANTLEN UNIVERSITY BREWING
AND BREWERY OPERATIONS

Kwantlen began offering this two-year diploma program at its Langley campus in September 2014. When I visited to give a guest lecture in November, the on-campus Brewery Instructional Laboratory (a complete brewery for teaching purposes) was nearly complete.

Visit www.kpu.ca/brew for more information.

SFU CRAFT BEER AND BREWING ESSENTIALS

This Continuing Studies certificate program will begin in September 2015 based at sfu Surrey, utilizing the original Central City brewpub as its teaching brewery.

Visit www.sfu.ca/beer for more information.

KEN BEATTIE—EUREKA BEER GUIDE

Ken Beattie, the executive director of the B.C. Craft Brewers Guild, teaches a variety of educational seminars under the Prud'homme Beer Certification banner, as well as his own very entertaining Beer 101 and History of Beer tasting events.

Visit www.eurekabeerguide.com for more information.

BEER FESTIVALS

....

MARCH
Victoria Beer Week
victoriabeerweek.com

APRIL
Okanagan Fest-of-Ale
(Penticton)
fest-of-ale.bc.ca

MAY
Great Okanagan Beer Festival
gobf.ca

Vancouver Craft Beer Week
vancouvercraftbeerweek.com

JUNE
East Kootenay Beer Festival
(Fairmont Hot Springs)
fairmonthotsprings.com

AUGUST
Canada Cup of Beer
(Vancouver)
canadacupofbeer.com

SEPTEMBER
Great Canadian Beer Festival
(Victoria)
gcbf.com

Whistler Village Beer Festival
wvbf.ca

OCTOBER
B.C. Craft Beer Month
bccraftbeer.com/events

Powell River Craft Beer Festival
camrapowellriver.ca

ACKNOWLEDGEMENTS

....

MANY PEOPLE HELPED me while I was researching and writing both editions of this book. I'd like to thank the tourism staff, public relations people and accommodation and restaurant partners who supported me as I travelled around B.C. conducting research over the past few years. Some breweries also assisted me directly by providing accommodation and/or meals while I was visiting their communities.

I would also like to thank Howard White, Anna Comfort O'Keeffe and Anna Boyar at Harbour Publishing first for resurrecting Douglas & McIntyre and then for believing in this project so completely. Cheers to you!

And here are some shout-outs to individuals who went the extra mile:

Shawn and Jessica—for encouraging me even when I didn't believe in myself, and for providing me a home away from home so many times.

John and Nancy—for pointing out what was obvious (and

for letting me win at squash once in a while, John.)

Glen—for the shared travels, the beer mug image, being my photographer—and for your photographic memory.

Enid and Linda—for your support, encouragement and interest, even though neither of you drinks beer.

Steve—for being my wing man on many brewery tours, providing me with a bed in Maple Ridge, and naming your excellent IPA after me.

Chris Labonté—for helping me take this from idea to reality.

Caroline Skelton—for jumping back into the fray and doing such a great job throughout, and doing it again a second time!

The beer geeks who always have answers for my questions: Mirella Amato, Stephen Beaumont, Chester Carey, Gerry Erith, Rick Green, Paul Kamon, Crystal Luxmore, and Paddy Treavor.

Some parts of this book have appeared in slightly different forms in various print and online publications. I am grateful to the print publications *BCBusiness*, *BC Craft Beer News*, *Beer West*, *Georgia Straight*, *The Growler*, *Northwest Brewing News*, *Taps*, *Taste*, *Toro*, *Vancouver View* and *WestEnder*, and the websites BCLiving.ca, HelloBC.com, OpenFile.ca and UrbanDiner.ca, for supporting my writing and indulging my obsession with beer.

REFERENCES

· ·

NOT ALL THE research for this book was conducted on a bar stool. There are several books I consulted, all of which I encourage interested folks to seek out.

Beaumont, Stephen. *Great Canadian Beer Guide*. Toronto: Macmillan, 1994.
Coutts, Ian. *Brew North*. Vancouver: Greystone, 2010.
Morrison, Lisa M. *Craft Beers of the Pacific Northwest*. Portland: Timber Press, 2011.
Moyes, Robert. *Island Pubbing II*. Victoria: Orca, 1991.
Oliver, Garrett (ed.). *Oxford Companion to Beer*. New York: Oxford University Press, 2012.
Sneath, Allen Winn. *Brewed in Canada*. Toronto: Dundurn, 2001.
Stott, Jon. C. *Beer Quest West*. Victoria: Touchwood Editions, 2011.

OTHER SOURCES
Brewer's Gold at www.chilliwackmuseum.ca

LIST OF
BREWERIES

• •

AUTHOR
NOTE

·····················

BEYOND THIS BOOK there are lots of other ways to stay in touch with me and keep up with the craft beer scene in B.C. I write the B.C. column for the *Northwest Brewing News*, which is distributed from California to Alaska. I also blog about craft beer for Tourism B.C. and am the beer columnist for CBC Radio's All Points West. Occasionally, I write articles about beer for magazines and newspapers, including *Taps*, the *Georgia Straight*, the *Vancouver Sun*, *BCBusiness*, and *The Growler*—look for links to those articles on my Thirsty Writer website. I tweet about beer often and provide regular updates to the information in this book on my Craft Beer Revolution Facebook page and website.

craftbeerrevolution.ca
facebook.com/BCCraftBeerRevolution
twitter.com/CraftBeerRevolu
twitter.com/thirstywriter
thirstywriter.com
blog.hellobc.com/author/joe-wiebe

INDEX

....